Foreign Investment and
NAFTA

Foreign Investment
and
NAFTA

edited by Alan M. Rugman

UNIVERSITY OF SOUTH CAROLINA PRESS

Copyright © 1994 University of South Carolina

Published in Columbia, South Carolina, by the
University of South Carolina Press

Manufactured in the United States of America

Library of Congress Cataloging-in-Publication Data

Foreign investment and NAFTA / edited by Alan M. Rugman.
    p.   cm.
    Includes bibliographical references and index.
    ISBN 0–87249–993–6 (acid-free paper)
    1. Free trade—North America.   2. Canada. Treaties, etc. 1992
Oct. 7.   3. Investments, Foreign—North America.   I. Rugman, Alan
M.
HF1746.F67   1994
332.67′3′097—dc20   93-48267
                                                   CIP

In memory of G. Robert Ross,
president of Western Washington University,
January 1983 to November 1987.

CONTENTS

PREFACE

This collection provides the reader with a unique overview and analysis of the key investment issues associated with the North American Free Trade Agreement (NAFTA). Three broad themes emerge from the authors' original research. The first is that, while NAFTA will undoubtedly accelerate economic change in North America, it is fundamentally a reflection of processes which are already underway. The second theme, related to the first, is that NAFTA can be interpreted as being part of an ongoing process of economic regionalization based on the Triad markets of the European Community (E.C.), Japan, and North America. This regionalization is driven by the strategic business activities of multinational enterprises (MNEs). The third theme concerns the anticipated distribution of benefits and costs associated with NAFTA. Here again, a clear consensus suggests that NAFTA will have a marginal impact in the United States and Canada but a much more significant impact in Mexico. Mexico stands to gain the most from this agreement, but must also be prepared for greater adjustment costs as well.

The book is divided into five parts. In part 1 four chapters explore the politics and economics of NAFTA. In considering the economics behind NAFTA, chapter 1 by Steven Globerman reviews the major economic studies which have analyzed various aspects of the agreement. These all identify welfare gains accruing to the three signatories. In addition, Globerman considers in detail the assumptions which underlie the type of modeling which had been done on NAFTA and finds that, to the extent that these studies are biased, the bias likely understates the gains which can be expected from NAFTA. As emerges in several other chapters in this volume, Globerman finds that

Mexico stands, in relative terms, to gain the most from this agreement. He also effectively debunks the popular but misguided critique of NAFTA as an agreement which will bring large adjustment cost to workers in Canada and the United States.

In chapter 2 Susan Liebeler brings the weight of her experience as a former chair of the U.S. International Trade Commission to her analysis of the politics of NAFTA. Liebeler first outlines the political economy of protectionism in the United States and details how political forces have polarized around NAFTA. Her paper brings insight and perspective to the politics surrounding the NAFTA debate in the United States, especially over the side agreements.

In chapter 3 Rugman and Gestrin explain the investment provisions of NAFTA, in particular the concept of national treatment. They provide an analysis of the sectors which have been exempted from the key investment provisions of the agreement. What the authors conclude is that, while the agreement does fall short in several areas (key sectors remain virtually closed to foreign investment, national investment screening policies are exempted, and decisions from the review procedures of the agreement are exempted), it is on balance a significant step forward, especially with regards to the opening of the Mexican market and the greater security for foreign direct investment (FDI) which the agreement brings to the NAFTA area. In chapter 4 Rugman and Verbeke develop an analytical framework to evaluate the investment provisions of NAFTA.

In part 2 the motives and expectations of each of the three signatories are examined in detail. An American perspective on NAFTA is provided by Edward Graham in chapter 5. A major theme explored by Graham is the apparent paradox reflected, on one hand, in the success on the part of U.S. negotiators in achieving the U.S. government's objective (and hence, presumably, in forwarding American interests) and, on the other hand, in the widespread opposition to the agreement at the grassroots level. Ultimately, Graham argues that the pro NAFTA forces have not backed their belief in open trade and investment with an equally energetic selling job.

In chapter 6 Nymark and Verdun report on the Canadian position during NAFTA's investment negotiations and the manner in which Canadian business will adjust to NAFTA in the future. Their focus is upon the competitiveness of Canadian business and the opportunities for investment in Canada after NAFTA.

In chapter 7 Edgar Ortiz offers readers an overview of the economic and political history which motivated the Mexican government to pursue NAFTA. Ortiz outlines Mexico's FDI position as it has evolved during the 1980s and looks closely at developments in the financial services sector.

The common theme of part 3 is clearly the disproportionate share of adjustment as well as opportunity which will be experienced in the Mexican economy relative to the adjustments anticipated in the United States and Canada. In chapter 8 Gestrin and Rugman explain why the impact of NAFTA will be neutral for large U.S. and Canadian multinationals.

Roberts and Vertinsky consider the impact of NAFTA on the forest products industry in chapter 9. In their study, they examine the makeup of the North American forest products sector in terms of the competitive advantages which particular regions of North America enjoy in subsectors of the industry. They conclude that NAFTA will offer significant new opportunities for exporters of lumber and pulp and paper products from the United States and Canada to Mexico in the short term, and that, with increased foreign investment, Mexico's forest products sector will become more competitive over time.

In their analysis of NAFTA's implications for the energy sector in chapter 10, Hagen, Henson, and Merrifield first outline in detail the energy provisions and exceptions of the agreement. They then describe the likely dynamics which will accompany Mexico's economic development in terms of energy demand and use and the implications of these changes for U.S. and Canadian energy producers. Ultimately, they point out that while NAFTA is restrictive in terms of the degree to which the Mexican energy sector is liberalized, Mexico's future development will likely suffer if better foreign investment access does not become de facto Mexican government policy.

In part 4 NAFTA is examined in terms of its likely impact upon "outsiders." The outsiders considered are Japan and the rest of Latin America. In chapter 11 Edgington and Fruin focus on the role and patterns of Japanese investment in North America—especially developments in the automotive sector. They identify important changes in Japanese corporate culture and strategy, in particular the abandonment of a strong home-country bias for more distinct region-based networks, which will have significant implications for Japanese investment patterns in North America.

In chapter 12 Gestrin and Waverman consider prospects for an extension of NAFTA to the rest of the Western Hemisphere. The authors find that, while political hurdles in the United States seem to mitigate against the widening of the agreement in the short to medium term, prospects for continued economics integration in the hemisphere are strong. More specifically, an expanding network of regional agreements within Latin America and the historically strong relationship between North and South America will likely form the basis of a strong process of economic regionalization during the 1990s.

Finally, in part 5 Robert Spich's rapporteur's comments consider the nature of the NAFTA debate and the need for a careful examination of the assumptions and biases which characterize it. Spich sees NAFTA not simply as an agreement on paper, but as a process which once underway will likely bring about considerable change, both from a neoclassical economic perspective as well as from a social perspective.

ACKNOWLEDGMENTS

This book contains original papers first presented at a series of seminars on the North American Free Trade Agreement (NAFTA), and a conference on the NAFTA and foreign investment held at Western Washington University in Spring 1993. The papers have been organized, revised, and edited to fit around the common theme of the investment implications of the NAFTA.

Funding for the seminars, the conference, and this book was provided by the G. Robert Ross Distinguished Professorship of Canada-U.S. Business and Economics Relations in the College of Business and Economics at Western Washington University. The chair, the first at Western, was established in memory of President Ross, and its endowment comes jointly from the government of Canada and the state of Washington. Additional sponsorship for the seminars was provided by the Intalco Aluminum Corporation and special thanks are extended to Mr. Jim Fredericks, the general manager of Intalco for his support.

As the first incumbent of the Ross visiting professorship I should like to acknowledge the help and support of Dean Dennis Murphy and his colleagues at Western Washington University. Invaluable assistance in the organization of the chair's activities and the preparation of this book was provided by Mrs. Kathryn Finn. Michael Gestrin of the University of Toronto was my main collaborator on this book. Without his help, insight, and dedication it would not have been possible. Editorial assistance was provided by Loretta Smith Backstrom of Western Washington University. The index was prepared by Rosemary Anderson.

Finally, this book is only as good as the chapters prepared by the authors and I should like to thank them for the exceptional quality of their work.

*Foreign Investment and
NAFTA*

PART 1

THE ECONOMICS AND POLITICS OF NAFTA

Chapter 1

THE ECONOMICS OF NAFTA

Steven Globerman

Introduction

On 17 December 1992 U.S. President Bush, Mexican President Salinas and Canadian Prime Minister Mulroney signed the North American Free Trade Agreement (NAFTA). At the time of writing, the Agreement is awaiting endorsement by the legislatures of the three countries; however, recently elected President Clinton has indicated a desire on his part to negotiate "supplemental" agreements in specific areas—most notably environmental protection and remediation safeguards against import surges and employment standards. At the present time, the precise nature of these supplemental agreements is unclear. Nor is it clear that any such agreements could be negotiated without reopening NAFTA itself.[1]

Supporters and critics of NAFTA can be found in all three countries, although they tend to focus on somewhat different issues. For example, opponents in the United States and Canada stress adverse effects on the environment along with downward pressure on real wages, especially wages of less skilled workers. Supporters argue that the faster resulting rate of growth in Mexico will lead to increased Mexican demand for high value-added goods and services from U.S. and Canadian producers. They also argue that higher real incomes in Mexico will mitigate many of the social and environmental pressures in that country.

Criticisms of the Agreement in Mexico have been relatively muted, although concerns have been raised about a substantial displacement of workers from the agricultural sector and a wave of bankruptcies of small, family-owned businesses. Supporters point to the benefits of institutionalizing Mexico's economic reforms and the increased inflows of foreign capital that will follow.

The debate surrounding NAFTA has spawned a host of studies on the likely impacts of the Agreement. The studies are generally consistent in their findings, thereby providing a basis for confidence in the median assessment of the impact of NAFTA. On the other hand, a nonbeliever in the reliability of economic research might conclude that mainstream economists, and the policymakers who listen to them, are in for a big surprise if and when NAFTA is implemented. In addition, several specific issues remain quite contentious, especially the impact of NAFTA on the environment and on specific industries and geographic regions.

This chapter has two major objectives: (1) to summarize and assess the literature dealing with the economic effects of NAFTA and (2) to identify and assess the major assumptions underlying many of the existing studies. By way of background, the next section briefly sets out the main provisions of NAFTA. The third section identifies the broad factors conditioning the economic impacts of free trade agreements generally and places them in the context of NAFTA. The fourth section summarizes a broad set of studies bearing upon the economic consequences of NAFTA and discusses the sensitivity of the mainstream findings to alternative assumptions about key economic relationships. Conclusions and policy recommendations are presented in the last section.

Overview of NAFTA

NAFTA is a massive document of thousands of pages, much of it quite technical. Hence, only a very general summary of its main features can be presented here.[2] In particular, the many exceptions to trade liberalization in the Agreement such as the investment reservations are not addressed.

First, and perhaps foremost, NAFTA provides for something approaching free trade in goods, including agricultural commodities, after a transition period that can range beyond fifteen years in some cases. Second, the coverage of investment in NAFTA is arguably broader than in the U.S.-Canadian Free Trade Agreement (FTA) given that the latter only covers foreign direct investment, whereas the former includes all investments. NAFTA provides investors with new dispute resolution procedures and safeguards against expropriation without compensation. It also conveys Most Favored Nation (MFN) status on investors—in other words, investors are to be treated no less favorably than investors of any other nation. Certain sectors, including those covered in FTA, are exempt from these investment provisions.

Rules of origin in NAFTA closely follow FTA rules with important exceptions. One such exception is the automotive goods sector. The threshold percentage of domestic content in NAFTA is 60 to 62.5 (depending on the product) compared to 50 in FTA. Moreover, under NAFTA, the automotive goods producer must trace all materials imported under specified tariff provisions. The domestic content can be averaged across broad categories of products, including parts, and in this sense liberalizes narrower categories for averaging under FTA.[3]

Rules of origin for textiles are even more complex and arguably more protectionist than for autos. The rule of origin is based on the principle of "yarn forward": a product must be made of yarns of NAFTA material, of textiles made of NAFTA yarn, and the products must be made of NAFTA fibers; however, preferential treatment up to a quota level is extended for yarns, fabrics, and apparel that do not meet the rules of origin.[4]

NAFTA contains a chapter on customs valuation which was not included in FTA. In it, the three countries agree to establish uniform regulations regarding the interpretation, application, and administration of rules of origin and embody these regulations in domestic law. The chapter also establishes procedures for producers and exporters to obtain advanced rulings, as well as a right to appeal customs decisions before domestic authorities.[5]

The basic institutional arrangements and procedures for dispute settlement established under FTA, both with respect to general dispute resolution and antidumping and countervailing duty actions are carried on in NAFTA. Appropriate allowances are made for multiple parties including recourse to arbitration, as well as the panel process under FTA. It also adds amendments to Mexico's unfair trade remedy legislation bringing the latter closer to U.S. and Canadian practices.[6]

Specific provisions in NAFTA affect environmental legislation and practices. For the most part, they reflect General Agreement on Tariffs and Trade (GATT) provisions. For example, NAFTA accords priority to specific international environmental agreements to which one or more of the parties is a member. Individual members are free to establish their own phytosanitary and related standards; however, those standards can be challenged by other members as being unjustifiable trade protectionist measures. The challenge would be dealt with by a dispute resolution process invoking scientific and other evidence. In what is a new provision in trade agreements, the members agree not to alter environmental legislation or enforcement practices in order to attract investment. Complaints brought under this latter provision would also go through a dispute resolution procedure.

Finally, there are provisions throughout NAFTA calling for the formation of committees or working groups to undertake additional work on aspects of the Agreement including outlining desirable qualities for the administration of antidumping and countervailing duty laws. Similar undertakings are included in FTA.

Potential Impacts Of Free Trade Agreements

The economic effects of trade liberalization generally, and free trade agreements specifically, are related to the following broad phenomena. First, these effects include a reallocation of resources across industries consistent with international patterns of comparative advantage. The resulting increases in allocative efficiency underlie traditional gains from trade. The second effect includes a reallocation of resources within specific industries consistent with increases in technical efficiency. Specifically, intensified competitive pressure from imports encourages domestic producers to rationalize production. This rationalization typically takes the form of increases in average plant size and increased product specialization.[7] And finally, these effects include changes in the overall quantity of resources available for production activity. This impact reflects a set of heterogeneous considerations related to deadweight costs of different origins.

An example of this phenomena would be the legislated elimination of tariffs and nontariff barriers that could discourage protectionist rent-seeking behavior to the extent that it reduces the probability of lobbyists receiving trade protection. On the other hand, increased import competition could lead some affected North American producers to intensify their efforts to raise the costs of imports from outside the free trade area, or indeed even within the area through use of antidumping and countervailing duty provisions, among other things. In principle, if the dispute resolution mechanism is working well, frivolous complaints, at least those directed at producers in other member countries, should be discouraged.

A second potentially important example relates to costs associated with the dislocation of workers and capital. In particular, resource requirements for retraining workers or transporting workers and capital to new geographic locations may be seen as deadweight costs associated with the relative price changes occasioned by free trade.

A third example is trade diverted to higher cost partners which might be partially offset by investment diversion to the free trade area from outside the area. In particular, the formation of a free trade area could encourage investment from outside by firms concerned about the competitive disadvantage associated with domestic content requirements.

A fourth example is the claim that free trade will lead to environmental degradation and its associated costs.[8] The direct (or indirect) costs associated with increased environmental damage, or the prevention of such damage, would legitimately be considered deadweight costs of trade liberalization. On the other hand, it can be argued that a free trade agreement such as NAFTA will reduce environmental pollution. The relationship between trade liberalization and the environment in the specific context of NAFTA will be addressed in a later section.

Finally, to the extent that free trade leads to a significant increase in the income inequality in one or more of the member countries, it could trigger fiscal programs to redistribute income. Such programs have their own deadweight costs, and the latter might be appropriately considered an indirect consequence of free trade.

In summary, there are a set of potential economic impacts conditioning the net benefits (or costs) of free trade. Beyond the well-known efficiency consequences, a set of more subtle impacts are receiving prominent attention in NAFTA debate. In fact, one might expect some interrelationships among the various factors. In particular, to the extent that trade liberalization has modest impacts on the reallocation of resources, either across sectors or within sectors, any adjustment costs associated with trade liberalization should also be modest. In a related fashion, the more prominent are interindustry reallocations relative to intraindustry reallocations, the more substantial adjustment costs are likely to be. The notion here is that it is less costly to retrain workers or relocate other resources when the relevant services are being redirected from one activity to another within the same industry. Specifically, embodied or disembodied expertise is arguably more fungible within industries than between industries.

Some A Priori Assessments of NAFTA's Impacts

As noted above, the reallocation of resources from comparatively disadvantaged to comparatively advantaged industries underlies the traditional allocative efficiency gains from freer trade. To the extent that potential trade flows associated with the elimination of existing trade barriers are relatively small, anticipated allocative efficiency gains might also be expected to be modest. Moreover, technical efficiency gains associated with increased foreign competition are likely to be mitigated by small (actual or potential) supply responses by foreign producers to reductions in domestic trade barriers.

Trade flows.   These simple propositions underlie arguments that NAFTA's impacts will be primarily experienced by Mexico, while the impacts on Canada and the United States will be quite modest. Specifically, table 1.1 reports recent estimates of exports and imports among the three countries. They show (among other things) that Canada's trade with Mexico is absolutely and relatively small. Consequently, they suggest that the addition of Mexico to the North American free trade area is unlikely, at least in the short run, to promote significant direct changes in the allocation of resources across and within Canadian industrial sectors. Likewise, tariff-free trade between Mexico and Canada is unlikely, by itself, to have significant implications for allocative and technical efficiency in Mexico.

The data in table 1.1 also show that the United States is the major market for Canadian and Mexican exports and is also the largest exporter to those markets. Over three-quarters of the trade done by Canada and Mexico is bilateral with the United States. To this extent, the accession of Mexico to the U.S.-Canadian free trade area may affect Canadian exports to the U.S. market. In particular, tariff-free access to the U.S. market might facilitate a substitution of Mexican for Canadian goods in that market; however, faster growth of the U.S. market could still result in an overall increase in the demand for Canadian goods.

More directly, a free trade agreement with the United States has the potential to encourage significant changes in resource allocation patterns in the Mexican economy. Conversely, Mexico is only the third largest (albeit rapidly growing) single country source of imports in the United States. This suggests modest impacts to the United States from a NAFTA beyond those already stimulated by FTA.

Trade Barriers.   It might be argued that existing trade flows are misleading indicators of the potential for increased trade flows associated with the formation of a free trade area. In

TABLE 1.1

Trilateral Exports and Imports, 1991
(U.S. billion dollars)

	United States		Mexico		Canada	
	Total $	% of Total	Total $	% of Total	Total $	% of Total
Canada:						
exports to	91.1	72.1	0.4	0.3	—	—
imports from	85.1	68.2	2.1	1.7	—	—
Mexico:						
exports to	31.2	80.3	—	—	2.1	1.9
imports from	33.3	79.7	—	—	0.4	0.9
United States:						
exports to	—	—	33.3	7.9	85.1	20.2
imports from	—	—	31.9	6.3	93.7	18.4

SOURCE: Adapted from IMF, *Direction of Trade Statistics Yearbook 1992.*

particular, it might be argued that Mexico's current modest role
as a trading partner reflects existing barriers to trade that would
be reduced significantly under a NAFTA. Without gainsaying
the potential for significant increases in trade volumes, one
should not overestimate the impact of existing trade barriers.
For example, the trade-weighted impact of Canadian tariffs is
around 10 percent, in line with that of Mexico, while the trade-
weighted impact of U.S. tariffs is around 5 percent.[9] A little less
than 10 percent of Mexican imports to the United States enter
duty free under the generalized system of preferences for less
developed countries. Forty five percent of U.S. imports from
Mexico are products from the maquiladora industries which pay
duty only on the value added in Mexico. All of Mexico's tariffs
are now within the range of 0 to 20 percent.[10]

The aforementioned numbers suggest that barriers to trade in
manufactures are already low; however, Mexican tariff rates are
incomplete indices of trade barriers given the continuation of

import licenses in areas such as automobiles, electronics, and pharmaceuticals. Similarly, Canadian and U.S. quotas on specific goods such as textiles and clothing, as well as de facto quotas imposed by health standards for agricultural products qualify the relevance of relatively low average tariff levels, at least on a sectoral basis. Hence, it is useful to look at studies which focus on individual sectors, and a number of such studies will be reviewed below.

It might also be argued that low levels of foreign direct investment in Mexico condition trade flows. Specifically, to the extent that trade among affiliates of multinational enterprises (MNEs) is more efficient than trade between countries, restrictions on foreign direct investment indirectly suppress trade flows. Symmetrically, eliminating restrictions on foreign direct investment could indirectly stimulate increases in trilateral trade. Given substantial historical restrictions on foreign direct investment in Mexico, other than in the maquiladora sector, the potential for increased direct investment in Mexico certainly exists; however, it is very difficult to predict the impact of NAFTA on direct investment flows.[11]

The impact of NAFTA on investment flows into Mexico is also potentially relevant inasmuch as investment flows affect the rate of growth of the Mexican economy. Empirical results underscore the sensitivity of results to assumed rates of income growth in Mexico. Given uncertainties about future capital formation rates in Mexico, there is also a substantial variance surrounding estimates of Mexico's real income growth.[12]

Sectoral Trade Concentration. As noted above, "average" results from trade liberalization may mask significant sectoral differences. In this regard, table 1.2 reports major SIC groups for manufactured exports. The table highlights the importance of the motor vehicle and parts industry and the machinery sector in the trinational trade context.

The data in table 1.2 also provide some insight into the potential for Mexican exports to compete with Canadian exports to the U.S. market. Specifically, they suggest that the United States is an important market for Canadian and Mexican exports in transportation equipment, machinery, energy, and metal products.

Whether Canadian and Mexican products are strong or weak substitutes depends upon the characteristics of the exports within these broad categories. As will be noted below, in the auto sector, Mexico tends to specialize in small cars, while Canada tends to specialize in large cars. In the energy sector, virtually all of Mexico's exports to the United States are petroleum or petroleum products. Almost two-thirds of Canada's energy exports to the United States comprise of natural gas. In machinery, there are differences across and within categories. For example, Canada exports relatively more telecommunications and related electronics equipment. In short, the inclusion of Mexico in a free trade area will have relatively benign impacts on Canada's exports to the United States.

Expected Environmental Effects. To the extent that the

TABLE 1.2

Major Manufactured Exports, 1991
(U.S. million dollars)

	United States		Canada	Mexico
	to Mexico	to Canada	to United States	to United States
Vehicles and Transport Equipment	2,218	19,136	28,595	4,345
Machinery	9,797	19,473	10,211	9,916
Chemicals	2,624	6,554	4,603	748
Petroleum and Natural Gas	844	886	10,353	4,876
Paper	776	1,536	6,352	124
Metal Products	2,800	4,861	6,557	1,469

Source: Author's calculations from OECD, *Foreign Trade by Commodities, 1991*, vol. 3 (Paris: OECD, 1992).

impacts of NAFTA on overall trade flows are significant for Mexico and modest for the United States and Canada, the environmental impacts of NAFTA are likely to be linked to the magnitude and nature of economic growth in Mexico. In this regard, critics of NAFTA have argued that faster economic growth in Mexico will exacerbate environmental damage, especially along the Mexican-U.S. border. On the other hand, it has been noted that higher incomes encourage an increased demand for a cleaner environment, and the net impact may well be lower emissions of many types of pollutants.[13]

While the impact of NAFTA on the environment will depend upon the overall rate of growth of the Mexican economy, it will also depend upon the pattern of growth. For example, to the extent that there is some dispersion of economic activity away from the border region, there will arguably be some mitigation of the environmental damage associated with congestion created by maquiladoras locating at the border. In principle, the extension of free trade status to the entire country should eliminate the incentive to locate in export processing zones near the border. On the other hand, the adoption of just-in-time production techniques, along with the employment of U.S. managers in Mexican plants and Mexican managers in U.S. plants, may perpetuate the locational advantage of border regions. Unfortunately, there is little available evidence on NAFTA's likely locational impacts on new investment.

Evidence On The Economic Impacts of NAFTA

The bulk of the quantitative evidence on the economic impacts of NAFTA consists of computable general equilibrium (CGE) models at the overall macroeconomic level or at the level of specific industries. Before reviewing the results, it is worth making several general observations about CGE models:

1. The available models were constructed and estimated, for the most part, prior to the actual details of NAFTA being released. To the extent that the assump-

tions underlying the models differ from the reality of the Agreement, the models' forecasts may need to be modified;

2. The models make assumptions about "exogenous" capital flows. To the extent that the assumptions are conservative, the impact of trade liberalization on income levels will be understated;

3. Most of these models do not incorporate changes in efficiency associated with increased competition and other manifestations of free trade. Again, ignoring these factors is likely to understate the income gains from free trade;

4. The models focus on manufacturing activities. While this is the sector where the elimination of trade restrictions will be primarily focused, there will be some liberalization in specific service sector activities, as noted above, which could add to the gains from trade;

5. The models incorporate import and export elasticities of demand that may or may not be reliable. To the extent that the elasticities used are biased downward, the impacts of NAFTA will again be understated.

Results From Macro Models

In short, the results of CGE models are more likely to understate than to overstate the impacts of NAFTA on the trading partners and, especially, Mexico. Bearing this disclaimer in mind, aggregate macroeconomic models support the notion that Mexico is likely to realize significant overall gains from trade liberalization, whereas the impacts on Canada and the United States will be trivial.

Many of the major studies are summarized in an article by Brown, Deardorff, and Stern.[14] The studies reviewed provide estimates of the impact of NAFTA on the overall percentage change in real income. The review concludes that there are fairly small welfare gains associated with bilateral and trilateral tariff removal. Even the welfare gain to Mexico is generally less than 0.5 percent of Gross National Product (GNP).

The impacts of removing nontariff barriers (NTBs) are more significant. Restrictions on foreign direct investment also seem to be an important source of welfare loss for Mexico. Specifically, comparatively small welfare gains from trade liberalization show much larger gains when physical capital in the form of foreign direct investment is assumed to flow freely into Mexico. For example, the income gains to Mexico given the elimination of nontariff barriers and barriers to inward direct investment increase to between 4 and 7 percent of GNP.

The bulk of the studies reviewed by Brown, Deardorff, and Stern conclude that the projected income gains to Canada and the United States amount to less than one percent of their respective GNPs. Several studies for the United States find a still relatively small income gain of up to 2 percent of GNP.

Existing studies also focus on the distributional effects of free trade. The expectation from the Stolper-Samuelson Theorem is that at least one factor of production will lose from NAFTA. The specific expectation in the Canadian and American cases is that the unskilled labor force will be the group most affected negatively by the Agreement. It should be noted that the Stolper-Samuelson Theorem ignores considerations such as changes in overall efficiency, as well as changes in a country's terms of trade which can lead to all factors of production gaining from free trade.

In fact, available studies suggest that the employment and wage impacts on unskilled workers in the United States may be positive or, at least, not negative.[15] The explanation is that other factors may offset the influence of increased (indirect) competition from unskilled workers in Mexico. In particular, the United States is expected to benefit from improved terms of trade (since it currently has lower tariffs than Mexico) which increases the demand for domestic labor. Improved efficiency in domestic industries also augments returns to all factors of production.

Whatever the overall impact of NAFTA on the distribution of

income in the United States and Canada, virtually all of the available evidence suggests that any changes will be relatively small.[16] The evidence is less clear-cut for Mexico where concerns have been expressed that NAFTA will lead to increased concentrations of income; however, the experience of Asian countries has been that export-led growth has contributed to increased equality in the distribution of income, and it seems plausible to conjecture the same will be true in the long-run for Mexico.[17]

Industry Studies

Concerns have also been expressed about differences across industries in the impacts of a NAFTA which could give rise to decreases in incomes and employment in specific industries or specific regions of the country, thereby necessitating trade adjustment programs. A review of the evidence on the impacts of NAFTA for specific industries is discussed below; however, it is unlikely that the small economy-wide effects identified for the United States and Canada are artifacts of an averaging of large positive and negative effects across industries. Moreover, evidence suggests that the bulk of the adjustments to trade liberalization take place within industries in the form of increased intraindustry trade.[18] This is likely to mitigate the displacement of specific factors of production from increased imports. Furthermore, the removal of tariffs over the relatively long time span of ten to fifteen years gives participants in affected industries time to adjust.

Transportation equipment is the single largest category in trilateral trade flows. Hence, evidence bearing upon NAFTA's impact on this industry is quite relevant. One CGE model of the assembly sector of the automobile industry suggests that Mexican consumers will be the major beneficiaries of economic integration in this sector, as inefficient plants close down and access to lower cost autos increases. There is a modest expansion of the assembly sector in the United States with the assembly sector in Canada, if anything, contracting marginally.[19]

A related CGE model focuses on both assembly and parts operations.[20] The authors conclude that assembling in Mexico by the Big Three will almost double, while it will increase slightly in the United States and decrease slightly in Canada. Counterbalancing this will be decreases by foreign firms in assembling in Mexico and the United States and increases in Canada. They also predict that Mexican production of parts will increase while production of engines will decrease. Parts production will decrease marginally in Canada and increase marginally in the United States. Engine production will increase by about 7 percent in the United States and by about 15 percent in Canada.

It might be argued that the CGE studies cited above do not reflect the more stringent North American content rules embodied in NAFTA compared to those in the U.S.-Canadian FTA. In particular, the higher domestic content requirements might affect the investment decisions of non-North American firms as well as their operations. Such changes would presumably affect the economic performances of the domestic industries of NAFTA members.

One possibility is that Japanese and other off-shore producers will increase their investments in North America in order to satisfy the higher domestic content requirements. Another is that they may find it unprofitable to make the incremental investments needed to satisfy the content requirements and (indeed) might move some North American operations "back home." To the extent that third country investors withdraw capacity from the North American industry, the increased domestic content levels could reinforce the protection afforded to domestic producers by existing tariffs. One possible consequence is that increases in the levels of efficiency contemplated by available CGE models may not materialize. Furthermore, the relatively long phase-in period for eliminating Mexican restrictions under the automotive decree might further contribute to smaller efficiency gains for Mexico than contemplated by existing CGE models of the industry.

The impact of NAFTA content requirements may also be geographically nonneutral. For example, Canada might be relatively hard hit by a reduction in capacity of Asian automobile assemblers and parts manufacturers given the elimination of duty drawback provisions. On the other hand, clarification of how the rules of origin are to be applied arguably reduces the uncertainty that producers in Canada, such as Honda, face in exporting to the United States. This latter consideration should make Canada a more attractive location for non-North American investors, all other things constant.

In summary, existing CGE models suggest that the major adjustments in the transportation equipment sector will be intraindustry in nature. That is, increased specialization will take place within the industry along national lines. This assertion is supported by a non-CGE study which concludes that Mexico will specialize in entry-level cars and trucks for the North American market, while Canadian and U.S. plants will continue to specialize in larger, more expensive vehicles.[21] There is no reason to believe that the actual details of the Agreement undercut this assertion.

The studies also suggest that the major welfare impacts will be experienced by Mexico. Output, employment, and welfare impacts on the United States and Canada will be quite modest, although they are highly leveraged to real income growth rates in Mexico. As noted above, both the forecasted overall economic effects, as well as their distribution across member countries, may be sensitive to the actual details of the Agreement as they apply to the automotive industry.

The results of CGE studies of the steel and textiles industries are broadly similar to those for the automobile and parts sector. Specifically, they show that liberalization in both sectors is jointly advantageous for the United States and Mexico with the majority of the identifiable welfare gains accruing to Mexico.[22] Small welfare losses are identified for Canada. Again, the CGE studies fail to identify changes in intraindustry trade patterns associated with increased specialization within countries. To this extent they may understate the welfare gains from free trade in the sector, in that they ignore efficiency gains associated with increased specialization. In this regard, there is some evidence that FTA has encouraged a significant increase in U.S.-Canadian intraindustry trade in the textiles and apparel sectors, and at least one study suggests that a similar pattern will characterize trilateral trade in these sectors following NAFTA.[23]

Continuing the theme, CGE studies of the agricultural sector conclude that the overall impact on all three countries will be modest. In particular, continuing domestic reforms in Mexico are much more important than NAFTA, per se, while developments in world agricultural markets and continued productivity growth are of dominating importance for the U.S. industry.[24] Increased specialization within the sector is predicted, particularly owing to differences in climatic and geographical conditions across countries; however, even where some substitutability exists between Mexican and U.S. produce, the impact of the Mexican-U.S. liberalization under NAFTA is expected to be modest with the possible exception of a potentially substantial contraction in the Mexican corn sector.

One of the identified advantages of FTA was its encouragement of greater north-south energy flows with an associated rationalization of production and transportation facilities. In particular, efficiencies were expected to result from increased sales of Canadian natural gas and electricity into specific U.S. markets and increased sales of U.S. petroleum and petroleum products and coal into specific Canadian markets. A similar rationalization on a trilateral basis might be hypothesized following the implementation of a NAFTA; however, one observer concludes that the impact of NAFTA on trade in energy commodities is likely to be de minimus given that FTA is already in place, that free trade in energy commodities already largely exists, and that severe restrictions persist in NAFTA on foreign investment in Mexico's energy sector.[25] Increased trilateral trade in petrochemical products along with increased specialization might be expected from NAFTA, although I am unaware of any studies that have attempted to model adjustments in this sector.

Summary of Empirical Findings

In summary, macroeconomic studies of NAFTA conclude that the overall income and employment effects for the United

States and Canada will be absolutely and relatively small, while the impacts will be more pronounced for Mexico. The conclusions with respect to the United States and Canada are somewhat sensitive to assumed Mexican real income growth rates. In relation, the results for Mexico tend to be quite sensitive to assumed rates of direct investment into that country. In this regard, provisions in NAFTA maintaining restrictions on foreign direct investment in Mexico's oil and gas sector should, on the margin, reduce the flow of inward direct investment compared to what might be expected had those restrictions been eliminated.

Individual industry studies tend to support conclusions drawn from aggregate studies in identifying Mexico as being most significantly impacted by NAFTA, albeit with relatively modest welfare consequences. They also identify increased intraindustry trade as an expected consequence of free trade. Depending upon the assumptions one makes about economies of scale from increased product specialization, at the margin, existing macroeconomic and industry-level CGE studies may underestimate the efficiency gains from increased intraindustry trade, either because they are too aggregated to identify the phenomenon or because they ignore or understate these economies.

One might therefore infer that any adverse distributional consequences and the deadweight losses associated with income redistribution schemes to compensate for those consequences will be relatively small, at least in the United States and Canada.

Implications For Services

It must again be emphasized that existing empirical studies focus on agriculture, natural resources, and (especially) manufacturing—both because trade data are readily available for these sectors and also (presumably) because direct trade in services is fairly limited to date. Ignoring the service industries could be potentially important given that service sector employment accounts for approximately 75 percent of total employment in the United States and Canada.

Given the fact that many services must be produced "on site," resource reallocations across countries and within industries will be associated with increased direct investment by service sector companies. As noted earlier, NAFTA arguably improves the investment regime in North America; however, many service industries are exempted from NAFTA investment provisions. Within the nonexempted sectors, increased direct investment might stimulate increased incomes in the "conventional" ways—by encouraging increased specialization in accordance with patterns of comparative advantage and by encouraging improved efficiency within domestic industries.

Since international production patterns of MNEs reflect firm-specific advantages at least as much, if not more, than country-specific advantages, the former impact is likely to be more relevant within the service sector than the latter. That is, foreign direct investment by service companies is likely to promote improved efficiency in host country service sectors as more efficient foreign-owned firms pressure domestic-owned firms to improve their efficiency.

One can only speculate about the magnitude and nature of production rationalization in nonexempt service industries pursuant to the implementation of a NAFTA. One would again expect the major impacts to be experienced by Mexico given the substantial barriers to inward direct investment that have characterized the Mexican economy; however, a substantial increase in demand for specific services could improve the terms of trade for American and Canadian producers with resulting income gains. In the short run, the latter impacts are unlikely to be substantial.

Implications For The Environment

Arguably the most contentious issue surrounding NAFTA is the magnitude of the deadweight costs associated with greater environmental damage. It is impossible in this chapter to provide a comprehensive evaluation of the theory and evidence surrounding this issue, although several brief points might be made[26]. One is that many forms of pollution decrease as income levels rise which reflects a positive income elasticity of demand for a cleaner environment and increased tax revenue for public sector enforcement of environmental legislation. A second is that costs associated with environmental regulations have hitherto been a relatively small share of all business costs in North America, and they do not appear to have influenced the locational decisions of firms affected except, perhaps, in the case of mining and metal fabricating.

It must be acknowledged that some forms of pollution, for example carbon dioxide emissions and solid wastes, tend to increase monotonically with real income levels. To this extent, if NAFTA encourages faster real economic growth, particularly in Mexico, there will be an intensification of some forms of pollution, other things constant. Moreover, if the United States and Canada move to impose substantially higher costs of environmental regulation on domestic businesses, the resulting mobility of investment to Mexico might be greater than one would predict based upon past experience.

Impacts On Multilateral Trade Environment

It is also not possible to consider the potential impact of a NAFTA on multilateral trade relations and, especially, on trade relations with the European Community and the Asia-Pacific countries. Some observers have expressed concern that there will be substantial trade and investment diversion associated with NAFTA which will provoke even greater trade friction among the Triad. If NAFTA were to contribute to increased trade intervention by European and Asian governments, the resulting deadweight costs for the United States and Canada could well exceed any income gains associated with NAFTA.

Other observers argue that trade and investment diversion associated with a NAFTA, per se, will be relatively small. Moreover, the threat of other countries acceding to NAFTA might stimulate recalcitrant bargainers at the GATT Uruguay Round (and any later rounds) to show some flexibility in their bargaining positions. Indeed, the stumbling bloc issues at the Uruguay Round are in no obvious way linked to the recent proliferation of regional trade agreements.

Conclusions and Policy Implications

It should be underscored that NAFTA does not call for free trade. It is shot full of protectionist exemptions and unseemly long periods before many tariffs are actually eliminated. As the small, open economy not yet within a free trade area, Mexico stands to experience the largest income gains from NAFTA and will also undergo the greatest industrial restructuring. Small income gains can be expected for the United States and Canada; however, the potential for upside surprises exists. Moreover, NAFTA arguably improves upon certain features of FTA which may reduce trade frictions and promote increased cross-border direct investment in service industries.

Large adverse income effects for unskilled American and Canadian workers, a fear which underpins many objections to NAFTA, may not materialize, or may be relatively modest. In any event, increasing competition from developing countries such as China, India, and Russia will continue to depress wages and employment prospects for low-skilled workers in developed countries. Another bogeyman of NAFTA opponents, greater environmental damage, may also be a chimera. Indeed, trade liberalization might itself promote greater expenditures on environmental protection and remediation.

Given the initial stance of the Clinton administration towards NAFTA, the main policy issue would seem to be whether and to what extent explicit or implicit harmonization of labor codes and environmental practices should be institutionalized in a "parallel" agreement. Again, a full consideration of this issue is beyond the scope of this chapter; however, it must be stressed that NAFTA is ostensibly about trade liberalization, not economic and political integration along the lines of the European Community.

Current critics of NAFTA, including President Clinton,

clearly have in mind a harmonization of labor codes and environmental practices presumably closer to U.S. standards.[27] Any "forced" harmonization will arguably be nonoptimal for one or more of the trading partners, or they would have voluntarily implemented those standards before. Hence, making the trade agreement contingent on some form of convergence or harmonization in these areas jeopardizes the Agreement itself, since, at some point, the welfare losses to Mexico associated with convergence or harmonization will exceed the benefits of the underlying trade agreement. Moreover, to the extent that convergence or harmonization is designed to equilibrate costs of production across borders for specific industries, it reduces the potential gains from trade by reducing the incentives for trade.

Perhaps most important, an insistence on convergence or harmonization in these two areas establishes a potential principle that any difference in national laws or regulations can be grounds for an appeal against "unfair" trade practices. The U.S. trade process is already highly corrupted by the politicization of trade laws and policy.[28] The rent-seeking behavior that has characterized the antics of trade lobbyists for a growing number of U.S. industries will receive further encouragement by an institutionalization of the notion that differences in legislation governing such things as unlawful dismissal, rights of striking workers, emissions standards, and the like are fundamental trade issues. This new fertile area for protectionist initiatives would pose a serious added risk factor to the already fragile liberalized trade environment.

Notes

1. For example, it has been reported that President Clinton wants more money spent on environmental clean-ups and a trinational environmental protection commission with powers to prevent and cleanup pollution. See "A Glance at the Clock," *The Economist*, 16 January 1993.

2. For an extensive discussion of the NAFTA along with an assessment of its economic implications, see the papers in Steven Globerman and Michael Walker, eds., *Assessing NAFTA: A Trinational Analysis* (Vancouver: The Fraser Institute, 1993). See also Gary Hufbauer and Jeffrey Schott, *North*

American Free Trade: Issues and Recommendations (Washington, D.C.: Institute For International Economics, 1992).

3. For details on the NAFTA as it affects the automotive sector, see Jon R. Johnson, "NAFTA and the Trade in Automotive Goods," in Globerman and Walker, 87–129.

4. Details on the Agreement as they relate to the textile and apparel industry are found in Eric Barry and Elizabeth Siwicki, "NAFTA: The Textile and Apparel Sector," in Globerman and Walker, 130–47.

5. A comprehensive overview of rules of origin is provided in Peter Morici, "NAFTA Rules of Origin and Automotive Content Requirements," in Globerman and Walker, 226–50.

6. See Gilbert Winham, "Dispute Settlement in NAFTA and the FTA," in Globerman and Walker, 251–70.

7. For an extensive discussion of the evidence surrounding trade liberalization and production responses, see Steven Globerman, *Trade Liberalization and Imperfectly Competitive Industries: Theory and Evidence* (Ottawa: Supply and Services Canada, 1988).

8. For an overview of the issues here, see Steven Globerman, "Trade Liberalization and the Environment," in Globerman and Walker, 293–314.

9. See Steven Globerman and Maureen Bader, "A Perspective on Trilateral Economic Relations" in Steven Globerman, ed., *Continental Accord: North American Economic Integration* (Vancouver: The Fraser Institute, 1991) 153–74.

10. See Roy G. Boyd, Kerry Krutilla, and Joseph McKinney, "The Impact of Tariff Liberalization Between the United States and Mexico: An Empirical Analysis," *Applied Economics* 25 (1993): 81–89.

11. See Alan Rugman and Michael Gestrin, "The Investment Provisions of the NAFTA" in Globerman and Walker, 271–92.

12. Contrast, for example, the estimates in Horacio E. Sobarzo, "A General Equilibrium Analysis of the Gains from Trade for the Mexican Economy of a North American Free Trade Agreement," *The World Economy* 15 (January 1992): 83–100 and Rogelio Ramirez de la O, "A Mexican Vision of North American Economic Integration," in Steven Globerman, *Continental Accord,* 1–30.

13. See Gene Grossman and Alan Krueger, "Environmental Impacts of a North American Free Trade Agreement," presented at a conference on the U.S.-Mexico free trade agreement, Princeton University, October 1991.

14. See Drusilla Brown, Alan Deardorff, and Robert Stern, "North American Integration," *The Economic Journal* (November 1992): 1507–18.

15. Ibid. In support of the conclusion that the impacts are likely to be negative and significant, see E. E. Leamer, "Wage Effects of a U.S-Mexican Free Trade Agreement," NBER Working Paper 3991 (Cambridge, Mass., 1992).

16. For a very recent study using a CGE model which reinforces this

conclusion for the United States, see Roy G. Boyd, Kerry Krutilla, and Joseph McKinney, "The Impact of Tariff Liberalization Between the United States and Mexico: An Empirical Analysis," *Applied Economics* 25 (1993): 81–89.

17. For a discussion of the potential impacts of NAFTA on the distribution of income in Mexico, see Diana Alarcon, "Trade Liberalization and Income Distribution in Mexico," El Colegio De La Frontera Norte, mimeo, 1992.

18. Some evidence that this has also been the case to date with respect to U.S.-Mexican bilateral trade is provided in Steven Globerman, "North American Trade Liberalization and Intra-Industry Trade," *Weltwirtschaftliches Archiv* 128, no. 3 (1992): 487–97.

19. See Linda Hunter, James Markusen, and Thomas Rutherford, "U.S.-Mexico Free Trade and the North American Auto Industry: Effects on Spatial Organization of Production of Finished Autos," *The World Economy* 15 (1992).

20. See Florencio Lopez-de-Silanes, James Markusen, and Thomas Rutherford, "The Auto Industry and the North American Free Trade Agreement: Employment, Production and Welfare Effects" (Cambridge: National Bureau of Economic Research, mimeo, September 1992).

21. See James P. Womack, D. T. Jones, and D. Roos, *The Machine That Changed The World* (Cambridge: MIT Press, 1990).

22. See Irene Trela and John Whalley, "Bilateral Trade Liberalization in Quota Restricted Items: U.S. and Mexico in Textiles and Steel," *The World Economy* 15 (January 1992).

23. See Eric Barry and Elizabeth Siwicki, "NAFTA: The Textile and Apparel Sector," in Globerman and Walker, 130–47.

24. See International Agricultural Trade Research Consortium, *The Implications of a North American Free Trade Area For Agriculture* (Vancouver: University of British Columbia, mimeo, November 1991) and Thomas Grennes, "Toward a More Open Agriculture in North America," in Globerman and Walker, 148–71.

25. G. C. Watkins, "NAFTA and Energy: A Bridge Not Far Enough?" in Globerman and Walker, 193–225.

26. For one such comprehensive assessment, see Steven Globerman, "The Environmental Impacts of Trade Liberalization," in Terry Anderson, ed., *Trade and the Environment* (San Francisco: Pacific Policy Research Institute, 1993).

27. The establishment of a trinational commission with legal powers to enforce a country's environmental or other legislation, while not strictly speaking harmonization, is a device to ensure that de facto standards in the target country are brought closer into line with those of its trading partners. It would be interesting to know if the U.S. administration would be willing to accept a "highest standards" threshold for harmonization, even when this turned out to be the Canadian standard in specific circumstances.

28. For a seminal discussion of the politicization of U.S. trade policy, see Alan Rugman and Andrew Anderson, *Administered Protection in America*, (Routledge: London and New York, 1987).

Chapter 2

THE POLITICS OF NAFTA

Susan W. Liebeler

Introduction

On 17 December 1992 the United States, Canada, and Mexico signed a landmark free trade pact. Building on the 1989 U.S.-Canadian Free Trade Agreement (FTA), the North American Free Trade Agreement (NAFTA) will create a $6.5 trillion market of 360 million people.

NAFTA is scheduled to go into effect on 1 January 1994—subject to ratification by the legislatures in all three countries. In Canada, the Agreement passed through Parliament in June 1993 and awaits royal assent. In Mexico NAFTA is before the Senate where passage is assured. In the United States, however, the Congressional approval process is complicated by the changing U.S. political landscape.

NAFTA was negotiated by a Republican administration which claimed to be committed to free trade. President Bush signed the Agreement shortly before leaving office; it has not yet been approved by Congress. Then-candidate Clinton expressed both support for NAFTA and concern that environmental, labor, and safeguard issues needed further attention.

If President Clinton means to requite his campaign support for NAFTA, he must convince Congress to approve it by implementing legislation. This task is made more difficult by the administration's relative lack of focus on trade policy and by a decidedly more protectionist attitude in Congress.

Before discussing the political aspects of NAFTA approval in

See below, p. 317, for an addendum to this chapter.

the United States, this chapter will review both the system by which trade agreements are negotiated and implemented in the United States and the U.S. postwar experience with tariff reduction and nontariff barriers. Finally the various political obstacles which must be overcome by the Clinton administration to secure Congressional approval of NAFTA will be examined.

The U.S. Trade Policy Process

In order to appreciate the difficulty of the task facing the Clinton administration, it is important to understand how U.S. trade agreements have been negotiated.[1] Trade agreements have historically involved reductions in U.S. tariffs in exchange for similar tariff concessions by our trading partners. Typically Congress delegated authority to negotiate trade agreements to the executive branch, subject to specified percentage limitations on the amount of reductions in U.S. tariffs. Since tariff reductions did not require legislative change, the president could implement the trade agreement by presidential proclamation. This system gave our trading partners confidence the deal they made would not be unraveled in Congress.

As trade negotiations began to focus on other barriers, the Congressional authorization process became more complicated. Unlike tariff negotiating authority which could easily be defined and limited by specific percentages, there was no simple way for Congress to provide the president advance authority to negotiate reductions of nontariff barriers (NTBs) and furnish assurance that what was promised our trading partners would actually become law. In the 1974 Trade Act Congress and the executive branch devised special delegation and legislative procedures, known as fast-track, under which the executive branch could enter into trade agreements covering NTBs and submit implementing legislation to Congress. Under the current negotiating authority, after consulting with the relevant Congressional committees, the president must give Congress at least ninety days notice before signing a trade agreement on NTBs.[2] Once the Agreement is signed, Congress has sixty days to act on the implementing legislation under rules limiting debate and prohibiting committee or floor amendments.[3]

Congress has given the executive branch fast-track authorizations through a series of successive statutes. In the 1988 Omnibus Trade and Competitiveness Act Congress extended the executive branch's fast-track authority to cover the Uruguay Round as well as bilateral negotiations. NAFTA was negotiated and signed prior to the 31 May 1992 expiration of the existing fast-track negotiating authority.[4]

Since the disastrous experience with the protectionist Smoot-Hawley tariffs of the 1930s, the United States has been party to a series of multilateral and bilateral trade negotiations aimed at expanding trade. Since its founding in 1947, substantial trade liberalization has been accomplished through the General Agreement on Tariffs and Trade (GATT). The GATT, based in Geneva, has grown from 23 to approximately 110 members who account for roughly 80 percent of all international trade. As a result of the seven previous rounds of negotiations, members' average tariff rates have fallen sharply from around 40 percent to about 4 percent. Not surprisingly, with tariff rates bound at fairly low levels, those demanding protection turned to NTBs.

Nontariff Barriers to Trade

A number of studies have shown substantial increases in the use of NTBs by developed countries.[5] For example, a 1988 World Bank Study found that from 1966 to 1986 the share of major developed countries' trade covered by NTBs had nearly doubled to 48 percent.[6] According to the Centre for International Economics, the protection afforded by NTBs could be as much as four to five times that of tariffs.[7] Perhaps most striking is a study by David Tarr for the Federal Trade Commission, which concluded the proliferation of NTBs on steel, automobiles, and textiles made the U.S. economy less open than it was in 1946.[8]

NTBs often take the form of "voluntary" quantitative restrictions, imposed through negotiations under the threat of other restrictions. NTBs can also take the form of standards, licensing requirements, content requirements, prohibitions and restrictions on foreign investment, and a thousand other forms. Sometimes these rules serve legitimate purposes but often they do not. They are sly and hidden ways of protecting parochial interests.

NTBs are far worse than the tariffs they replaced. Although tariffs are generally applied equally to imports from all countries, NTBs are usually imposed in a discriminatory manner. For example, with quantitative restrictions, each exporting country is usually assigned an explicit amount. The most pernicious aspect of NTBs is their lack of transparency. Unlike tariffs, which have a direct and obvious impact on purchasers, NTBs are hidden taxes—their effects are often difficult to quantify and can be well concealed.

Since World War II there has been a move toward an integrated trading world. Open markets benefit all nations, and the more open the markets the greater the benefit. The Centre for International Economics in Australia found that by reducing tariffs and NTBs by 50 percent, the world stands to gain nearly three quarters of a trillion dollars each year.[9] This would be an increase in real wealth: cutting trade restraints in half would increase world incomes by 5 percent per year. Yet this gain is unlikely to be realized in the near future; the trend in certain highly developed countries is towards increased protection, not away from it, especially in the European Community (E.C.) and the United States, the two largest economies where NTBs are proliferating.

Market Reforms in Mexico and Developing Countries

It is ironic that the proponents of free trade have been losing ground in the United States while they are having some of their biggest successes internationally. In the international arena it has become abundantly clear that although there are many ways of organizing an economic system, the one which provides the highest standard of living also provides the most freedom—the market economy. Accordingly, nations are turning away from centrally planned economic systems to more open ones.

The biggest success is Eastern Europe. After suffering under communism's yoke for forty-five years, the nations of Eastern Europe are throwing open their economies to foreign investment and trade in an attempt to achieve the kind of economic prosperity enjoyed in the West.

Another example is Mexico, which suffered many years of rampant inflation and lackluster economic growth under a highly regulated, closed economy—until it recently turned to trade liberalization. Since 1986 Mexico has been opening its borders by lowering tariffs,[10] cutting its average tariff rate from 40 to 10 percent, and eliminating import licenses for most products. With surprising speed, Mexico reduced tariffs, trade barriers, and restrictions on foreign investment; controlled inflation; lowered taxes; and has undertaken the task of reprivatizing government-owned enterprises in key industries—including airlines, mining, telecommunications, and banking. Mexico is liberalizing trade and investment restrictions in order to spur economic growth.

Although Mexico has removed many trade barriers, some restrictions remain. Import licensing requirements still cover about 7 percent of the value of U.S. exports, including auto parts, wood, and wood products. Also, 60 percent of U.S. agricultural exports still require import licenses. Mexico also has discriminatory government procurement policies, standards, testing, and certification requirements, and limited intellectual property protection in certain areas. Often the import licensing, testing, and certification procedures are unclear. There are also restrictions and barriers applicable to particular sectors or specific commodities such as the automotive, computer, and pharmaceutical industries. The average Mexican tariff is 2.5 times higher than the average tariff in the United States and tariff rates as high as 20 percent still protect certain Mexican products including beer and beverages, tobacco products, home appliances, and automobiles. Foreign investment is still restricted in certain industries, especially the energy sector. The United States also has tariff and nontariff barriers. These are used to protect producers of agricultural products, steel, machine tools, textiles and apparel, trucks, and if the U.S. auto industry accomplishes its desire, minivans would be added to the list.

The Rationale for NAFTA

NAFTA negotiations presented an excellent opportunity to eliminate these tariffs and barriers to trade and investment. The Agreement makes considerable progress in reducing tariff and barriers to trade, but in some cases the tariffs and barriers will not disappear for another ten or fifteen years. In addition, in many cases NAFTA establishes new rules of origin imposing high North American content requirements on goods which can be sold duty free in North America. For example—for autos, light trucks, and engines—the North American content requirement, calculated on a net cost basis, is 56 percent beginning in 1998 and 62.5 percent beginning in 2002.[11] In a few cases, an entire industry was exempted from NAFTA and trade barriers remain.[12]

If the benefits from free trade are so enormous, why then does NAFTA not immediately provide it? The answer is while free trade increases total wealth, it does so unevenly. Workers and industries which will not fare well under increased competition invested time and money to protect their position. NAFTA represents a political compromise among the competing interests of exporting firms seeking greater access to the North American market and import-competing domestic firms seeking to protect and expand their share of the domestic market. Thus, NAFTA is not perfect and is by no means a full free trade arrangement. It does, however, provide for freer trade and removes many NTBs to investment and trade. NAFTA immediately eliminates many tariffs, offers new trade and investment opportunities, and opens Mexico's government procurement and services market. It also provides for increased intellectual property protection throughout North America. One can anticipate substantial economic benefits to the entire North American region through a more efficient allocation of resources.

There have been numerous studies of the effects of NAFTA.[13]

Most have concluded it will result in net aggregate gains to all three countries. From a U.S. perspective, the studies predict net gains in U.S. exports and aggregate employment and positive effects on real gross domestic product (GDP) and national income. For example, a study by the Institute for International Economics predicts that by 1995 NAFTA will create a net gain of over 130,000 U.S. jobs (242,000+; 107,000-); a doubling of U.S. exports to Mexico from $25 to $58.6 billion; creation of 609,000 new jobs in Mexico; and an 8.7 percent rise in real wages for Mexican workers.[14]

The Politics of NAFTA

Although NAFTA will provide net benefits to the North American region, and in particular to Mexico and the United States, some industries will not prosper under NAFTA. Freer trade means there will be adjustment costs to owners and workers in these industries. Not surprisingly, there is strong and well-organized opposition to NAFTA by special interests in industries which will not fare well under competition.

When focussing on the political aspects of NAFTA, it becomes obvious that the political and economic aspects are intertwined. Those who have something to gain by suppressing import competition will use any argument they can to defeat or dilute the Agreement.

Many opponents have overstated the likely impact of NAFTA by predicting that scores of U.S. factories will close their doors and move south where they can minimize pollution abatement costs and exploit low-cost Mexican workers. In the 1992 U.S. presidential debates, Ross Perot predicted a "giant sucking sound" as U.S. jobs are siphoned into Mexico.

These claims are clearly exaggerated. If lower wages and lax environmental enforcement guaranteed competitive advantages, Detroit would be complaining that India, not Japan, is dumping cars in the United States. Although German salaries are much higher than salaries in Portugal, one does not see firms fleeing Hamburg for Lisbon. In the case of Mexico, a substantial percentage of Mexican exports already enter the United States duty free under the Generalized System of Preferences (GSP)[15] or through the Maquiladora programs, while the rest enter at low duty rates. Yet U.S. firms have not engaged in wide-scale relocation of factories and jobs to escape U.S. environmental regulations and high labor rates. Many other factors contribute to competitiveness, including technology, infrastructure, the skill and education of the work force, and productivity.

Opponents of NAFTA are lobbying the U.S. Congress, raising a variety of labor and environmental concerns. Several Congressional leaders have indicated their opposition to NAFTA unless adequate provision is made to protect American workers and address environmental problems. Senators Max Baucus (D-Mont.) and Daniel P. Moynihan (D-N.Y), House Majority Leader Richard A. Gephardt (D-Mo.), and other Congressional leaders have suggested assessing a user fee on goods and investments crossing the border to finance border environmental cleanup.

The Side Agreements

As a candidate and as president, Clinton indicated his support for NAFTA provided it is accompanied by side agreements covering environmental and labor matters and import surges. Clinton also pledged to provide increased adjustment assistance and training programs for U.S. workers adversely affected by NAFTA. These side agreements are encapsulated below.

Environment.   Environmental concerns are particularly useful issues for special interests opposed to freer trade. These special interest groups claim that U.S. firms will rush to Mexico where they can freely pollute and ruin the global environment. Mexican environmental laws and regulations are similar to U.S. and Canadian ones, but their enforcement is not up to U.S. and Canadian standards. NAFTA is unique among trade agreements in that it contains several environmental provisions. It preserves existing national and international requirements and reserves to the parties the power to maintain or adopt more stringent safety and environmental regulations, as long as the requirements are not discriminatory and have a scientific basis.[16] In addition the parties agree not to lower health, safety, or environmental standards to attract investment. Finally, the signatories promise to work jointly to protect the environment and human, animal, and plant life and health. In response to environmental concerns, the United States and Mexico conducted parallel environmental negotiations alongside NAFTA negotiations. In 1992 these parallel efforts resulted in a U.S.-Mexico joint environmental plan whereby the U.S. government pledged $379 million and the Mexican government $466 million for environmental cleanup along the border.

An environmental side agreement is unnecessary. NAFTA is the ''greenest'' trade agreement to date, and it will improve the environment by encouraging Mexican prosperity. As incomes rise, Mexican citizens will prefer cleaner air and water and many types of pollution will decrease. In addition, increased tax revenue will permit the Mexican government to increase environmental enforcement. Finally, NAFTA is designed to lower tariffs and trade barriers. An environmental tax on imports is equivalent to raising tariffs and would inhibit rather than enhance trade. It would also increase transaction costs on GSP or Maquiladora imports which currently are not taxed.

Labor.   There is no need for a labor sidebar to provide additional protection or adjustment assistance for American workers. Mexico already has strong labor laws which are comparable to those in the United States and Canada, although Mexico's enforcement is not up to U.S. or Canadian standards.

As for the need for additional adjustment assistance, the United States can spend whatever it wants on adjustment assistance; it does not need an international agreement to undertake job retraining programs. In any case, NAFTA has built-in adjustment mechanisms for workers in import-sensitive industries: a gradual phaseout of tariffs and trade barriers.[17] Indeed, for some sensitive industries, such as sugar, the tariff reduction transition period is fifteen years.[18] Thus, many of the U.S. workers who will be adversely affected by NAFTA are in junior high school.[19] In addition, NAFTA does not affect any party's unfair trade laws. If a NAFTA signatory were to dump cheap imports into the United States, U.S. workers and firms can petition for antidumping duties under U.S. trade laws.

The Clinton administration claims the labor and environmental side pacts are an opportunity to harmonize environmental and labor standards. The labor proposals call for Mexico to adopt U.S. labor, safety, and health standards; to copy U.S. rules for trade unions; to upgrade Mexico's pay scales; and otherwise adopt the U.S. labor agenda. Yet, specialization and comparative advantage would seem to suggest harmonizing labor and environmental standards is not efficient. If higher or different labor standards were efficient for Mexico, they would already have adopted them. Each country has certain comparative advantages and cheaper labor is Mexico's. Harmonizing labor standards would reduce the incentives and gains from trade.

Such differences in labor and environmental laws should not be viewed as trade issues. Protectionists will seize the opportunity to complain about these differences in an attempt to defeat NAFTA. In addition, it is not clear the United States has optimal labor and environmental regulations. Harmonization suggests the United States would pass along the bad as well as the good features of the U.S. regulatory scheme. For example, many economists and policymakers believe private causes of action for failure to meet government standards are a bad idea. Yet the United States is already pressing Mexico and Canada to accord private parties the right to bring litigation to address environmental problems.

Safeguards.   Promising a side pact to provide additional protection from import surges was another bad idea. Safeguards provide for temporary tariffs or import relief when imports increase too rapidly, thereby providing the affected industry more time to adjust and in some cases more time to accomplish an orderly withdrawal from the industry. Safeguards were developed as a political expedient to soften opposition to trade liberalization from import-sensitive industries. These political compromises are never efficient. Import protection is addicting and causes firms to postpone painful adjustments. Industries become competitive by competing, not by gaining additional protection from imports.

NAFTA already contains adequate safeguard provisions which permit a party to take bilateral safeguard action during the NAFTA tariff reduction transition period. On a particular good the safeguard can only be for three years with one additional year for extremely sensitive goods such as textiles. The safeguard may be either a temporary suspension of further tariff reductions or a snap back to the Most Favored Nation (MFN) rate in effect prior to NAFTA. Compensation in the form of trade concessions is called for if safeguards are utilized. While parties are still permitted to use global safeguard actions under the GATT escape clause, as in the Israel and U.S-Canadian Free Trade Agreements, NAFTA parties will be excluded unless they are one of the top five suppliers of the merchandise by import share during the most recent three year period. Furthermore, imports from a party must be an important cause of serious injury and they will be deemed not to be if their growth rate is lower than the growth rate from all other sources.

Moreover, the United States should not be in the business of encouraging its trading partners to use trade remedies against U.S. exports. The United States is more likely to be the target of safeguard relief than to use it. The United States is the leading exporter into Mexico and many U.S. exports enter Mexico at significant duty rates. On the other hand, the U.S. economy is much larger and more open than that of Mexico and Mexican imports are but a small portion of U.S. total imports. As noted earlier, a large proportion of Mexican imports already enter duty free under GSP or the Maquiladora program. Thus, safeguards are more likely to be used against the United States than vice versa.

Unfortunately, President Clinton seems reluctant to abandon his commitment to negotiate a sidebar on import surges and one can only hope the safeguards side agreement will be innocuous. In May of 1993 U.S. negotiators were considering a proposal for a trilateral NAFTA Safeguards Committee to monitor imports and the use of safeguards. Thus far, the United States has not proposed tightening NAFTA safeguard provision. The U.S. negotiators have indicated they will wait until agreements have been reached on the environmental and labor pacts before presenting Canada and Mexico with a safeguards proposal.

Capturing the Trade Policy Process

Special supplementary NAFTA side pacts are unnecessary. The problem with the side agreements as well as the trilateral commissions is they are likely to be captured by special interests who seek to renegotiate their NAFTA deals. Reopening any one of these arrangements will be an incentive for other industries to complain and attempt to cut a better deal.

The side agreements also raise interesting legal issues. If these side agreements require special implementing legislation, it is unclear whether the implementing legislation can be submitted to Congress under fast-track procedures. Former President Bush signed NAFTA before the expiration of the president's fast-track negotiating authority. The text submitted to Congress did not contain sidebar agreements, but it did include the president's report on labor and environmental issues, as requested by Congress. Arguably, new side pacts will require an extension of fast-track negotiating authority or sidebar implementing legislation will be considered by Congress under its normal rules.

If Congress can attach any number of riders and amendments to sidebar legislation, the side pacts could become the vehicles for unraveling NAFTA. The Clinton administration will try to avoid this thorny legal issue by including any sidebar legislation within the general NAFTA implementing legislation which it plans to submit to Congress in August of 1993.

The Side Agreement Negotiations

As part of its negotiating strategy the Clinton administration promised it will deliver strong side pacts which would make NAFTA acceptable to Congress. Of course, Mexico and Canada may not agree to such agreements and tough negotiations may take place during the summer of 1993.

The Clinton administration promised to deliver sidebars with strong trilateral environmental and labor commissions, yet vacillated on whether the commissions should have the power to issue subpoenas or impose trade sanctions. The U.S. Trade Ambassador Mickey Kantor first testified in favor of a North American Commission on the Environment which would monitor and investigate environmental problems and report regularly. Initially Kantor testified that the commission should not have enforcement or subpoena power. After floating a series of trial balloons on sanctions and subpoena power, the Clinton administration decided not to seek subpoena power for the commissions but to insist on giving them power to issue trade sanctions for persistent violations of laws protecting workers and the environment.

In May of 1993 the United States tabled a proposal for trilateral environmental and labor commissions which would not have subpoena power but would have the power to impose trade sanctions. The U.S. proposal would permit private individuals and nongovernmental organizations to petition the commissions for an investigation. If a commission finds persistent violations of environmental or labor laws, it can send the issue to an arbitration panel if two of the three countries agree. If the arbiters affirm the charges of persistent violations, the other two countries would have the power to impose trade sanctions. Not surprisingly, Mexico and Canada oppose giving enforcement power to a trilateral authority as an intrusion on national sovereignty. They are concerned that new trade sanctions will be used as a trade barrier against them and will be captured by special interests in the United States. Canadian International Trade Minister Michael Wilson has suggested as a compromise that the trilateral commissions might issue fines against individual companies instead of trade sanctions. In addition, Mexico and Canada are reluctant to permit employees, unions, and other private organizations to petition the trinational tribunals without the support of their government.

Anti-NAFTA Forces

The Clinton administration faces an uphill battle in getting NAFTA through Congress. Well-organized NAFTA opponents have orchestrated an effective anti-NAFTA campaign. Presidential candidates Ross Perot and Jerry Brown opposed the Agreement and Ross Perot continued his NAFTA-trashing through television appearances and specials. Perot and others often refer to a highly suspect study by Pat Choate to the effect that NAFTA will jeopardize 5.9 million U.S. jobs. This unscientific claim is derived by counting all U.S. jobs in which labor costs account for at least 20 percent of total costs and in which wages exceed seven dollars per hour. Perot never explains why this job flight has not already occurred, why it will not occur without NAFTA, or why the United States would be worse off if U.S. firms locate offshore assembly or production facilities in Mexico rather than Asia.

On 13 May 1993 twenty-four members of the House of Representatives formed an anti-NAFTA caucus, announcing they will not support NAFTA no matter what the side pacts contain. Organized labor has also been a consistent critic and has worked hard to defeat the pact. In the November 1992 elections, the AFL-CIO reportedly conditioned financial support to several Congressional candidates on their willingness to oppose NAFTA. In May 1993 the AFL-CIO launched a "nix it or fix it" advertising campaign to pressure President Clinton to abandon or renegotiate the Agreement signed by former President Bush.

During the first one hundred days of the Clinton administration NAFTA opponents gained ground as the administration failed to develop a strategy for getting NAFTA approved by Congress. Representative Robert T. Matsui (D-Calif.), the principal House whip for NAFTA, and other leading NAFTA supporters repeatedly warned that its opponents were ahead and the administration lacked the votes to get NAFTA through Congress. In April 1993 published reports quoted Leon Panetta, office of management and budget director, as stating NAFTA "is dead for now" because it lacks sufficient Congressional votes for approval. Panetta's gloomy prognosis appears to have galvanized the Clinton administration and NAFTA supporters into action.

Pro-NAFTA Forces

The president and his cabinet began to speak out in favor of NAFTA in public speeches and testimony, emphasizing job and export growth as among its positive aspects. In an attempt to preempt Ross Perot's 30 May 1993 televised thirty minute anti-NAFTA "infomercial," the U.S. Council of Economic Advisors Chair Laura Tyson, Labor Secretary Robert Reich, and U.S. Trade Representative (USTR) Mickey Kantor held a joint press conference defending NAFTA on 28 May 1993. Kantor announced the formation of Elected Officials for NAFTA, a bipartisan group of state and local leaders who will work to generate support for NAFTA.

Other pro-NAFTA groups have been organized. The U.S. Alliance for NAFTA, USA-NAFTA, a coalition of state governors, local officials, and over one thousand private firms has established a $2 million budget to promote passage of NAFTA. The Mexican government has hired several Washington firms to lobby for Congressional approval of the Agreement.

As the supporters of NAFTA begin to mobilize, NAFTA critics have responded by attacking NAFTA support groups. For example, the Center for Public Integrity,[20] whose board members include the presidents of the UAW and the AFL-CIO, reported that since 1989 Mexico has spent $25 million in the United States to lobby for fast-track extensions and NAFTA and is likely to spend as much as an additional $10 million in 1993, an amount the Center claims is the largest sum ever spent by a foreign government on one piece of legislation. No sooner did Kantor announce the formation of Elected Officials for NAFTA, then the anti-NAFTA Congressional caucus demanded a General Accounting Office investigation to ensure funds appropriated to USTR are not used to lobby Congress.[21]

Getting NAFTA Through the U.S. Congress

The Clinton administration's strategy for obtaining Congressional approval of NAFTA seems to be based entirely on negotiating strong environmental and labor sidebars. There are several problems with this strategy.

First, by attempting to mollify environmental and labor critics with promises of strong trinational commissions and side pacts, President Clinton reinforced the notion that under NAFTA U.S. firms will flock to Mexico to exploit cheap labor and pollute the environment. So far, the Clinton administration has let the critics set the agenda and allowed the debate to center on jobs. For the most part they have responded by praising NAFTA more for what it is not, than what it is.

President Clinton has not convinced the American people NAFTA is good for them or countered NAFTA critics' highly effective media campaign that NAFTA is bad business. While Ross Perot has reached millions of viewers with his thirty minute national television program on 30 May 1993, the administration's press conference, a somewhat feeble attempt to preempt Perot, did not have the same reach. The administration did not permit reporters to tape it for television or radio.

Unfortunately, more people believe Perot. According to a CNN and *Time Magazine* poll conducted on 26 May and 27 May 1993, only one in four Americans believe NAFTA would create U.S. jobs, while 63 percent think Perot is correct in saying the trade pact would encourage U.S. firm to move jobs to Mexico.

Another problem with the sidebar strategy is that strong side pacts and trinational commissions may alienate NAFTA supporters who fear the side pacts will diminish NAFTA's gains. Many champions of NAFTA are wary of the sidebar negotiations and in particular the U.S. proposals to create strong labor and environmental commissions with power to issue sanctions. The U.S. Chamber of Commerce wrote Ambassador Kantor on 29 April 1993 warning that creation of multinational bureaucracies with enforcement authority to investigate private interests or impose sanctions against private interests would jeopardize its members continued support for NAFTA.

On 28 April 1993 Senate Minority Leader Robert Dole and twenty-six Republican Senate colleagues wrote President Clinton of their willingness to approve NAFTA as is, without any sidebar agreements and cautioned the president against weakening NAFTA through side agreements. In particular, they objected to the creation of trinational commissions with broad investigatory and enforcement powers. On 28 April 1993 eighteen Republic Congressional members wrote President Clinton seeking bipartisan consultation on the sidebar negotiations and raising several questions about the powers of any trinational commissions, the level of public participation, and whether the labor sidebar would require changes in U.S. law. As a follow-up, on 24 May 1993 nine House Republicans, including House Minority Leader Robert Michel (R-Ill.) and Minority Whip Newt Gingrich (R-Ga.), wrote President Clinton to object to the U.S. environmental and labor side pact proposals. They indicated they could not support NAFTA's approval which creates trilateral environmental and labor bureaucracies with little accountability, sweeping mandates, and the ability to impose trade sanctions to compel enforcement of U.S. laws. They also objected to any cross-border transaction tax to fund NAFTA projects by opposing any public works, labor, or environmental projects which are not funded from existing revenues and are exempt from the appropriations process.[22]

President Clinton cannot afford to lose these votes. He needs a simple majority vote in both the House and the Senate. His biggest problem is in the House where approximately 25 percent of the members are undecided. According to a 14 May 1993 survey of Congressional opinion by the Wexler Group for USA-NAFTA, 91 members of the House strongly support NAFTA and another 91 members lean toward supporting NAFTA, while 44 members are opposed, 103 members lean toward opposing NAFTA and 103 are undecided. This means the Clinton administration must win the votes of a substantial number of undecided members.

Conclusion

The president and Ambassador Kantor have a tough job ahead. Appeasing NAFTA's critics with promises of strong side pacts on the environment, labor, and safeguards gave credence to claims that NAFTA would cause massive U.S. job loss and environmental catastrophe. The administration must now refute these claims.

So far President Clinton has kept a relatively low profile on NAFTA and has yet to bring to bear his rather considerable campaign skills to sell Congress and the American people an agreement he did not negotiate and might have done differently or not at all. At the same time, he must take care not to weaken or endanger NAFTA through expansive side pacts. While expansive labor and environmental pacts might please some Congressional critics, such pacts could alienate NAFTA supporters as well as jeopardize the benefits of NAFTA.

Notes

1. For an excellent analysis of the political history of U.S. trade policy, see I. M. Destler, *American Trade Politics,* Institute for International Economics with the Twentieth Century Fund, 2d ed. (1992).

2. 19 U.S. Code §2902.

3. The fast-track procedures under which Congress considers legislation implementing trade agreements are found in 19 U.S. Code §2191.

4. In April 1993 the House Ways and Means Trade Subcommittee approved an extension of the administration's fast-track negotiating authority for the Uruguay Round until 16 April 1994, but increased the required Congressional notification period from 90 to 120 days. As a practical matter, this would mean that the Uruguay Round must be concluded by 15 December 1993.

5. See studies cited in Centre for International Economics, *Western Trade Blocks: Game, Set or Match for Asia-Pacific and the World Economy?* (Australia, 1990) 12.

6. Sam Laird and Alexander J. Yeats, *Trends in Non-tariff Barriers of Developed Countries*, 1966-86 (World Bank, Wash. D.C., 1988).

7. *Western Trade Blocks: Game, Set or Match for Asia-Pacific and the World Economy?* Centre for International Economics, (Australia 1990): 72.

8. David G. Tarr, *A General Equilibrium Analysis of the Welfare and Employment Effects of U.S. Quotas in Textiles, Autos and Steel,* Bureau of

Economics Staff Report to the Federal Trade Commission, (Washington, D.C., 1989) This report uses a computable general equilibrium (CGE) model to estimate the costs to the U.S. economy, which in a CGE model are the same as costs to U.S. consumers, of import quotas on textiles, steel autos, and apparel in 1984. Tarr finds the combined costs of the three quotas to be equivalent to a general 25 percent tariff on all U.S. imports. This tariff rate is higher than even the average tariff under Smoot-Hawley.

9. Centre for International Economics, 72.

10. Upon joining the GATT, Mexico waived the usual transition period and immediately dropped its tariff barriers.

11. This will supersede lower domestic content requirements in the U.S.-Canadian FTA. The domestic content requirement for refitted or new North American plants which produce autos of a new class, marque, or size and underbody, is reduced to 15 percent for two and five years, respectively, under the North American content requirement.

12. For example, pursuant to the Mexican Constitutional provision reserving ownership of basic energy resources to the state, NAFTA reserves to the Mexican state goods and investments in the oil, gas, refining, petrochemicals, nuclear, and electricity industries. NAFTA does, however, open certain limited downstream activities in some energy sectors to greater foreign investment.

13. For a review of these studies, see *Potential Impact on the U.S. Economy and Selected Industries of the North American Free-Trade Agreement*, USITC Pub. 2596 (January 1993) 2–1 to 2–7.

14. Gary C. Hufbauer and Jeffrey J. Schott, *North American Free Trade: Issues and Recommendations* (Institute for International Economics, Washington D.C., 1992).

15. The Generalized System of Preferences (GSP) describes the temporary tariff preferences industrialized nations afford to a variety of exports of developing countries in order to promote their advancement. The statutes authorizing U.S. participation in the GSP are found at 19 U.S. Code §2461–66. For a discussion of GSP eligibility and withdrawal criteria, see Peter B. Feller, *U.S. Customs and International Trade Guide* §11.07 Matthew Bender (1993).

16. NAFTA provides that in the event of inconsistency between NAFTA and trade obligations set forth in specified international and bilateral environmental agreements, those agreements apply—not NAFTA. The international and bilateral agreements include the Convention on International Trade in Endangered Species, the Montreal Protocol on Ozone Protection, the Basel Convention, the U.S.-Canada Bilateral Treaty on Transboundary Movement of Hazardous Waste, and the U.S.-Mexican Agreement on Improvement of the Environment in the Border Area.

17. NAFTA provides four different phaseout periods for tariffs:

A: Immediate. Duty free as of the effective date.
B: 5 year phaseout period.

> C: 10 year phaseout period.
> C +: 15 year phaseout period.

18. Import sensitive industries which are protected by fifteen year tariff phaseouts include U.S. peanuts, sugar, and frozen concentrated orange juice and Mexican corn, dry beans, and nonfat dry milk.

19. Because of the transition period, import-sensitive industries will postpone rationalization and hire these students who otherwise would have found employment elsewhere, thereby creating additional demand for adjustment assistance and protection.

20. The Center is reported to receive 10 percent of its funding from organized labor.

21. 18 U.S. Code §1913 prohibits the use of appropriated funds for any services, advertisements, letters, or other means or devices intended to influence a member of Congress to favor or oppose any legislation, except by express Congressional authorization.

22. Specifically, the Congressional members opposed (1) procedures for trade sanctions against practices with no relationship to NAFTA and no demonstrable trade or economic impact on the United States; (2) an independent trinational bureaucracy to investigate wide-ranging environmental and labor issues whether or not related to NAFTA and which can set the agenda by determining which issues receive priority.

Chapter 3

NAFTA's TREATMENT OF FOREIGN INVESTMENT

Alan M. Rugman and Michael Gestrin

Introduction

The North American Free Trade Agreement's (NAFTA) thorough treatment of investment reflects the extent to which international economic relations are increasingly characterized by foreign direct investment (FDI) relative to trade. This chapter will look at the provisions of NAFTA that pertain to investment and their impact upon the North American investment regime. NAFTA will encourage more liberal international investment flows in North America as well as a more efficient allocation of productive resources throughout the continent.

This chapter is organized as follows. The second section will place North America within the context of triad FDI patterns during the 1980s. The third section will explain in broad terms the main parts of the Agreement which will affect FDI. The fourth section will consider in detail areas and sectors which NAFTA did not substantially liberalize and the last section concludes with an overall evaluation of NAFTA from an international investment perspective.

Changing FDI Patterns in the Triad

During the 1980s FDI patterns within the triad have undergone two remarkable and related changes. First, the E.C. replaced the United States as the largest source of FDI, increasing its stock of FDI by 170 percent between 1980 and 1989 (see table 3.1). Indeed, the U.S. share of the Triad's outward FDI stocks fell from 50 percent in 1980 to 35 percent in 1989. Second, the United States maintained its status as the largest single host country for FDI, accounting for 24 percent of the world total in 1990. As a group, the E.C. accounted for a larger share, at 40 percent in 1990. However, over the period 1980 to 1990, the average annual rate of growth of FDI stocks into the United States, at 16.9 percent, surpassed that for either the E.C. or Japan, at 13.2 and 11.6 percent, respectively.[1] What these data highlight is the degree to which North America has become a more significant host environment for FDI, and hence, the motivation for a strong investment chapter in NAFTA.

While the FDI stocks among the triad members experienced considerable change during the 1980s, FDI patterns within North America have also undergone some substantial variations. Table 3.2 provides details of the values of the six FDI relationships in North America over the 1981 to 1990 period. From this table it is noticeable that Canada's FDI in the United States grew three times as fast as U.S. FDI in Canada, which in 1990 had a book value of $68 billion. By 1990 the stock of Canadian FDI in the United States was worth $46 billion, about 60 percent of the stock of U.S. FDI in Canada. Canadian FDI into the United States grew by an annual average of over 12 percent from 1981 to 1990, while U.S. FDI in Canada grew by only 4.4 percent a year over the same period. The other key point in table 3.2 is the negligible amount of Mexican outward FDI—$1 billion in 1990 with under $4 million in Canada. Conversely, the growth of Mexico's FDI stocks in Canada and the United States, at 51 and 32 percent, respectively, surpasses the average annual growth rates of any other outward stock within the region. By comparison, the average annual growth rates of outward FDI stocks for all developing countries between 1980 and 1990 was 14.4 percent.[2]

While FDI stocks among the triad members experienced considerable change during the 1980s, FDI patterns within North America have also undergone some substantial variations. Table 3.2 also reveals the symmetrical economic dependence of both

TABLE 3.1

Outward Stocks of Triad FDI

Country/Region	1980 (U.S. billion dollars)	% of world	1989 (U.S. billion dollars)	% of world
United States	220	42	380	28
EC*	203	39	549	41
Japan	20	4	154	12
Triad	443	85	1,083	81
All Others	81	15	259	19
World	524	100	1,342	100

*Data for the EC's FDI include intra-EC FDI, and the 1989 figures are only for the United Kingdom, Germany, France, the Netherlands, and Italy.

SOURCES: Data for 1980 are from United Nations Centre on Transnational Corporations, *World Investment Report 1991: The Triad in Foreign Direct Investment*, August 1991; Data for 1989 are provided by Policy and Research Division, United Nations Centre on Transnational Corporations, September 1991.

Canada and Mexico on the United States in terms of FDI. There is a similar dependence in the trading relationships of the three countries. In 1990 the United States accounted for 62 percent of all FDI in Canada and 63 percent of the stock of FDI in Mexico. In 1990 the E.C. stock of FDI in Canada was 23 percent and Japan's was 4 percent. In earlier years Canada's dependence on U.S. FDI was even greater. For example, in 1981 U.S. FDI accounted for 68 percent of FDI stocks in Canada. Similarly, in 1981 the United States accounted for 69 percent of the FDI in Mexico.

Conversely, the growth of Mexico's FDI stocks in Canada and the United States, at 51 and 32 percent, respectively, surpasses the average annual growth rates of any other outward stock within the region. By comparison, the average annual growth rates of outward FDI stocks for all developing countries between 1980 and 1990 was 14.4 percent.[3]

There is an asymmetry between Canada and Mexico, however. Canada has significant outward FDI, of which 61 percent

TABLE 3.2

Stocks of FDI by Canada, the United States, and Mexico 1981–1990, U.S. million dollars

	Canada's FDI in:		U.S. FDI in:		Mexico's FDI in:	
	U.S.	Mexico	Canada	Mexico	Canada	U.S.
1981	18,012	187	46,957	6,962	0.97	163
1982	17,036	195	43,511	5,019	5.13	259
1983	18,481	207	44,339	4,381	6.80	244
1984	29,497	255	46,830	4,568	5.13	308
1985	35,008	198	46,435	5,087	5.50	520
1986	39,189	195	50,629	4,623	4.72	841
1987	41,809	179	57,783	4,913	4.95	903
1988	42,356	172	62,656	5,712	3.84	858
1989	43,967	168	65,548	7,280	3.64	1,251
1990	45,674	n/a	68,431	9,360	n/a	n/a
Average annual						
% change	**12.1**	**−0.7**	**4.4**	**4.9**	**51.2**	**32.3**

SOURCES: Figures for U.S. FDI are from U.S. Department of Commerce, *Survey of Current Business*, August 1982, 1986, 1991; figures for Canada's FDI are from Statistics Canada, *Canada's International Investment Position*, (1981–1986, 1988–1990). Figures for Canada's FDI have been changed from Canadian dollars to U.S. dollars using exchange rates from IMF, *International Financial Statistics Yearbook* (1990); figures for Mexico's FDI are from two sources: FDI in Canada are from Statistics Canada (Ibid.); FDI in U.S. are from U.S. Department of Commerce (Ibid.).

of its total is in the United States.[4] In contrast, Mexico's outward FDI is negligible since it has few multinationals. Canada's outward FDI reflects the maturity of its industrial and service sectors and the size of large multinational enterprises such as Northern Telecom, Noranda, Alcan, Bombardier, and Seagram.

Table 3.3 reports the stocks of FDI by the E.C. and Japan in the three North American countries. By 1990 a huge amount of the E.C. FDI, about $230 billion, was in the United States. In addition, $83 billion of Japanese FDI was in the United States. In contrast, E.C. FDI in Canada is about one tenth that of its U.S. FDI, while Japanese FDI in Canada is about one twentieth that of its FDI in the United States.[5] Neither the E.C. nor Japan have much FDI in Mexico; the total in 1989 was under $6 billion. However, with increased regional economic integration, it is likely that the E.C. and Japan will expand their FDI in the North American region in the next decade. The key issues for North America in terms of future FDI patterns are twofold; first, what will happen to FDI entering North America in response to NAFTA, and second, what will happen to FDI patterns among the three signatories of the Agreement? To answer these questions one must examine NAFTA to determine in what specific ways the Agreement will either encourage or discourage FDI, both generally, as well as in particular sectors. The next section considers the Agreement's overall impact upon the North American investment environment.

NAFTA's Investment Provisions

The investment chapter of NAFTA picks up where FTA investment chapter left off. The principal provisions of the latter have been maintained and several important additions have been made. These changes to the rules governing investment patterns in North America are important because, as mentioned above, they will affect not only intra-NAFTA FDI but also all FDI entering NAFTA area from outside.

The most notable changes to the actual rules governing FDI

TABLE 3.3

Stocks of FDI in North America by the EC and Japan 1981–1990, U.S. million dollars

	EC's FDI in:			Japan's FDI in:		
	U.S.	Canada	Mexico	U.S.	Canada	Mexico
1981	64,145	10,349	n/a	7,697	977	n/a
1982	74,012	10,645	n/a	9,677	1,219	n/a
1983	82,286	10,821	n/a	11,336	1,379	n/a
1984	96,555	12,768	2,032	16,044	1,627	816
1985	106,004	13,987	2,461	19,116	1,833	895
1986	127,221	17,299	3,203	26,824	2,224	1,038
1987	161,061	18,998	3,878	34,421	2,531	1,170
1988	188,342	22,438	4,038	51,126	2,976	1,319
1989	216,132	24,365	4,642	67,319	4,217	1,356
1990	229,913	n/a	n/a	83,498	n/a	n/a
Average annual % change	15.4	11.5	18.3	30.7	20.4	10.8

SOURCES: Figures for FDI in the United States are from U.S. Department of Commerce, *Survey of Current Business*, August 1985, 1986, 1991; figures for FDI in Canada are from Statistics Canada, *Canada's International Investment Position* (1986, 1988–1990); figures for Mexico are from Executive Secretariat of the National Foreign Investment Commission, Mexico, and reproduced in Investment Canada, "Canada-U.S.-Mexico Free Trade Negotiations: The Rationale and the Investment Dimension," December 1990. These data are not directly comparable to the other data used, since the Mexican Commission defines FDI as "authorized by the Commission," not the actual stock of FDI; figures for the EC's FDI in Mexico are based on the United Kingdom, West Germany, France, the Netherlands, Italy, and Spain.

in North America include: (1) the scope of coverage of the investment rules has been considerably expanded to include minority shareholders; (2) the application of Most Favored Nation (MFN) treatment to investments and investors; and (3) new rules and procedures have been established to deal with disputes concerning FDI in North America, including the opportunity for investors to take their disputes to binding international arbitration.

Where Mexico is concerned, the investment regime has been radically liberalized—the government has acknowledged the need to pay full and fair compensation for expropriated investments and has undertaken to move the Mexican business environment towards a legal framework which would see appropriate constraints established against uncompetitive practices and protection ensured for intellectual property rights. Where the United States and Canada are concerned, NAFTA mainly serves to maintain the benefits and advantages established during FTA negotiations.

Another notable feature of NAFTA is the addition of a series of seven annexes for each country. These list the particular exceptions which each signatory plans to maintain to various provisions of the Agreement. On balance this is a positive development. Previously, article 1607 of FTA (the "grandfathering" clause) simply identified all preexisting, nonconforming legislation as being exempt from the Agreement. Now the exceptions to the rules which each country wants to maintain must be made explicit, which, in theory, introduces greater transparency to each party's protectionist regime.

Table 3.4 describes each annex in terms of the chapters of the Agreement to which it applies, the specific articles which it covers, and the extent of the coverage. Annex 1 covers chapters 11 and 12, or those dealing with investment and services, respectively. The reservations in this annex can deal with any combination of five provisions in these chapters. These include: national treatment (articles 1102, 1202), MFN treatment (articles 1103, 1203), local presence (article 1205), performance requirements (article 1106), and nationality requirements (article 1107). Annex 1 lists existing, nonconforming measures held by federal,

TABLE 3.4

The NAFTA Annexes

Annex Number	Chapter(s) Covered	Articles Covered	Extent of Coverage
1	Investment (11) and Services (12)	National treatment (1102, 1202), MFN (1103, 1203), local presence (1205), performance requirements (1106), and nationality requirements (1107)	Existing, nonconforming measures maintained (2 years for states and provinces to add their own restrictions)
2	Investment (11) and Services (12)	Same as above	Existing, nonconforming measures maintained and reservation of right to adopt new or more restrictive measures in sectors and activities listed
3 (Mexico only)	Investment (11) and Services (12)	Blanket coverage	Constitutional restrictions reserving complete control of certain sectors for the Mexican state

Continued on next page

Table 3.4—*Continued*

Annex Number	Chapter(s) Covered	Articles Covered	Extent of Coverage
4	Investment (11)	MFN (1103)	Existing international agreements, any international agreements negotiated within two years, and any future agreements dealing with aviation, fisheries, maritime matters, and telecommunications
5	Investment (11) and Services (12)	none	Existing, nondiscriminatory measures which the parties commit to trying to liberalize (1 year for states and provinces to add restrictions)
6	Services (12)	Cross-border provision of services (1208)	Commitments to liberalize particular preexisting restrictions on cross-border services
7	Financial Services (14)	Cross-border trade (1404), establishment (1403), national treatment (1405), senior management (1408)	Indeterminate maintenance of preexisting exceptions

SOURCE: Alan M. Rugman and Michael Gestrin, "The Investment Provisions of NAFTA," in Steven Globerman and Michael Walker, eds., *Assessing NAFTA: A Trinational Analysis* (Vancouver: Fraser Institute, 1993) 271–92.

provincial, or state levels of government up to an indefinite period (although in some cases phasing-out schedules apply).

Annex 2 covers the same chapters and articles as annex 1, but extends the coverage beyond the maintenance of existing non-conforming measures. Annex 2 lists "sectors, subsectors or activities" against which nonconforming measures are maintained by each party, and against which each party reserves the right to add more restrictive measures at any time.

Annex 3 is unique to Mexico, covering as it does sectors from which foreign investors are barred by the Mexican constitution. These areas include: petroleum and related petrochemicals, electricity, nuclear power and treatment of radioactive materials, satellite communications, telegraph service, radiotelegraph services, postal services, railroads, issuance of currency, control over inland ports, and control of airports and heliports.

Annex 4 constitutes a reservation on the part of all three NAFTA countries to the application of article 1103 (MFN treatment) to existing international agreements. The annex covers both existing and future agreements in the areas of aviation, fisheries, maritime matters (including salvage), and telecommunications.

Annex 7 deals exclusively with financial services. The main provisions affecting investment covered by reservations in the annex include "establishment," (article 1404) and national treatment (article 1407). This annex permits the maintenance of preexisting, nonconforming measures.

Therefore, in sum, annexes 1, 2, 3, 4, and 7 contain discriminatory measures affecting investment. Of these, annex 2 can be made more restrictive in the areas already listed insofar as each party reserves the right to "adopt new or more restrictive measures . . . (which) may derogate from an obligation relating to" one or more of articles 1102, 1202, 1103, 1203, 1205, 1106, and 1107. Annexes 1 and 7 will have more measures, taken from existing legislation, added by the states and provinces within two years of the Agreement coming into effect. It seems likely that the states and provinces will add a significant number of measures.

Table 3.5 provides a breakdown of the number of reservations which each NAFTA country has included in annexes 1, 2, and 7. For each of these a breakdown of reservations by article is also provided. Annex 3 will be discussed as a special case later in this section, constituting as it does a list of highly discriminatory measures unique to Mexico. Annexes 4, 5, and 6 are not included in table 3.5 as their discriminatory impact upon investments is either negligible (annex 4), or nonexistent, (annexes 5 and 6).

Under the name of each country are two columns. The first column starting on the left gives the number of times the country in question has listed a reservation to a particular article. The second column shows the distribution of reservations to articles in particular annexes among the total number of reservations taken by a particular country in annexes 1, 2, and 7. In this way one sees, for example, that reservations to article 1403 (Establishment of Financial Institutions) account for 13 percent of Mexico's investment reservations in the three annexes. It is critical to note that the purpose of table 3.5 is not to use a count of reservations in the annexes as a proxy for the economic significance of these. Rather, its purpose is to introduce the reader to the overall structure of the three annexes.

In terms of absolute numbers, Mexico has the largest number of reservations to investment articles, with eighty-nine, followed by the United States with fifty, and Canada with forty-eight. The most frequently used annex is annex 1, with eighty-eight reservations between the three countries, followed by annex 2, with fifty-nine reservations, and then annex 7, with forty reservations.

Several patterns emerge in table 3.5 which are worthy of consideration. The first concerns the concentration of reservations in annexes 1 and 2 against national treatment (article 1602) and MFN (article 1103) by all three countries. Since these provisions constitute the cornerstone of nondiscriminatory treatment in NAFTA, reservations to articles 1102 and 1103 are more significant than reservations to the performance requirements provision (article 1106) or the senior management provision (article 1107). Almost 60 percent of Canada's reservations to investment articles in annexes 1 and 2 deal with national

TABLE 3.5

Distribution of Investment Reservations Between Canada, Mexico, and the United States by Article

Annex	Article	Number of Reservations by:						Total Number of Reservations Per Article
		Canada		Mexico		United States		
		Number	Share of Canada's Total	Number	Share of Mexico's Total	Number	Share of U.S. Total	
1	1102	11	23%	31	35%	9	18%	51
	1103	3	6%	3	3%	5	10%	11
	1106	4	8%	8	9%	1	2%	13
	1107	5	10%	7	8%	1	2%	13
Annex 1 Total		23	48%	49	55%	16	32%	88
2	1102	9	19%	6	7%	8	16%	23
	1103	5	10%	4	4%	6	12%	15
	1106	4	8%	0	0%	2	4%	6
	1107	7	15%	3	3%	5	10%	15
Annex 2 Total		25	52%	13	15%	21	42%	59
7	1403	0	0%	12	13%	0	0%	12
	1405	0	0%	13	15%	8	16%	21
	1406	0	0%	1	1%	3	6%	4
	1408	0	0%	1	1%	2	4%	3
Annex 7 Total		0	0%	27	30%	13	26%	40
Totals:		**48**	**100%**	**89**	**100%**	**50**	**100%**	**187**

SOURCE: Alan M. Rugman and Michael Gestrin, "The Investment Provisions of NAFTA," in Steven Globerman and Michael Walker, eds., *Assessing NAFTA: A Trinational Analysis* (Vancouver: Fraser Institute, 1993).

treatment and MFN, 71 percent in the case of Mexico, and 76 percent in the case of the United States. What this suggests is that where Canada, Mexico and the United States do have legislation or measures which are discriminatory and which they wish to maintain, these are usually of a broad nature as opposed to the specific forms of discrimination associated with derogations to articles 1106 and 1107.

Another interesting feature of table 3.5 is the discrepancy, both in relative and absolute terms, of the use by Mexico versus the use by Canada and the United States of annex 2. Annex 2 is much more restrictive than annex 1 because it allows the parties to make the discriminatory measures already listed in this annex even more restrictive at any time (the reservations in annex 1 are fixed). Canada lists almost twice as many reservations in annex 2 than Mexico, while the United States lists 62 percent more than Mexico. Furthermore, Canada and the United States each have more reservations to investment articles in annex 2 than in annex 1. Mexico exhibits the reverse pattern, with only thirteen reservations in annex 2. This difference may reflect a negotiating dynamic whereby Mexico, with several significant reservations in its unique and absolutely restrictive annex 3, probably felt pressure to compensate for this by less liberal use of annex 2 than either Canada or the United States.

Finally, table 3.5 also includes annex 7. This is the only annex of the seven which deals with a particular economic sector, the financial services sector. This reflects the significance of this sector in the negotiations. The summary of the annex 7 reservations to provisions relating to investment in table 3.5 indicates three things. First, this is an area of economic strength for Canada, as indicated by the lack of a single reservation by Canada to the articles listed. Second, Mexico's investment regime in financial services is still very restrictive as indicated by the numerous reservations to articles 1403 and 1405, which concern establishment and national treatment. Third, one sees reflected in the reservations for the United States a partially restrictive regime with no discriminatory restrictions against establishment but numerous reservations to the national treatment provisions (article 1405), reflecting the decentralized nature of the U.S. financial system.

Table 3.5 provides an overall guide to the character of annexes 1, 2, and 7, and the use which each country has made of them. However, counting reservations does not give a complete picture of the scope of the discrimination which has been carried over into NAFTA. This is due to the fact that the reservations range widely in terms of the economic value of their coverage. Some reservations will target specific economic subsectors (duty-free shops) while others will apply to areas which are highly significant from an economic perspective (automotive industry). Obviously, the former should not be given the same weight as the latter when it comes to analyzing their economic significance.

The Impact on the North American Investment Regime

To what extent will NAFTA actually liberalize the North American investment regime? In the previous section the impact of NAFTA on the rules and norms which will characterize the North American investment regime once the Agreement comes into effect was considered. This section analyzes NAFTA's likely impact upon specific sectors of the North American economy. Within this context, the specific sectoral effects of the Agreement in the economies of the three signatories, the probable impact of the tit for tat reservations, the treatment of investment review in NAFTA, and the discriminatory features of U.S. industrial policy will be outlined.

The Sectoral Reservations

Each of the NAFTA signatories has signaled its sensitive sectors by listing various derogations in the first three annexes. These derogations are summarized in the appendices for this chapter. The United States and Canada have more or less maintained the status quo in terms of the areas in which discriminatory measures will be maintained. Mexico, on the other hand, will have long lists of exceptions to various provisions of NAFTA when the Agreement comes into effect, with most of these having phase-out schedules. Mexico's investment regime will therefore undergo a one-time massive liberalization when the Agreement begins and subsequently undergo a second open-ing-up as most of the country's remaining discriminatory mea-sures are phased-out during the first ten years of the Agreement (with a few notable exceptions discussed below).[6]

The United States and Canada.   Canada's sectoral reser-vations (see appendix 3.1) are concentrated in three areas. The first is natural resources, where the government has made one weak reservation in agriculture and five relatively more restric-tive reservations in energy and fishing.

The second general area is social services. All three NAFTA signatories have exempted social services and minority affairs from the Agreement. Canada has also exempted all policies and measures related to aboriginal peoples.

The third major area of Canadian exclusion is transportation. Canada's reservations here include the exclusion of foreign interests from all forms of air transport along with heavy restric-tions on foreign interests from all forms of cabotage and heavy restrictions upon foreign involvement in the maritime sector. There is also a tit for tat reservation designed to give the Canadian government the right to treat U.S. investors in Cana-dian water transport as unfairly as Canadian investors in this sector are treated in the United States. It should be noted, that transportation has long been one of the most restricted sectors in North America and was completely excluded from the provi-sions of FTA. As restricted as this sector remains, its inclusion in NAFTA and the liberalization of some of its subsectors constitutes a substantial step forward.

The two areas in which the highest concentration of U.S. reservations are found are transportation, especially maritime transportation, and social services (see appendix 3.2).

Mexico.   Mexico's lists of reservations (see appendix 3.3) are the most extensive in NAFTA. The types of reservations held by Canada and the United States are repeated: energy and social services are essentially limited to domestic control, while the transportation sector is subject to numerous discriminatory measures. Like Canada, Mexico has protected its cultural industries, but it has done so by using the annexes to place restrictions on foreign involvement in radio, television, the cinema, and newspaper publishing.

Mexico's annex listings differ most from those of Canada and the United States by the large number of reservations applied to various manufacturing sectors. These include reservations in the automotive and automotive parts sector, the Maquiladora industries, manufacturing subject to the PITEX Decree (related to export and import requirements), and basic petrochemicals. Many of these reservations, however, have phase-out schedules, which will see most Mexican manufacturing completely liberalized during the ten years following implementation of the Agreement.

Tit for Tat Reservations

The several tit for tat reservations in NAFTA annexes are an interesting by-product of the negotiation of the negative lists. These reservations state that restrictions upon foreign investment in another party's territory will be met with mirrored treatment for the offending party's investors in the home country's same sectors. Indeed, tit for tat reservations suggests that retaliation may go beyond equivalent commercial effect to substantially greater commercial effect.

The effect of tit for tat measures on non-NAFTA entities contemplating North American investments should be considered. If domestic discriminatory measures inhibit the free flow of foreign investment to a particular sector of the Canadian or Mexican economy, the addition of a tit for tat reservation by the United States against the country holding this measure will reinforce the original disincentive to invest in the economy in question. Indeed, to give one example, NAFTA will raise the price Canada pays for protecting cultural industries, such as newspapers and cable television systems, since the United States has reserved for itself the right to discriminate against

Canadian investors, as well as foreign investors in Canada who seek to expand their operations into the United States from a Canadian base, by applying the same discriminatory rules as Canada.

As already mentioned, Canada has a tit for tat reservation in the maritime sector against the United States. Mexico also has one also against the United States in the area of legal services. And the United States has a total of six reservations covering mining, rights of way for pipelines across federally owned lands, and leases on the Naval Petroleum Reserves; indirect air transportation activities ("air freight forwarding and charter activities other than as actual operators of the aircraft"); specialty air services; the provision of cable television services; newspaper publishing; and Canadian ownership of oceanfront land. It is not clear whether or not the provinces and states will try to use tit for tat reservations in their lists.

It should come as no surprise that the United States is using tit for tat reservations more than Mexico and Canada. It is interested in overcoming barriers to its investors in foreign investment markets, and a smaller country has a strong incentive to liberalize when retaliation could go beyond commercial effect.

It should be noted in this regard that the culture provision of FTA (article 2005) will remain in force once the NAFTA comes into effect. What this article states is that where Canada takes measures to protect its cultural industries, U.S. retaliatory measures are limited to "equivalent commercial effect" (article 2005.2). The cultural sector is therefore an exception to the "greater than commercial effect" implicit in the tit for tat measures adopted by the United States.

Investment Review

The investment review procedures and the outcomes of these in all three NAFTA signatories are not subject to review under the terms of the Agreement's dispute-settlement procedures. Canada and Mexico accomplish the exclusion by using reservations in NAFTA annexes. The Canadian investment review process applies special criteria in a few limited sectors, such as cultural industries. Otherwise, only acquisitions worth more than $150 million can be reviewed. Mexico applies a range of thresholds and restrictions to several categories: activities reserved exclusively for the Mexican state (listed in annex 3); activities reserved to Mexican nationals and companies that exclude foreign participation; activities that limit foreign participation to 34, 40, or 49 percent (based upon lists of sectors); and activities in which majority foreign participation is allowed with prior approval of the National Commission on Foreign Investment (NCDI).

The United States, in contrast to Canada and Mexico, does not list any investment review procedures in its reservations. The reason is that U.S. investment review procedures are based on national security criteria and, as such, are excluded from the provisions of NAFTA (article 2102). This should be of particular concern to all investors considering acquisitions in the United States since the current criteria, established by the 1988 Exon-Florio legislation and its subsequent revisions, for determining whether or not an investment represents a threat to national security, are extremely vague and are likely to be interpreted differently by successive administrations. Furthermore, it is widely acknowledged that whereas the trends in investment review in Canada and Mexico indicate a wane in interventionist practice, the Committee on Foreign Investment in the United States (CFIUS) has yet to demonstrate how much enthusiasm it will exercise in wielding the new powers bestowed on it in 1988.

The Exon-Florio amendment (section 721) to the U.S. Omnibus Trade and Competitiveness Act of 1988 gave the president of the United States the authority to review and block foreign acquisitions of U.S. firms on the basis of "national security" considerations. The CFIUS is the body responsible for carrying out such reviews and for making recommendations to the president. Amendments to Exon-Florio in 1992 identified the need for U.S. technological leadership in sectors related to defense as a legitimate basis for blocking foreign takeovers.

Much of the ambiguity surrounding the discriminatory potential of CFIUS can be traced to the growing importance to national competitiveness of the huge development costs of new technologies, which are usually dual-use (they have both domestic and military applications). Under these conditions, combined with the current trend toward greater global corporate concentration in high-technology production, the activities of CFIUS seem likely to increase. Therefore, the exclusion of review processes from NAFTA's dispute-settlement procedures, combined with the lack of even the most basic guidelines to ensure fair, nondiscriminatory review procedures in all three countries, is likely to prove, in the medium term, to be one of the investment chapter's main weaknesses.

The U.S. High-Technology Consortia

Another deviation from the letter and spirit of NAFTA's investment provisions are the high-technology consortia in the United States which are funded by the U.S. government and which informally exclude foreign investors. Two notable examples of this discrimination are Sematech, a high-technology consortium established in 1985 and funded by the Pentagon, and the awards of Pentagon funding, beginning in 1988, to develop an indigenous high-definition television industry. Yet this overt discriminatory behavior with respect to foreign investors and investments does not even appear in the annexes, again because it is ostensibly linked to national security concerns.

The omission of the high-technology consortia and of the American investment review mechanism constitutes a loose interpretation of what should be excluded from the provisions of NAFTA on security grounds. Unfortunately, matters that fall under the national security clause of the Agreement are not subject to dispute resolution. Therefore, any policies or decisions associated with national security concerns, as defined by national governments, are not subject to challenge.

Overall Impact

Two points need to be made with respect to the sectoral impact of NAFTA. First, the investment regimes of the United

States and Canada are not changing substantially. Sectors that have been excluded or protected from foreign investment under FTA will continue to be protected under NAFTA. A few modest gains were achieved in the transportation sector. Although it will remain highly restricted overall, phase-out schedules on reservations in certain limited segments promise some liberalization. More important, transportation will be covered by the dispute-settlement provisions of the investment chapter, whereas the sector is wholly excluded from the provisions of the FTA.

The second point is that Mexico's sectoral reservations highlight the degree to which that country's investment regime is becoming liberalized. Although Mexico has listed many reservations, a high percentage of these will be completely phased out, most within ten years of the Agreement coming into effect.

Conclusion

This chapter has considered the institutional provisions of NAFTA and the changes to the North American investment regime to which NAFTA will give rise. The most positive contributions are greater transparency in the rules governing the treatment of foreign investments in North America and the impetus the Agreement supplies for the continuing liberalization of the Mexican investment regime. NAFTA does not, however represent any significant liberalization of the Canadian or U.S. investment regimes. In future negotiations NAFTA will need to be extended to establish guidelines for either investment review procedures as well as the adoption of discriminatory policies ostensibly based upon national security criteria.

APPENDIX 1

Canada's Reservations From NAFTA Investment Provisions, annexes 1 and 2

Sectors	Derogation	Phase-Out
ANNEX 1		
1. Agriculture	Loans from the Farm Credit Corporation are reserved for Canadians.	None
2. All sectors	Review procedures and performance requirements allowed by the *Investment Canada Act* are excluded from the agreement.	None
3. All sectors	The federal and provincial governments maintain the right to limit the ability of foreign interest to acquire assets or equity interests in state enterprises when such assets are being sold or otherwise disposed of.	None
4. All sectors	The ownership of shares in federally incorporated corporations is constrained.	None
5. All sectors	A "simple majority of the board of directors, or of a committee thereof, of a federally-incorporated corporation must be resident Canadians."	None
6. All sectors	Non-Canadians' ownership of land in Alberta may be limited.	None
7. All sectors	Foreign ownership of seven companies involved in air transportation, energy, and high technology is restricted.	None
8. Automotive	Waivers on customs duties are linked to performance requirements.	None

Sectors	Derogation	Phase-Out
9. Customs broker- ages and brokers	Senior management has nationality restrictions.	None
10. Duty free shops	Ownership of shares and licensing are limited to nationals.	None
11. Oil and gas	Production licenses for "frontier lands" and "offshore areas" can be held only by entities that are at least 50 percent Canadian-owned.	None
12. Oil and gas	Approval of projects may be linked to technology transfer, domestic re- search and development expendi- tures, and local presence.	None
13. Oil and gas	"Benefit plans" and technology transfer requirements can be im- posed in conjunction with the *Hiber- nia Development Project Act.*	None
14. Uranium	Foreign ownership of a uranium min- ing property is limited to 49 percent.	None
15. Fish harvesting & processing	Foreign vessels excluded from Can- ada's Exclusive Economic Zone. The ownership of more than 49 per- cent of a fish processing enterprise and the acquisition of a commercial fishing license are mutually exclu- sive rights for foreign interests.	None
16. Air transportation	Domestic air routes and particular scheduled international routes are reserved for firms at least 75 percent Canadian-owned.	None

ANNEX 2

17. Aboriginal affairs	Rights accorded to aboriginal peo- ples are not subject to any provi- sions.	*

---

*Phase-outs do not apply to annex 2 which specifically lists reservations that allow for future increases in discriminatory treatment.

Sectors	Derogation	Phase-Out
18. All sectors	Any measures can be adopted with respect to the ownership of ocean-front land.	*
19. Telecommuni-cations**	Canada reserves right to adopt any measures in this area.	*
20. Securities	Canada reserves right to adopt any measures with respect to the acqui-sition or sale of securities issued by any level of government in Canada.	*
21. Minority affairs	Canada reserves the right to adopt any measures in this area.	*
22. Social services	Canada reserves the right to adopt any measures in this area.	*
23. Air transportation	Canada reserves the right to adopt any measure that restricts foreign ownership of specialty air services to no more than 25 percent.	*
24. Water transporta-tion	Canada reserves the right to adopt any measures in this area.	*
25. Water transporta-tion	This is a tit for tat reservation in re-sponse to a U.S. reservation.	*

*Phase-outs do not apply to annex 2 which specifically lists reservations that allow for future increases in discriminatory treatment.
**Telecommunications transport networks and services, radio communications, and submarine cables.

APPENDIX 2

The U.S. Reservations From NAFTA Investment Provisions, annexes 1 and 2

Sectors	Derogation	Phase-out
ANNEX 1		
1. All sectors	Foreign firms (except Canadian firms) must use a longer form to register securities issued and do not qualify for the less costly standards that U.S. and Canadian firms enjoy.	None
2. Atomic energy	License to "transfer, manufacture, produce, use or import any facilities that produce or use nuclear materials" cannot be issued to an entity owned or controlled by foreign interests.	None
3. Telecommunications (enhanced or value-added services)	Firms with more than 20 percent foreign-owned stock must "submit" copies of all operating agreements granted by foreign governments and evidence of refusal by foreign governments to grant operating agreements.	None
4. Agricultural chemicals	Limits upon information which foreign firms of MNEs may obtain from the Environmental Protection Agency.	None
5. Mining	This is a tit for tat reservation. Foreign entities can be denied the right to "acquire right-of-way for oil or gas pipelines" or to "acquire leases of interests in certain minerals" such as coal or oil if U.S. citizens are similarly denied in the foreign entity's home country.	None

Sectors	Derogation	Phase-out
6. Public administration	Overseas Private Investment Corporation and loan guarantees are not available to some foreign enterprises.	None
7. Air transportation	Cabotage limited to U.S. nationals (maximum of 25 percent voting stock of a firm can be held by nonnationals). This reservation also contains a tit for tat clause that applies to "indirect air transportation activities."	None
8. Air transportation	Foreign firms require special licenses to carry out specialty air services and can be denied such licenses if more than 25 percent voting stock is foreign owned. Cross-border services of this kind are allowed but are subject to phase-in schedules. This reservation contains a tit for tat clause.	None
9. Land transportation	There are limits on establishment of bus or truck services or enterprise in U.S. to carry out distribution of international cargo.	None
10. Customs brokers	To receive a customs broker's license, a foreign corporation must have at least one officer who is a U.S. citizen and also holds a customs broker's license.	None
11. Waste management	Grants for treatment plants can be tied to domestic sourcing requirements.	None

ANNEX 2

12. All sectors	This is a tit for tat response to Canadian limits on ownership of ocean-front land.	*

---

*Phase-outs do not apply to annex 2, which specifically lists reservations that allow for future increases in discriminatory treatment.

Sectors	Derogation	Phase-out
13. Cable television	This is a tit for tat reservation concerning operation of cable television systems.	*
14. Telecommunication**	Federal government reserves right to adopt any measures in this sector.	*
15. Social services	Federal government reserves right to adopt any measures in this sector.	*
16. Minority affairs	Federal government reserves right to adopt any measures in this sector.	*
17. Legal services	Federal government reserves right to adopt any measures in this sector with regard to the provision of such services by Mexican nationals.	*
18. Newspaper publishing	This is a tit for tat reservation concerning restriction on foreign ownership of newspaper operations.	*
19. Water transportation	Federal government reserves right to adopt any measures in this sector.	*

---

*Phase-outs do not apply to annex 2, which specifically lists reservations that allow for future increases in discriminatory treatment.
**Telecommunications transport networks and services, radio communications, and submarine cables.

APPENDIX 3

Mexico's Reservations From NAFTA Investment Provisions, annexes 1, 2, and 3

Sector	Derogation	Phase-out
ANNEX 1		
1. Agriculture, live-stock, forestry	Canadian and U.S. investors may only own 49 percent of shares in land in these sectors.	None
2. All sectors	Foreign interests may develop or use land or water along a kilometer strip of Mexico's border only by arranging that a Mexican financial institution acquire, through trust, title to the real estate in question.	None
3. All sectors	Criteria to be used in reviewing investment proposals are employment, training, technological contribution, contribution to industrial productivity, and competitiveness.	None
4. All sectors	The threshold for investment are $25 million until 1 January, 1997; $75 million until 1 January, 2003; and $150 million thereafter.	None
5. All sectors	Only 10 percent of persons in a Mexican cooperative may be foreigners.	None
6. All sectors	Foreign investment is not permitted in "microindustry enterprise," which is defined as an enterprise with up to fifteen workers that has sales regulated by the Mexican government.	None
7. Entertainment services**	There are licensing requirements to import radio or television programming in any form.	None

**Broadcasting, multipoint distribution systems, and cable television.

Sector	Derogation	Phase-out
8. Entertainment services**	Non-Mexican radio or television announcers require special authorization.	None
9. Entertainment services**	Spanish language must be used in advertising.	None
10. Entertainment services** (cable television)	Maximum foreign ownership in a cable television firm is 49 percent.	None
11. Entertainment services (cinema)	30 percent of screen time (annual basis) in every theater is reserved for Mexican films.	None
12. Telecommunications (enhanced on value-added services)	Foreign ownership of videotext or enhanced packet switching services is limited to 49 percent.	1/7/95*
13. Transport and telecommunication	Foreign state enterprises and governments are barred from investments in these sectors.	None
14. Construction	Foreign investors must have special permission to own more than 49 percent of a construction firm.	None
15. Construction	Risk-sharing contracts are prohibited. Foreign participation in nonrisk sharing contracts involved in drilling limited to 49 percent.	None
16. Private schools	Foreign interests may not own more than 49 percent of an establishment.	None
17. Petroleum products	Foreign ownership is barred from "the distribution, transportation, storage, or sale of liquified petroleum gas and the installation of fixed deposits."	None

*When a date is given in the phase-out column, it represents the complete removal of the constraint in question.
**Broadcasting, multipoint distribution systems, and cable television.

Sector	Derogation	Phase-out
18. Petroleum products	Foreign interests are excluded from acquiring, establishing, or operating detail outlets for fuel.	None
19. Fishing	Foreign ownership of a fishing enterprise is limited to 49 percent.	None
20. Auto parts industry	There are limits on foreign ownership in this sector.	1/1/99*
21. Automotive	There are limits on foreign owner-ship.	
22. Maquiladora	Access to domestic market is limited to 55 percent of value of exports in previous year.	Yes
23. Manufacture of goods	Export requirements apply to certain firms.	1/1/01*
24. Manufacture of goods	Export requirements apply to certain firms.	1/1/01*
25. Artificial explosives, fireworks, firearms, and cartridges	Foreign ownership of a firm is limited to 49 percent. Membership on the board of directors limited to Mexican nationals.	None
26. Extraction and ex-ploitation of miner-als	Foreign ownership of a firm is limited to 49 percent.	1/1/99*
27. Newspaper publish-ing	Foreign ownership of a domestic newspaper is limited to 49 percent.	None
28. Professional serv-ices	Foreign involvement and investment in legal practice is limited.	None
29. Specialized (com-mercial) public no-taries	Limited to Mexican nationals.	None

*When a date is given in the phase-out column, it represents the complete removal of the constraint in question.

Sector	Derogation	Phase-out
30. Specialized services	Fiat to be public notaries is limited to Mexican nationals.	None
31. Sale of nonfood products in specialized establishments	Foreign ownership in a store selling firearms and the like is limited to 49 percent.	None
32. Religious services	The representation of religious associations in Mexico is limited to Mexican nationals.	None
33. Air transportation	Foreign ownership of an enterprise in this sector is limited to 25 percent. Only Mexican enterprises may perform cabotage, "scheduled international services," and "nonscheduled international services."	None
34. Specialty air services	Foreign ownership of an enterprise engaged in specialty air services is limited to 25 percent.	None
35. Air transportation	Foreign ownership of an enterprise engaged in the construction or operation of airports or heliports is limited to 49 percent.	None
36. Land transportation	Ownership and operation of bus and truck terminals is limited to Mexican nationals.	Yes
37. Land transportation	Foreign participation in local bus services, school bus services, and taxi or other collective transportation services is prohibited.	None
38. Land transportation	Foreign ownership in industry classifications CMAP 711201 through 204 and 711311 and 711318 is prohibited.	Yes
39. Land and water transportation	Foreign participation in the construction or operation of marine or river works or roads for land transportation is forbidden.	None

Sector	Derogation	Phase-out
40. Specialized personnel	Foreign participation in customs brokerage is forbidden.	None
41. Water transportation	Subsidies for Mexican vessels are contingent upon their doing repairs and maintenance operations in Mexico.	None
42. Water transportation	Foreign participation in cabotage forbidden. Foreign ownership of an enterprise performing international maritime transport is limited to 49 percent.	None
43. Water transportation	Foreign participation in an enterprise engaged in support services for the maritime sector is limited to 49 percent.	None
ANNEX 2		
44. All sectors	There are restrictions on debt securities issued by any level of government in Mexico.	
45. Entertainment services	Mexico reserves right to adopt any measures with regard to investments in broadcasting, MDS, uninterrupted music, and high-definition television services	†
46. Telecommunications	Mexico reserves right to adopt any measures regarding air navigation.	†
47. Telecommunications transport networks	Mexico reserves right to adopt any measures in this area.	†
48. Professional services	Tit for tat measure against the United States in the area of legal services.	†
49. Social services	Mexico reserves the right to adopt any measures in this area.	†

† Phase-outs do no apply to annex 2, which specifically lists reservations that follow for future increases in discriminatory treatment.

Sector	Derogation	Phase-out
ANNEX 3		
50. Petroleum, other hydrocarbons, and basic petrochemicals	Exclusive domain of Mexican state.	‡
51. Electricity	Exclusive domain of Mexican state.	‡
52. Nuclear power and treatment of radio-active materials	Exclusive domain of Mexican state.	‡
53. Satellite communications	Exclusive domain of Mexican state.	‡
54. Telegraph services	Exclusive domain of Mexican state.	‡
55. Radio-telegraph services	Exclusive domain of Mexican state.	‡
56. Postal services	Exclusive of Mexican state.	‡
57. Railroads	Exclusive domain of Mexican state.	‡
58. Issuance of currency	Exclusive domain of Mexican state.	‡
59. Control of maritime and inland ports	Exclusive domain of Mexican state.	‡
60. Control of airports and heliports	Exclusive domain of Mexican state.	‡

---

‡ Phase-outs do not apply to annex 3, which specifically lists sectors that the Mexican Constitution reserves to the state.

Notes

1. John Rutter, "Recent Trends in International Direct Investment," U.S. (Washington: U.S. Department of Commerce, August 1992) table 6.
2. Ibid., table 1.
3. Ibid.
4. See Alan M. Rugman, *Multinationals and Canada-United States Free Trade* (Columbia: University of South Carolina Press, 1990).
5. For a discussion of the relative lack of Japanese FDI, see Alan M. Rugman, *Japanese Foreign Direct Investment in Canada* (Ottawa: Canada-Japan Trade Council, 1990).
6. For a more detailed discussion of these reservations, see Michael Gestrin and Alan M. Rugman, "The NAFTA's Impact on the North American Investment Regime," *C. D. Howe Institute Commentary*, No. 42 (Toronto: C. D. Howe Institute, March 1993).

Additional References

Hill, Roderick and Ronald J. Wonnacott. "Free Trade with Mexico: What Form Should It Take?" *C. D. Howe Institute Commentary*, No. 28 (Toronto: C. D. Howe Institute, March 1991).

Lipsey, Richard E. "Canada at the U.S.-Mexico Free Trade Dance: Wallflower or Partner?" *C. D. Howe Institute Commentary*, No. 20 (Toronto: C. D. Howe Institute, August 1990).

Wonnacott, Ronald. "U.S. Hub and Spoke Bilaterals and the Multilateral Trading System." *C. D. Howe Institute Commentary*, No. 23 (Toronto: C. D. Howe Institute, October 1990).

Chapter 4

FOREIGN DIRECT INVESTMENT AND NAFTA: A CONCEPTUAL FRAMEWORK

Alan M. Rugman and Alain Verbeke

Introduction

In this chapter the investment provisions of the North American Free Trade Agreement (NAFTA) are analyzed using a conceptual framework developed to classify government policies towards inward foreign direct investment (FDI). It is demonstrated that NAFTA investment reservations are made for public goods reasons, or to provide shelter (protection) for domestic producers. Using this new framework, the investment provisions of NAFTA are analyzed with a focus on the exemptions from national treatment—the equal treatment of foreign and domestic firms under domestic law—obtained by each of the three signatories: Canada, Mexico, and the United States. It is found that many of the exemptions need to be viewed as the result of a sheltering process which will be of benefit to protected domestic producers at the expense of both foreign producers and domestic consumers.

Shelter Through the Regulation of Foreign Direct Investment

Rugman and Verbeke have developed the theory of shelter which argues that both firms and government agencies may pursue strategies that do not aim to exploit existing Firm Specific Advantages (FSAs) or develop new ones.[1] Shelter implies that artificial costs are imposed on foreign rivals without positively affecting the core competencies and long-term natural competitiveness of the firms benefiting from shelter. The authors have argued that both firms and government agencies may attempt to have their sheltering strategies perceived by taxpayers or others as welfare increasing. For example, unfair trade laws may be used to protect inefficient domestic producers.[2] This is made possible through a decision process that portrays the sheltering measures as being required to achieve a level playing field—for example, fair trade. In other words, it is argued that a public good, similar to national security, is provided.

A similar situation was observed in the area of "strategic trade policy" which is supposed to lead to dynamic internal economic effects (superior profits associated with learning curve advantages resulting from preemptive government intervention) and dynamic external economic effects (technological spillovers). The application of strategic trade policy may lead to perverse effects.[3] For example, if the perception exists that firms or industries which allegedly have the potential to achieve superior profits or technological spillover effects should be supported by government, this provides an incentive to firms and industries to achieve the status of "strategic trade policy candidate." Here again, this status may be perceived as the basis of some type of public good or externality.

Yet it is difficult to assess the comparative strengths of firms and sectors regarding profits or technological spillovers. Hence, firms and sectors may use false, or at least nonobjectively verifiable, information to receive government protection. This shelter may be meant primarily to hinder competition by foreign rivals but it is again rationalized by public good or externality arguments. Again, both domestic consumers and foreign producers may suffer from shelter provided to domestic producers.

In the two cases described (unfair trade laws and strategic trade policy), the possibility of creating false images regarding public good or externality outcomes associated with government shelter, may vary according to: (1) the attitudes prevailing in government about discriminating against foreign firms in favor of domestic ones; (2) the discretion prevailing in the regulatory process to take into account subjective rather than objective parameters.

Rugman and Verbeke have emphasized the danger of political or bureaucratic discretion in regulatory decision processes, when a strong bias in attitude exists against foreign firms.[4] In such cases, domestic firms may misuse the public good and positive externality argument in an attempt to persuade public policymakers that protectionist regulations will prevent the import of foreign efficiency. In practice, prevailing domestic inefficiency is maintained by such sheltering.

The theory of shelter can be applied to the regulation of FDI. Two dimensions are required, as illustrated in figure 4.1. At the most general level, government policy regarding inward FDI can be discriminatory or nondiscriminatory as compared to policies affecting investments by domestic companies. A discriminatory attitude towards FDI, in principle, could take the form of intentional additional incentives, as compared to domestic investment because of institutional competition for FDI. A nondiscriminatory attitude towards foreign firms would mean the expansion of national treatment. The decision process through which investments by firms are assessed and possibly restricted can be rules-based, or can be discretionary. The latter is a process with ample opportunity for discretionary behavior by bureaucrats and/or politicians.

Figure 4.1 describes the four categories of FDI policies, based upon the use of the two parameters described above. A rules-based decision process, associated with a nondiscriminatory attitude in government regarding inward FDI (quadrant 1) does not favor shelter-based strategies of firms. In contrast, as government policy moves closer toward quadrant 4, with quadrants 2 and 3 being intermediate stages, the danger of shelter-based strategies favoring domestic producers at the expense of consumer welfare increases.

These two parameters form the substantive basis for a host country's "incentive system," and its "administrative system" regarding inward FDI.[5] Several authors, including Encarnation

Figure 4.1

Generic Categories of Government Policies Toward Inward FDI

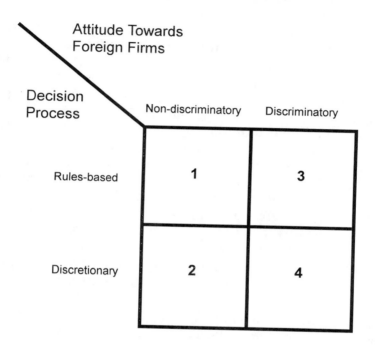

and Wells[6] and Lecraw and Morrison[7] have suggested that discretionary decision processes regarding the regulation of inward FDI may lead to important policy problems. A central administration unit may be biased by narrow goals that do not include wider objectives relevant to national interests. In addition, it may suffer from the requirement of managing conflicting constituencies. In contrast, a decentralized system may lead to conflicting policies pursued by various public agencies.

It is interesting to observe, however, that these authors completely neglect the possible impact of shelter-based policies by domestic firms in the regulatory process. Lecraw and Morrison even argue that a rules-based system whereby host nations have "a set of clear, uniform requirements that they apply to all projects" is not to be recommended in spite of its efficiency, clarity, and objectivity because it would "limit flexibility, a critical requirement in turbulent international environments."[8] Such an interpretation is inconsistent with the logic of figure 4.1.

Graham has demonstrated that asymmetrical investment policies (with one liberal country and one restrictive country) will always benefit large producers in the more restrictive country, mostly at the expense of both global interests and overall national interests of the country imposing restrictions.[9] As the author argues "These policies ultimately reflect producers' interests more than those of any constituency and it is almost surely producers' interests that dominate in any nation that actually imposes them."[10] This finding is based on a model where all firms face constant marginal costs, where economies of scale and learning are present, and where one assumes the existence of differential technological accumulation leading to complementarity in the case of foreign acquisitions.

This view is consistent with the concept of rent-seeking as "the collusive pursuit by producers' of restrictions on competition that transfer[s] consumers' surplus into producers' surplus."[11] The societal costs associated with rent-seeking reflect: (1) the costs of the rent-seeking process itself, which may include the use of an inefficient production technology imposed by the government as a compensation for protectionist measures and (2) the output that would have been generated if the same resources had been used productively, possibly by foreign multinational enterprises (MNEs).

In the pursuit of shelter the outcomes of rent-seeking behavior must be packaged in such a way that they appear to be in the public interest. It could be argued that the public at large must at least get the impression that restrictions on inward FDI reflect more than a pork barrel outcome.

In a related vein, Dunning has argued that the impact of MNEs on a nation state may be different from the impact of a uninational firm in six ways:

1. The transfer of resources (technological capacity);

2. The control of resources;

3. The impact of sourcing on markets;

4. The impact on domestic competition;

5. The distribution of the benefits of value-added activities;

6. The impact on the international allocation of resources.[12]

Hence, domestic firms can attempt to emphasize these differences when lobbying with government agencies in order to obtain discriminatory regulations in their favor. In theory, a host country government, driven by welfare economic objectives, could ask the question whether the social return of inward FDI (as expressed in a conventional way for example by value added minus profits accruing to foreign owners) is larger than the opportunity cost of capital. In practice, firms operate within clusters or business networks so a correct analysis would require taking into account spillover effects on factors of production, demand, related and supporting industries, and rival firms.[13]

Given the imperfect information available to public policy-makers on the likely impact of inward FDI, it is not surprising to observe that domestic firms, threatened by possible foreign entries, may attempt to exclude such entries through sheltering measures. For example, in a high technology industry, the argument could be used that foreign MNEs will destroy the local innovation capacity. This argument may or may not be factually correct, but it is difficult to verify, and depends upon a number of assumptions. Dunning has argued that the following four elements may be important in these respects:

1. If inward FDI is not allowed, will this investment be undertaken in an other proximate nation, leaving the country with restrictive FDI policies worse off? This occurs in the European Community (E.C.) where restrictive policy in one E.C. nation diverts FDI to

another E.C. nation, followed by exports to the nation with restrictions.

2. If FDI is associated with the use of domestic resources which can therefore not be deployed elsewhere in the economy, the question is whether these resources could have been used more productively by domestic firms.

3. Foreign MNEs could, in theory, destroy a host nation's innovation capability. However, they may become a core player in an industry cluster or even the flagship firm in a host country network, as a result of setting up local research and development centers or by transferring nonlocation bound FSAs to the host nation that may lead to technological diffusion.[14]

4. Even if foreign investors drive out local innovation capabilities, these domestic resources will likely be usefully redeployed elsewhere in the domestic economy.[15]

Given that it may be very difficult for public policymakers to assess the preceding elements, abundant possibilities exist for the pursuit of shelter by domestic firms. Justification for such arguments would be focused on the alleged high contribution to the local economy by domestic firms jeopardized by foreign entries.

Government regulation of inward FDI, discriminating against MNEs, whether rules-based or discretionary-based in the implementation stage, may be characterized by different types of scope in terms of breadth (general or sectoral) and impact (limitations on control of assets or reduction in expected value of benefits, given a specific control structure of assets).

These four options are pictured in figure 4.2. Quadrant 1 includes government policies related to screening all foreign investment across sectors (possibly above a particular amount in terms of expected "performance"). Quadrant 2 reflects policies aimed at restricting foreign sourcing, foreign content, negative trade balance effects, domestic market access, and other

Figure 4.2

Scope of Inward FDI Regulation

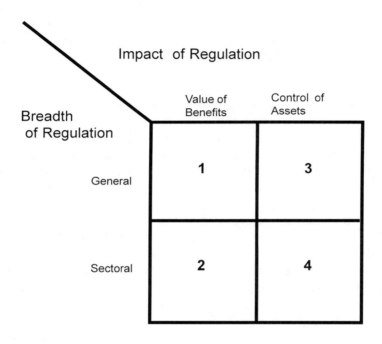

such items. Quadrant 3 and quadrant 4 are related to limitations regarding ownership aimed to "unbundle" the contribution of MNEs to the domestic economy. In quadrant 3, foreign control in the form of majority equity participation may be prohibited, but elements related to technology transfer may be deemed valuable. Finally, in quadrant 4, foreign control is restricted in specific sectors in order to pursue public policy goals such as the infant industry argument; strategic trade policy arguments; dangers associated with a potential subsequent withdrawal of foreign firms leaving a domestic industrial desert; or the Trojan-horse argument, where foreign FDI would lead the to destruction of domestic clusters and to impacts which would go far beyond the negative effects on immediate domestic rivals.[16]

In the last section of this chapter, the significance of NAFTA in terms of changes in government policies toward inward FDI (as described by figures 4.1 and 4.2) is analyzed. A new analytical framework is developed which explains the possible reasons for investment exemptions in NAFTA, building upon the concepts of shelter and public goods discussed above.

The Conceptual Basis for Investment Exemptions in NAFTA

NAFTA can be viewed as an institutional device resulting from political exchange. It is designed primarily to reduce both the production costs and transaction costs associated with economic exchange among the three partner countries. The possible production cost effects and related business behavior have been analyzed in a wide variety of studies.[17]

The value of a complex agreement such as NAFTA to each of the three signatories depends on the value given to each of the attributes of the Agreement as compared to the situation without the Agreement. Two problems arise, however, regarding the assessment of the net benefits that will accrue to each partner nation.

First, NAFTA contains several measures difficult to evaluate, not only in monetary value, but even in quantitative physical terms. These include effects related to the relocation of economic activity for reasons other than production costs (proximity to large markets or an innovative environment); costs associated with new requirements imposed on production factors (retraining workers, redirection of capital and assets to other sectors); or external effects such as those on the environment.[18]

Second, each country's negotiators normally have a substantial information advantage over the negotiators from the partner nations, as far as domestic effects are concerned. Hence, even if the partners in a negotiation are driven primarily by the goal of increasing national consumer welfare or gross national income, information asymmetries could still lead to opportunistic behavior. This occurs because each partner nation has an incentive to push for specific measures *only* if the outcomes of these measures are valued positively by public policymakers in that partner nation as compared to a situation without NAFTA.

These outcomes may include: (1) an international reallocation of resources across industries according to the principle of comparative advantage; (2) an international intraindustry restructuring according to the competitive advantages of firms in each industry (higher efficiency may be achieved as a result of the elimination of X-inefficiency, the specialization of particular firms, scale economies, or the exit of inefficient firms); and (3) the elimination of transaction costs associated with international economic exchange, for example, through the reduction of uncertainty associated with operating in a partner country.

Each partner country would like to avoid two types of attributes related to a full liberalization of economic exchange. The first are measures that would be detrimental to public goods such as national culture, social programs, and the environment. In a number of cases, the value of alleged public goods to public policymakers may reflect these policymakers' own goals, not societal goals, but in the case of a democratic system of government it can be assumed that limits exist on the possibility for public policymakers to pursue their own goals.

The second are measures that would eliminate shelter benefiting sectors or firms considered important due to following: the monetary or other contributions to these policymakers, the voting power they represent, the political or social problems associated with forced relocation or destruction of labor and productive assets, personal relationships between managers or owners and policymakers, and the affected firms' symbolic significance for a region or nation.

In this context, it should be emphasized that the value of many of the public goods mentioned above cannot be quantified in monetary terms. In addition, the defense of public goods is generally more credible in market driven economic systems than is the defense of inefficient domestic firms. These firms have an incentive to use public goods arguments when calling for exemptions to investment liberalization.

Each nation participating in the creation of an institutional structure that will liberalize economic exchange in terms of trade and investment is thus faced with its own transaction costs at two levels. At the level of negotiations with the other nations it is confronted with bounded rationality because it had comparatively limited information on the effect of specific measures on the partner countries. It also faces the opportunism of the other countries' negotiators who may want exemptions based on the alleged existence of public goods. In this context the concept of the "strategic importance of sector X" is often employed. It is unclear whether such claims accurately reflect the actual value of public goods, or whether these public goods really exist.

The situation is comparable to a used car salesperson who knows much more about the value of each attribute of the product than potential buyers know.[19] Buyers will focus primarily on visible attributes or information conveyed by the seller, but given that opportunism can be expected, the value of the exchange will be reduced.

In the case of NAFTA, each negotiating party has an incentive to conceal or misrepresent information on the effects of particular measures in the Agreement in order to maximize payoffs related to it. In economic exchange among firms, opportunism is inevitably perceived as negative by the affected parties and may even lead to changes in institutional boundaries (vertical and horizontal integration).[20] This, however, is not necessarily the case in political exchange—often the success of government is measured by elements such as the achievement of a negotiated outcome with several attributes, including the absence of resistance by pressure groups and general satisfaction by the public at large.

At the level of negotiations with domestic constituencies, to whom the measures need to be sold, government also faces bounded rationality and opportunism problems. Both producers and other interest groups may attempt to portray their narrow interests as highly valuable public goods. It is very difficult for government to assess the border between demands for shelter and demands for public goods as well as the value of these public goods. In addition, the public at large may focus on only those specific attributes of an agreement that could entail a loss of public goods, without having the information processing capabilities to correctly assess all costs and benefits associated with the Agreement. This may create political problems for the negotiators.

However, public policymakers in each of the partner countries can also take advantage of information asymmetries to facilitate political exchange. Given the difficulties faced by partner nations in assessing the impact of particular liberalization measures on the domestic economy, public policy makers can negotiate exemptions with these partner nations. These negotiations are based on the nonverifiable value of public goods and externalities. In addition, they can attempt to sell an overall agreement negotiated with the partner countries to domestic constituencies and the public at large by emphasizing the impact of attributes with positive potential effects and downplaying the possible negative effects of other attributes.

In political exchange, the existence of high information costs related to assessing the effects of all the specific attributes of an agreement has the advantage that negotiations are facilitated at the two levels described above. This situation could be termed "benevolent ignorance." This benefit, however, is at least partially offset by the negative economic effects, both in an efficiency sense and distributional sense, given that specific producers' interests are maintained and some public goods overvalued through exemptions.

In accord with North it could be argued that political institutions do not generally lead to a maximization of economic output.[21] This is because public policymakers try to avoid conflict with other powerful political or economic actors, and because an efficient system may be detrimental to achieving specific public goals such as a more easily controllable economic structure.

From a political perspective, NAFTA with its multitude of investment exemptions should be viewed as effective. Each of the partners has consciously accepted sheltering strategies disguised as concerns about public goods and overvalued public goods of the two others, in exchange for the (implicit) right to engage in similar behavior. The "benevolent ignorance" of the actual nature and value of the goods and externalities obtained through exemption demands by the partners has allowed each nation to retain exemptions that satisfy powerful domestic constituencies, while simultaneously providing a "good story" for the domestic public at large on how valuable "crown jewels" were excluded from the Agreement.

NAFTA thus creates three outcomes. The first outcome is a public good resulting from the institutionalization of an economic exchange system that allows free investment flows. It is also this public good that will make possible changes in economic behavior leading to higher economic efficiency. The second outcome is the public goods (and positive externalities) through institutionalized exemptions from a free investment regime. These public goods are nonexclusive, which means that all citizens and firms of the affected nations share the same level of provision. The problem is that the value of these public goods is difficult to assess. They are not readily quantifiable and their value depends upon subsequent behavior of economic agents (the value of a governance structure that allows free FDI or that prohibits FDI, for example, in national security industries that depend upon the strategic behavior of the affected or exempted firms as compared to behavior expected under an alternative institutional structure). Since the citizens of the affected countries cannot directly express their preferences about the agreement, and if a referendum had taken place, would probably not have been able to perform a correct assessment of the value of all the Agreement's attributes, then the value of these public goods would remain unknown. In addition, given that government has a monopoly on the provision of the Agreement, no comparison is possible with the outcome of alternative institutional systems. Finally, the third outcome is the shelter for those firms and sectors that were able to have their narrow producers' interests viewed as a public good benefiting all citizens of the nation involved.

The bounded rationality and opportunism issues described

above explain why it is possible to integrate such sheltering measures in a system of exemptions based on the public goods concept.

The Model and the Investment Exemptions of NAFTA

NAFTA, which is supposed to come into effect on 1 January 1994, contains detailed investment provisions reflecting the growth of economic activities by MNEs. A careful analysis of the differences with the U.S.-Canadian Free Trade Agreement (FTA), which came into effect on 1 January 1989 can be found in Gestrin and Rugman.[22] The key carry-overs from FTA include the principle of national treatment for investment; the Canadian threshold for review of American direct acquisitions at $150 million; the threshold of $5 million for direct acquisitions and $50 million for indirect acquisitions in cultural industries, certain energy sectors, financial services, transportation; and the discriminatory application of Investment Canada provisions against foreign investment.

The main improvements of NAFTA compared to FTA include:

1. The application of the Most Favored Nation (MFN) treatment to investment coming from the partner nations, which is especially important for sectors exempted from the national treatment provisions;

2. An extension of FTA provisions to portfolio investment;

3. Additional restrictions on performance requirements (especially technology transfer, domestic sourcing, export performance, and requirements that a firm act as ''exclusive supplier'' to specific regions or markets);

4. Limits on the imposition of nationality requirements and a provision on denial of benefits which outlines the conditions to be fulfilled for one of the countries to deny NAFTA benefits to non-NAFTA investors seeking to expand from a base in one of

NAFTA countries (Japanese investors in Canada, seeking to establish operations in the United States);

5. A dramatic liberalization of the Mexican investment regime, including the need to pay full and fair compensation in the case of expropriated investments;

6. The introduction of detailed procedures for the resolution of international investment disputes through binding arbitration panels.

NAFTA implies, in terms of the conceptual framework developed in the first section of this chapter, that the regulatory system regarding inward FDI has moved closer to quadrant 1 of figure 4.1—a nondiscriminatory attitude toward foreign firms from the partner nations combined with a more rules-based decision process. It could be argued that Canada and the United States were already largely in this quadrant as a result of FTA, but for Mexico NAFTA implies a significant move from a position relatively close to quadrant 4 towards quadrant 1.

In spite of the general shift towards quadrant 1, substantial sections of the economy clearly remain in quadrants 3 and 4 of figure 4.1. NAFTA includes seven annexes which list the exemptions each signatory plans to seek.[23] The annexes will replace the grandfathering provisions of FTA. These grandfathering provisions implied that all nonconforming measures in existence when FTA was signed would be maintained. This would have allowed substantial discretionary discrimination in quadrant 4 of figure 4.1, given Mexico's protectionist heritage regarding inward FDI. In contrast, the annexes force the three partners to make explicit all the existing discriminatory measures maintained through exemptions.

This process of making explicit exemptions constitutes, in itself, a shift toward a more transparent rules-based regulatory regime, positioned in quadrant 3 of figure 4.1, which is especially important for inward FDI in Mexico.

Given that the investment exemptions reflect either public goods or shelter-based strategies of domestic firms in each partner nation, the explicit list of exemptions makes clear which benefits were actually obtained by each partner. This allows each of the partners to assess if benefits obtained by others are broadly equivalent to the benefits obtained for oneself. In other words, these lists reflect the institutionalization of reciprocal opportunism.

It is interesting to observe, however, that the level of opportunism of each party implicitly permitted by the other parties has been restricted through the use of so-called tit for tat reservations. Here restrictive practices will be met with a mirrored treatment for the offending party's investors in the same sectors. Canada has one reservation against the United States in the maritime sector. Mexico also has one against the United States in the area of legal services. The United States has six reservations related to mining, rights of pipelines across federally owned lands, leases to naval petroleum reserves, indirect air transportation activities, specialty air services, cable television services and newspaper publishing, and the ownership by Canadians of oceanfront land. This instrument is obviously much more useful to the United States than the other nations for curbing opportunism given the much larger commercial effect on the partner nations' firms that could result from it.

In this context, the following elements related to the lists indicate a danger of increasing shelter, representing a move toward quadrant 4 in figure 4.1:

1. The federal governments of Canada, Mexico, and the United States will be able to add more nonconforming or restrictive measures to annex 2;

2. Annex 4 allows each government to negotiate international agreements, whether bilateral or multilateral that may run counter to the MFN provisions—including aviation, fisheries, maritime matters, telecommunications, transport networks, and transport services. Such future agreements could embody a protectionist component against outsiders, in this case, the other parties in NAFTA;

3. Annex 5 describes nondiscriminatory quantitative restrictions. It lists service sectors to be exempted for each nation which can be broadened at any time

by one of the parties, as long as the other parties are notified of the new measures;

4. The actual exemptions listed in the annex by the signatories are substantial and all have negotiated exemptions in each of the four quadrants of figure 4.2.

For Canada, the performance requirements allowed by the Investment Canada Act are clearly positioned in quadrant 1. This exemption is valid across sectors and may affect the value of benefits accruing to foreign investors. The rights of federal and provincial governments to limit foreign interests in the acquisition of state assets reflects a quadrant 3 measure that is valid across sectors, but relates to the control of assets. Several measures can be positioned in quadrant 2, such as project approvals in the oil and gas industry made conditional upon technology transfer, domestic research and development expenditures, and local presence. Finally, limitations on foreign ownership, for example, a maximum of 25 percent in air transportation, can be placed in quadrant 4 of figure 4.2 as the control of assets is restricted in this specific sector.

The United States has not presently listed many exemptions across sectors which would be positioned in quadrants 1 and 3 of figure 4.2. It should be emphasized, however, that the United States retains its rights to review investments based on national security criteria. This national security argument (which is a public goods argument) simultaneously keeps foreign investors out of high technology consortia funded by the Pentagon, where national security concerns also prevail.

At the sectoral level, the nonavailability of Overseas Private Investment Corporation insurance and loan guarantees to some foreign firms is an example of quadrant 2 policy which reduces the value of benefits to foreign firms. The limitation of foreign ownership to 25 percent in firms engaged in air transportation cabotage can be placed in quadrant 4 of figure 4.2.

Mexico clearly had retained the largest list of protectionist measures both at the general and sectoral level. In quadrant 1 of figure 4.2, Mexico will retain the use of criteria such as employment, training, technical contributions, contributions to industrial productivity, and competitiveness across sectors. It is quite possible this may substantially decrease the benefits of FDI by MNEs from the partner countries.

In quadrant 3, foreign involvement is not allowed in microindustry enterprises—enterprises with up to fifteen workers and which have sales regulated by the state. The sectoral reservations are extensive. The export requirements for certain manufacturing firms can be placed in quadrant 2, while the bulk of protectionist measures is located in quadrant 4. The control of assets through foreign ownership is restricted or even excluded in a variety of sectors including agriculture, entertainment, transportation, telecommunications, construction, petroleum products, auto parts, mining, and energy.

The outcome of NAFTA can hardly be called a fully liberalized investment regime. There are many exclusions which take the form of both asset control and value of benefit restrictions, both cross-sectoral and sectoral.

Given the conceptual framework developed in the second section of this chapter, figure 4.3 can be developed as a useful way to classify investment exclusions according to their economic significance. Two possible reasons exist for investment exclusions: a shelter-based one and a public goods-based one. This distinction is shown on the vertical axis of figure 4.3. The investment exemptions can also be classified according to their geographic locus which can be trilateral, national, and subnational. In practice it is not easy to distinguish between shelter-based and public goods-based reasons for investment exclusions when in-depth insights into the actual decision processes leading to the exclusions are lacking. Nevertheless, valid reasons may exist to protect telecommunications, cultural industries, or national security related industries without intent to protect narrow producers' interests. In contrast, the prevailing view in each nation to protect sectors such as agriculture and air transportation seems to be related to producers' interests. For some sectors, such as the Mexican petroleum production and the Canadian fish industry, shelter-based reasons for exclusions are clearly national and cannot be found in other nations.

Figure 4.3

NAFTA and the Investment Exclusions

Geographic Locus of Reservations

Rationale for Investment Exclusions	Trilateral	National	Sub-National
Shelter-Based	**1** Air Transportation Maritime Transportation	**3** Mexican Petroleum Canadian Fish	**5** To Be Announced
Public Goods-Based	**2** Telecommunications Social Services	**4** Canadian Culture U.S. Atomic Energy Mexican Entertainment	**6** To Be Announced

Finally, it should be noted that the fifty U.S. states, thirty-one Mexican states, and ten Canadian provinces may add their own restrictions to annex 1 within two years after NAFTA will have come into effect. The danger of opportunistic behavior by these subnational bodies has been eliminated because they may not add new restrictions to the lists, only existing ones. One of the reasons for this situation may obviously be that subnational levels are now heavily involved in institutional competition to attract as much inward FDI as possible rather than in attempts to reduce FDI.

Conclusion

NAFTA should be viewed as an institutional structure aimed at reducing the discriminatory attitude of the signatories towards inward FDI from the partner nations. It also limits the possibilities of using discretionary regulatory processes against foreign firms.

However, each of the partner nations has retained a substantial number of exemptions, both sectoral and cross-sectoral, that are related to both the value of benefits and control of assets by foreign MNEs. Nevertheless, from a transaction cost perspective, these exemptions may have facilitated the political exchange process leading to NAFTA. Benevolent ignorance of the actual level of opportunistic behavior by partners engaging in this cooperative relationship and the possibility of reciprocal opportunism have undoubtedly contributed to the creation of a political governance structure to facilitate international economic exchange. This governance structure may have serious limitations, but it constitutes a public good in itself. The process of negotiating the investment reservations in NAFTA has made them more transparent and erected targets for future negotiators to shoot at.

Notes

1. Alan Rugman and Alain Verbeke, *Global Corporate Strategy and Trade Policy* (London and New York: Routledge, 1990) and Alan Rugman and Alain Verbeke, "Shelter, Trade Policy and Strategies for Multinational Enterprises," in *Research in Global Strategic Management* vol. 3: *Corporate Response to Global Change,* Alan M. Rugman and Alain Verbeke, eds. (Greenwich, Conn.: JAI Press, 1992), 3–25.

2. Alan Rugman and Alain Verbeke, "Mintzberg's Intended and Emergent Corporate Strategies and Trade Policy," *Canadian Journal of Administrative Sciences* 8, no. 3 (September 1991): 200–8.

3. Alan Rugman and Alain Verbeke, "Strategic Trade Policy is Not Good Strategy," *Hitotsubashi Journal of Commerce and Management* 25, no. 1 (December 1990): 75–97.

4. Rugman and Verbeke, *Global Corporate Strategy* and Rugman and Verbeke, "Strategic Trade Policy," 75–97.

5. See Donald Lecraw and Alan Morrison, *Transnational Corporations— Host Country Relations,* South Carolina Essays in International Business No. 9 (1991).

6. D. J. Encarnation and Louis T. Wells, "Sovereignty en garde: Organizing to Negotiate with Foreign Industry," *International Organization* 39 (1985): 47–58.

7. Lecraw and Morrison.

8. Ibid., 23.

9. Edward M. Graham, "Government Policies Towards Inward Foreign Direct Investment, Effects on Producers and Consumers," in Peter J. Buckley and Mark Casson, eds., *Multinational Enterprises in the World Economy: Essays in Honour of John Dunning* (Aldershot, U.K.: Edward Elgar, 1992), 176–94.

10. Ibid., 193.

11. Gordon Tulloch, "The Costs of Special Privilege," in James E. Alt and Kenneth A. Shepsle, eds., *Perspectives on Positive Political Economy* (New York: Cambridge University Press, 1990), 199.

12. John H. Dunning, *Japanese Participation in British Industry* (London: Croom Helm, Routledge, 1986) 285.

13. Michael E. Porter, *The Competitive Advantage of Nations* (New York: Free Press, Macmillan, 1990) and Joseph R. D'Cruz and Alan M. Rugman, "Business Networks for International Competitiveness," *Business Quarterly* 56, no. 4 (Spring 1992): 101–7.

14. For an analysis of nonlocation bound FSAs, see Alan Rugman and Alain Verbeke, "A Note on the Transnational Solution and the Transaction Cost Theory of Multinational Strategic Management," *Journal of International Business Studies* 23, no. 4 (December 1992): 761–71 and Alan Rugman and Alain Verbeke, "Multinational Enterprise and National Economic Policy," in Peter J. Buckley and Mark Casson, eds., *Multinational Enterprises in the World Economy: Essays in Honour of John Dunning* (Aldershot, U.K.: Edward Elgar, 1992), 194–211.

15. John H. Dunning, *Multinational Enterprises and the Global Economy* (Reading: Addison-Wesley, 1993) 318.

16. See John H. Dunning, *Japanese Participation in British Industry* (London: Croom Helm, Routledge, 1986).

17. See Steven Globerman and Michael Walker, *Assessing NAFTA: A Trinational Analysis* (Vancouver: Fraser Institute, 1993) and Gary C. Hufbauer and Jeffrey J. Schott, *NAFTA: An Assessment* (Washington D.C.: Institute for International Economics, 1993).

18. See Steven Globerman, "The Economics of NAFTA," in *Foreign Investment and North America Free Trade,* Alan M. Rugman, ed. (Columbia: University of South Carolina Press, 1993).

19. See G. Akerlof, "The Market for Lemons," *Quarterly Journal of Economics* 84 (1970): 488–500.

20. See Alan M. Rugman, *Inside the Multinationals: The Economics of Internal Markets* (New York: Columbia University Press, 1981) and Alan M. Rugman, *Multinationals and Canada-United States Free Trade* (Columbia: University of South Carolina Press, 1990).

21. Douglas C. North, *Structure and Change in Economic History* (New York: Norton, 1981) and Douglas C. North, "Institutions and a Transaction-Cost Theory of Exchange," in James E. Alt and Kenneth A. Shepslem, eds., *Perspectives in Positive Political Economy* (New York: Cambridge University Press, 1990), 182–94.

22. Michael Gestrin and Alan M. Rugman, "The NAFTA's Impact on the North American Investment Regime," *C. D. Institute Howe Commentary,* No. 42 (Toronto: C. D. Howe Institute, March 1993).

23. For a detailed analysis, see ibid.

PART 2

COUNTRY STUDIES

Chapter 5

NAFTA, FOREIGN DIRECT INVESTMENT, AND THE UNITED STATES

Edward M. Graham

Introduction

This chapter addresses the investment provisions of the North American Free Trade Agreement (NAFTA) from the perspective of the United States. It is very difficult to determine what is, or even what should be, the perspective. The overall reaction of the U.S. public towards NAFTA has been ambivalent, and there is a real danger at the time of this writing that the U.S. Congress will fail to ratify the Agreement. The tactics of the Clinton administration to date (June 1993) may have increased the probability of nonratification, this in spite of President Clinton's unequivocal support of the Agreement.[1] Despite this, in the end the treaty will likely squeak through the ratification process by a narrow margin, but in the meantime the difficulty persists in defining what exactly is the U.S. viewpoint with respect to NAFTA.

The U.S. public seems to be ambivalent toward the Agreement. Indeed, there is a basis for this ambivalence. NAFTA is littered with provisions that tilt towards domestic (or incumbent) interests in the three North American countries. The U.S. public is much more concerned that the Agreement is too little protective of incumbent interests rather than too much so.

Why is there concern toward the Agreement? One reason lies in the nature of U.S. society. The United States is a very heterogeneous society which shows every sign of becoming more so. It is also, in many ways, a troubled society with a large disparity between the well-off and the not-so-well-off. However, the diversity of a heterogeneous society spawns a creative energy that in turn propels an economy in a very dynamic manner. Much, if not most, of the dynamic strength of the U.S. economy comes from innovative and entrepreneurial activities; these activities derive from, or at least are reinforced by, the diversity of the society.

Living within a country with a dynamic economy, many Americans not only endure their society's shortcomings, but actually manage to prosper in the face of them. But this prosperity is not at all universal. A large social underclass exists and the plight of persons caught in this segment of U.S. society, by many measures, is worsening. Moreover, the gap between those who are doing well in the U.S. economy and those who are not seems to be widening.

It is probably because of this gap that, in spite of its dynamic nature, the U.S. economy is not one that adapts easily or painlessly to change. That the U.S. economy is both dynamic and resistant to change is paradoxical, but the paradox is not an illusion. Schumpeter's "winds of creative destruction" blow particularly strong in the United States, and it is a good thing that they do: without them, the economy would experience little growth, and with little growth, the social problems likely would become overbearing. Nonetheless, structural changes in the U.S. economy are doubtlessly one factor behind the economic disparities of U.S. society. Furthermore, the geographical sprawl of the U.S. economy, resulting social and economic costs of relocation that must be borne by individuals when they are forced to change the means by which they earn their livelihood and the inadequate "social safety net" to protect the interests of those who are caught short by such changes are additional factors.

Many Americans not of the underclass are highly resistant to change. Much political capital therefore is invested each year in efforts to preserve this status quo. These efforts have over the years been partly successful—witness the long history of protection granted to the U.S. textile and apparel industries—and the resulting inefficiencies have doubtlessly contributed to the rather sluggish growth of the U.S. economy over the past two decades. Inevitably in a heterogeneous society, the politics of preservation of the status quo has led to divisiveness and to public policies which can be inconsistent both cross-sectionally and longitudinally. A heterogeneous society has great difficulty reaching consensus on major public policy issues, and the consequence can be a process to achieve choice that is circuitous at best and fractious at worst.

These aspects of both U.S. society and the political process by which choices are made must be borne in mind when one examines NAFTA and U.S. reaction to it. First is the examination of some of the important investment provisions of NAFTA with a view toward determining how well these satisfy the negotiating objectives of the U.S. government. This review is not intended to be exhaustive of all provisions in NAFTA that bear upon foreign direct investment (FDI) or the activities of multinational firms, but rather to establish the point with respect to investment, that the U.S. government largely received what it wanted from the NAFTA negotiations. Next, the question of why there is so much discomfiture with the Agreement is evaluated, as expressed by a number of Congressional members reflecting the doubts of numerous U.S. constituencies.

Formal Investment Provisions of NAFTA: A U.S. Official Perspective

It is safe to say that the formal investment provisions of NAFTA, as articulated in chapter 11 of part 5 of the draft agreement, embody substantial elements of a long-standing U.S. official agenda and hence the U.S. government should be particularly satisfied with this chapter.[2] The U.S. government, when it has entered into discussions or negotiations in such for a as the Organisation for Economic Cooperation and Development (OECD) and the General Agreement on Tariffs and Trade (GATT), has long sought agreement on principles that would enable business activities to operate across national boundaries (agreed rules or principles pertaining to rights of establishment, transfer of funds, standards for expropriation, national treatment for business entities under the control of foreign entities, restrictions on governmentally mandated performance requirements, or protection of intellectual property). Many of these goals have been achieved in NAFTA.

The national treatment provision of NAFTA embodies right of establishment and obligates the signing parties to accord to investors (and investments of investors) of other signing parties treatment "no less favorable that it accords, in like circumstances, to its own investors (investments) with respect to the establishment, acquisition, expansion, management, conducts, operation, and sale or other disposition of investments."[3]

Importantly, and in contrast to the OECD National Treatment Instrument, the relevant NAFTA provision (article 1102) forces states and provinces to also grant national treatment to investors (and investments of investors) of the other signing parties. Efforts mounted in 1990 in the OECD to develop a strengthened national treatment instrument failed over European insistence that the instrument be binding on state and provincial governments and U.S. and Canadian resistance to these provisos. Exactly why these two countries were able to agree upon such provisos in the context of NAFTA but not in the OECD is not known.[4]

National treatment in NAFTA is further strengthened by Most Favored Nation (articles 1103 and 1104) and minimum standard of treatment (article 1105) provisions, whereby respectively signing parties must grant investors and investments of other signing parties treatment no less favorable than that granted to investors and investments of nonsigning countries and that provided for under international law. The national treatment provisions do not apply, however, to local governments or to procurement by state agencies (thus, for example, the "buy American" laws of U.S. states are largely unaffected), and these provisions are tempered by a number of reservations and exceptions that are detailed in annexes to the draft agreement.

The national treatment provisions of NAFTA apply only to the investors and investments of countries that are parties to

NAFTA. Such investors and investments include, however, members of a party that are under the control of investors of a nonparty, but with important exceptions that are spelled out in article 1113. Thus, for example, if a U.S. firm were to be under the control of a Japanese firm and this U.S. firm were to hold a subsidiary in Mexico or Canada, that subsidiary and its immediate parent (the U.S. firm) would be accorded national treatment by Canada and Mexico unless the exceptions of article 1113 applied. This would be so even though NAFTA does not require the United States to offer national treatment to either the U.S. firm or its Japanese parent. However, all parties to NAFTA—Canada, Mexico, and the United States—have the right to "multilateralize" the national treatment provision, in other words, to extend NAFTA provisions to investors and investments of non-NAFTA nations.

The U.S. government has since the late 1970s sought to limit investment incentives and performance requirements granted to and/or placed upon international investors and investments by host countries. On the former (investment incentives) no headway has been made in any international negotiation, including NAFTA, possibly because there really is no consensus anywhere (even in the United States itself) over the desirability of such limitations (U.S. states routinely grant them, and U.S. multinational firms can benefit from them) and hence the issue has never been pushed very hard.[5]

On the latter (performance requirements) by contrast, there has been progress on a number of fronts—the Trade Related Investment Measures (TRIMs) agreement in the still ongoing Uruguay Round and the U.S.-Canadian Free Trade Agreement (FTA). The proposed TRIMs agreement is by almost all counts a disappointment—only the most overt trade-related performance requirements would be regulated—but FTA is much more satisfactory in that it bans a number of new performance requirements (and phases out old ones) in categories that are not strictly "trade-related." NAFTA provisions (article 1106) go still further in that the ban on new performance requirements (and phaseout of old ones) not only would cover all categories already agreed to in FTA but would also cover some additional categories that continue to be permitted under FTA.

Article 1106 of NAFTA applies to performance requirements placed on any investment, and not simply investments of a country that is party to NAFTA. From an economic perspective, restrictions on performance requirements make great sense, because these act in much the same manner as traditional trade restrictive devices.[6] However, in some instances NAFTA provisions are less than ideal. In particular, NAFTA phases out Mexican performance requirements placed on automotive manufacturers at a slower rate for new entrants than for incumbent firms, and thus is biased in favor of the former. As alluded to previously, NAFTA contains a number of biases in favor of incumbent firms, and the bias in favor of incumbent auto firms is but one of many. The pro-incumbency bias apparently was introduced in order to gain the acceptance of the relevant firms (the U.S. Big Three plus Nissan and Volkswagen), which in turn was seen as necessary for political reasons. The blemish caused by this provision is, however, a fairly minor one relative to certain other pro-incumbency biases, especially those created by rules of origin.

Expropriation and compensation for expropriated properties has long been a festering issue between the United States and Mexico (indeed, it has been a festering issue between the United States and most other Latin American nations and, in recent times, between Canada and certain Caribbean and South American countries). NAFTA provisions pertaining to expropriation and compensation (article 1110) basically forbid expropriation except for a public purpose, and then it must be done without discrimination, with due process, and entail prompt payment at fair market value in a G-7 currency. It is difficult to see how U.S. negotiators could have crafted language more to their liking on this issue.[7] However, it should be noted that this is one of a number of issues on which the Mexicans were prepared to undertake reforms irrespective of NAFTA negotiations.[8]

Likewise, the issue of transfers of capital (including profit and royalty remittances) has long been a sore issue between the United States and Mexico, and again U.S. negotiators achieved an outcome to their satisfaction on this issue without really having to try particularly hard as the Mexicans were prepared to undertake unilateral reform. Thus, NAFTA basically allows no restrictions on such transfers except for those required for balance of payments reasons or where issues pertaining to bankruptcy and creditors' rights, criminality, and other exceptional circumstances are extant (article 1109).[9]

Section B of chapter 11 of NAFTA establishes a set of procedures for resolving investment disputes. This section, encompassing articles 1115 through 1138, is arguably one of the most innovative and desirable features of the Agreement. The most striking feature is a mechanism by which an investor (but not an investment) may seek arbitration of a dispute against a government that is party to NAFTA. In other international dispute settlement mechanisms—those of FTA and the GATT—the only parties that have "standing" are governments. Hence an investor must seek a government (usually the investor's home government) to represent it to pursue any claim it might have against a host government. Under NAFTA, however, an investor can pursue claims on its own behalf or on behalf of its investment if the claim involves breach by a signing party (where a "signing party" includes obviously any of the governments of Canada, Mexico, and the United States, but apparently can also include a state or provincial government of any of these nations as well) of obligations under section A of chapter 11 or certain other articles of NAFTA.

Under the procedures established by these articles, an effort must be made to solve the dispute first by means of consultation and negotiation, but if this fails the dispute can be submitted to binding arbitration under the rules of the World Bank (ICSID Convention) or the United Nations (UNCITRAL). The tribunal (arbitration panel) can order interim measures to protect the rights of the disputing investor, but may not enjoin application of a measure alleged to constitute a breach of NAFTA. A final award made by the tribunal can include monetary damages (but not punitive damages) and/or restitution of property, where the damages can include applicable interest. If the claim is made by an investor on behalf of an investment, any award granted by the tribunal is made without prejudice to any right the investment might have relief under in domestic law.

The main significance of the dispute settlement procedure from a U.S. perspective, apart from its innovative aspects and the precedent that it potentially sets, is that it resolves a longstanding dispute between the United States and Mexico over the so-called "Calvo Doctrine." Under the Calvo Doctrine, Mexico and other Latin American nations have held that the sole means for resolving a dispute between a sovereign state and an investment within the territory of that state is judicial proceedings in local courts. In the eyes of U.S. investors and the U.S. government, these proceedings have often been other than fair and impartial. The suspicion is that the Mexican government has been dissatisfied with the Calvo Doctrine as well, given that in practice disputes between U.S. investors and Mexico have been subject to often heavy-handed diplomatic pressures from Washington. Thus, one suspects that Mexico once again was quite willing to offer reforms in this area, and might indeed have done so unilaterally. But whether or not this in fact has been the case, the U.S. government has much reason to be satisfied with NAFTA, part 5, section B.

The United States has long objected to the investment screening activities of the Canadian and Mexican governments, but under NAFTA both Canada and Mexico are given a "green light" to continue with such screening. This green light is contained in article 1138.2, by which decisions taken by Canada under the Investment Canada Act with respect to whether an acquisition should be allowed to proceed and taken by Mexico by the National Commission on Foreign Investment are not subject to the disputes settlement mechanism. Under article 1138, this exclusion also extends to actions "taken by a party pursuant to Article 2102." Article 2102 is a national security "carve out" that allows the signing parties to deviate from NAFTA's obligations in the name of national security. This carve out allows parties to NAFTA to take "any action that it considers necessary for the protection of its essential security interests . . . relating to the traffic in arms, ammunition, and implements of war and to such transactions in other goods, material, services and technology undertaken directly or indirectly for the purpose of supplying a military or other security establishment'' (article 2102, section 1, subsection b). Article 1138 thus would render decisions taken by the United States to block Canadian or Mexican acquisitions of U.S. firms under the Exon-Florio provision of the Trade Act of 1988 not subject to the disputes settlement mechanism if the United States claimed that its action was in accordance with 2102.1b. Whether the implicit U.S. tolerance to investment screening by Canada and Mexico was an explicit U.S. concession to gain Canadian and Mexican tolerance for language that effectively sanctifies Exon-Florio is not known, but such a conclusion does not seem to be wildly implausible.

NAFTA contains many reservations and exceptions to the provisions of chapter 11, spelled out in the annexes. These reservations and exceptions—including those of the United States itself, as well as those of Canada and Mexico—were seen by U.S. negotiators as intrinsically undesirable but pragmatically necessary in order to establish the principles. But once established, it might be argued by the negotiators, the principles become de facto irrevocable, while the reservations and exceptions are subject to liberalization in future negotiations.

From an official U.S. point of view, the most objectionable of the exceptions is the continuing exclusion of the petroleum sector from FDI. The reason for this exclusion is that Mexico chooses to continue to reserve its important petroleum sector for the state-owned monopoly PEMEX. From an economic perspective, this choice is even less than satisfactory for Mexico itself, because PEMEX is widely acknowledged to be rife with inefficiency, backwardness, and out-and-out corruption. However, Mexico's choice is based more on political (and emotional) factors than economic ones, and for U.S. or Canadian negotiators to have pushed hard on the issue of FDI in this sector would likely have derailed the whole negotiation.

But, aside from petroleum, with respect to the opening of sectors formerly closed to FDI, Mexico has done better than the United States or Canada. Mexico has opened (at least partially) two sectors that were formally closed to this investment—

electricity generation and distribution and petrochemicals. The United States and Canada by contrast have chosen not to open any sectors that have for historical reasons not been open to foreign ownership. This is true in spite of the fact that, whatever the reasons for the closure historically might have been, many of these reasons have almost surely lost most of their potency with the passage of time. Thus, for example Canada and the United States refuse to allow the other's citizens, or those of Mexico, to own air transport services in their territories. Mexico has a similar exception.

The full lists of reservations, exceptions, and sectors reserved for the state are contained in annexes 1 to 4 of NAFTA and, excluding purely explanatory pages and title pages, run to a total of 197 pages. Out of this total, 58 pages are devoted to the reservations and exceptions of Canada, 102 pages to those of Mexico, and 37 pages to those of the United States. No effort will be made here to attempt to summarize them.[10]

To sum up this section, NAFTA formal investment provisions constitute a triumph for U.S. negotiators (and, possibly, for Canadian and Mexican negotiators as well). This is true in spite of a number of blemishes that have been identified and discussed. The blemishes are very real, but they should not detract from the overall highly satisfactory outcome of negotiations on the investment provisions, when this outcome is judged against the U.S. government's original objectives (and, indeed, when this outcome is judged against economic criteria).[11]

FDI Provisions Not Found in NAFTA

Much the same statement can be made as was made in the final sentence of the previous section, but more cautiously, with respect to provisions in NAFTA pertaining to investment but not located in chapter 11. Part 6 of NAFTA, containing just chapter 17 (intellectual property), for example, is largely aimed towards bringing Mexican law and practice with respect to intellectual property roughly into line with U.S. law and practice. (The United States officially has had very little problem with Canadian law and practice, with the exception of Canada's "cultural industries" exemption, which seems to be widened in NAFTA relative to the equivalent provision in FTA.[12]) Much of this chapter is in fact designed to lock in reforms in Mexican law that Mexico had already taken unilaterally. Some steps are taken to extend this law.[13] The main reason for caution is that it really remains to be seen how well the new laws will be enforced. Before the current reforms were introduced into Mexican law, the U.S. government had sought better enforcement of existing law in Mexico, but often with disappointing results. Only time will tell whether results post-NAFTA will be significantly better than those pre-NAFTA.

Chapter 17 provides for national treatment with respect to intellectual property, but with some exceptions. National treatment in this instance is to be interpreted slightly differently than as in chapter 11. In the present context, the term implies that nationals of signing parties operating within the jurisdiction of another signing party, and enterprises under the control of such nationals, are accorded the same rights and privileges pertaining to intellectual property as are nationals of that signing party.

In the case of Mexico, the main exception pertains to who holds the copyright in a live performance. Under Mexican law it is automatically the performer or performers, but not necessarily so under Canadian or U.S. law. Hence this category is subject to reciprocity.

In the case of Canada, it is held by U.S. firms operating in the affected industries that Canada's "cultural industries" exemption is tantamount to denial of national treatment, and it is rumored that these firms will seek U.S. legislation for Canadian (or Canadian-controlled) firms operating in these industries to be subject to a reciprocity standard.

The exceptions and qualifications notwithstanding, chapter 17 represents a major achievement of U.S. negotiating goals. Certainly relative to what has been tentatively negotiated in the domain of intellectual property in the GATT Uruguay Round, this chapter is highly satisfactory from the perspective of the U.S. government.

A necessary evil in any free trade agreement is a set of rules of origin. Such rules are necessary because they determine whether a product produced (or at least claimed to be produced) in a nation party to the Agreement qualify for preferential treatment when sold in another party nation. The rules are "evil" because, inevitably, they will introduce some element of welfare-reducing trade diversion into the picture.

The rules of origin, as laid out in chapter 4, are complex to the point of being an accountant's delight. In particular, the "roll-up" provisions of FTA are eliminated. The new rules were clearly crafted to protect the interests of certain incumbent firms, especially those in the textile and auto sectors (where, to qualify as North American, a very high regional content must be demonstrated).

With respect to the activities of multinational firms, the reason why these rules can be pro-incumbent is that newly established operations (or, in NAFTA parlance, "investments") of such firms tend to source significantly more inputs from home nations than do long established firms. The evidence would suggest that over time, the local content of the output of such operations tends to rise. Thus, operations of multinational firms from home nations outside of North America would tend to be at a disadvantage relative to incumbent firms if they cannot initially meet rules of origin requirements. The same may not, however, apply to newly established operations of a firm based in another party nation, whose inputs would most likely come from a nation within NAFTA.

The likely effect of the discriminatory nature of these rules is not, however, so much to inhibit FDI as to divert it. In particular, if a firm based outside of North America were to determine that its optimal location for production under completely free trade were to be in Canada or Mexico but that the majority of the output of this site would be sold in the United States, then this firm might find that the rules of origin biased its location decision towards the United States. To put this point in more general terms, rules of origin would tend to cause production location decisions to be more weighted by the locus of the market and less by the locus of the lowest cost of production, and hence because of its much greater size, the United States would tend to receive more investment under NAFTA rules of origin than if these rules were to be less stringent. This bias might be seen as one that shifts benefits to the United States from Canada or Mexico (and, indeed, this might be the case), but it should also be noted that the bias works against economic efficiency and hence penalizes consumers in all three countries.

Thus, NAFTA rules of origin implicitly (but, according to a number of sources, intentionally) discriminate against new investments of firms not domiciled within the region. The exact amount of this discrimination is dependent upon the value of the preferential measures. The value of these in turn depends upon the outcome of the still ongoing Uruguay Round of multilateral trade negotiations. For example, if the outcome of this round were to be globally liberalized trade in textiles and apparel, then rules of origin applying to these sector will have less value than if the outcome is continued high levels of protection.

One might note that restrictive rules of origin not only discriminate against investments of non-North American multinational firms, but they can implicitly discriminate against some North American producers as well. Suppose, for example, firm A, located in Mexico, is a potential competitor to firm B, located in the United States, where most of the market for the product of these two firms is located. Suppose further that both firms source an important component from outside of North America and that the value of this component is high enough that, by virtue of its not being North American, the final product does not meet rules of origin. Finally, suppose that North American suppliers of this component cannot meet the cost or quality of the non-North American supplier. Under these circumstances, the Mexican firm (firm A) might find that it is not competitive against firm B because its (firm A's) product, although produced in Mexico, is not considered to be "North American" under the rules of origin and hence does not qualify for preferential treatment under NAFTA.

For these reasons, the rules of origin should be seen as one of the least desirable features of NAFTA, even if they doubtlessly do meet the goal of protecting certain incumbent U.S. interests. The purpose of a free trade agreement is, after all, to stimulate

commerce and to make firms more competitive, not the opposite. But the pro-incumbency biases of NAFTA are more likely
to do the opposite. That is, they will make North American
firms less competitive, and restrict commerce, rather than serve
the ultimate purposes of the free trade agreement.

To close this section, one more issue in NAFTA that affects
FDI should be discussed. This is the very short chapter on
competition policy, monopolies, and state enterprises (chapter
15). Article 1501 of this chapter indicates that each nation party
to NAFTA "shall adopt or maintain measures to proscribe
anticompetitive business conduct and take appropriate action
with respect thereto, recognizing that such measures will enhance the fulfillment of the objectives of this Agreement." This
worthy language does enable fulfillment of one important goal,
the creation by Mexico of a competition (antitrust) law and
enforcement agency. This law is very recent and its creation
was doubtlessly done to meet NAFTA requirement. As a result,
it is much too early to assess its impact.

Chapter 15 goes on to sanction state monopolies (article 1502)
and state-owned enterprises (article 1503) and to create a working group on trade and competition (article 1504) which is
charged with making recommendations within five years of the
date of entry into force of NAFTA on "further work as appropriate."

While chapter 15 clearly meets one important U.S. goal, one
should note that competition policy is nonetheless one of the
weakest areas of NAFTA. In contrast to the rather tentative
language of NAFTA, the Treaty of Rome establishing the European Common Market contains strong language to prohibit
monopolies, cartels, and abuse of dominant firm position. This
Treaty also provides for rather stringent limitations on state aid
to industry, including to state-owned enterprises. And, most
importantly, the Treaty of Rome grants to the European Commission significant powers to enforce these provisions. NAFTA,
by contrast, goes little beyond exhortation. Competition policy
represents an important venue by which the benefits of a free
trade agreement can be realized (or, perhaps by which action
can be taken to ensure that actions of private firms and/or

governments do not impair the benefits of free trade), and it is to be hoped that stronger competition policy measures might be introduced into NAFTA at some future time.

Conclusion

The exposition of the past two sections of this chapter lead one to conclude that, viewed from an official U.S. perspective, NAFTA is quite good. Goals for the United States in the investment area have been met, and indeed the outcome surpassed the expectations of most persons familiar with the U.S. negotiating position.

But if the outcome is so good, then why are not Americans all for it? Why, for example, is there considerable resistance to NAFTA in Congress, to the point where some analysts have suggested that it might not be ratified?

To begin, one must note that opposition within the United States is not focused on the investment provisions of NAFTA, but rather on the whole agreement. This is not to say that investment has nothing to do with this opposition; it almost surely does, figuring especially in fears that U.S. firms will rush en masse to invest in Mexico, destroying U.S. jobs in the process. Nonetheless, one must look at NAFTA as a whole in order to understand U.S. attitudes towards it.

Second, one must also note that one reason why NAFTA might be in trouble within Congress is that the Clinton administration has sent out signals that are somewhat ambiguous. In particular, as a candidate Clinton distanced himself somewhat from NAFTA by suggesting that his support for it was conditional upon negotiation of certain side agreements. Then, as resident, Clinton has decided that it is indeed necessary to proceed with these additional negotiations.

However, it must be noted that there is almost surely more to the Congressional opposition to NAFTA (or, to put it somewhat more accurately, opposition on the part of certain elements within Congress) than that fueled by the administration. What seems to lay behind this is a tremendous fear of change on the part of certain constituencies within the United States. Exacerbating this fear is a resurgence of the "pauper labor" argument, which is, in essence, that U.S. workers will never be able to compete with Mexican workers who on average (in the manufacturing sector) are compensated at less than 15 percent the amount per hour as their U.S. counterparts.[14] This argument is easily shown to be fallacious both on grounds of logic (in fact U.S. workers are paid seven times their Mexican counterparts because on average U.S. workers are seven times more productive and hence are able to compete)[15] and on grounds of evidence (if the argument were to be true, the United States would already be losing ground to Mexico because the existing trade and investment barriers between the United States and Mexico are not great enough to compensate for a seven to one trade differential, all else being equal). In fact, loss of U.S. competitiveness has been most marked against Japan, where on average wages are now higher than in the United States. Additionally, the United States currently enjoys a large trade surplus with Mexico. Nonetheless, the pauper wage argument seems to ring true to persons already nervous about their own economic security.

Questions are certainly being asked by many Americans as to who exactly set the U.S. goals for NAFTA negotiations and, more fundamentally, whose interests are perceived to be served by these goals? In general, the average American's answer will be the large multinational firms—not usually thought to have interests coincidental with general U.S. society.

In other words, NAFTA was negotiated with other peoples' interests in mind—not the average American's. In this context, the interests of the large multinationals can be taken to mean something to the effect that "whatever interests NAFTA serves, it isn't my interests." That NAFTA might serve a broad range of interests, including those of at least most Americans, is not a possibility that is seriously considered, and those that do often are suspicious that lurking behind it all is a plot by the multinationals to take away jobs from Americans and give them to Mexicans.

As alluded to in the introduction, a "me versus them" approach to politics is probably inevitable in a society as hetero-geneous and querulous as that of the United States, at least if that society is governed by a democratic process. A familiar outcome of such a process is that special interests, if they are loud and powerful enough, will have their interests catered to.

But another outcome that is more relevant to this study is that the strategy of the nation with respect to international trade and investment issues is likely to lack coherence. This lack is partic-ularly evident in the early days of the Clinton administration, where U.S. officials seem intent on pushing forward with multi-lateral agenda (the Uruguay Round as well as NAFTA), but simultaneously pursue bilateral and even unilateral actions that often tend to corrode the very underpinnings of the multilateral system. These actions are often the result of special interest brokering but, increasingly, they reflect a lack of consensus as to exactly what is normatively the right strategy for the United States. Will this lack of consensus result in the United States increasingly pursuing a bilateral or unilateral approach to trade and investment issues? One cannot say for sure, of course, but a good guess would be that the U.S. strategy will remain some-what incoherent, with elements of a multilateral approach often vying with elements of bilateral and unilateral approaches to cross purposes.

Under these circumstances, it is important that public debate on major public policy issues be informed and rational if the outcome is to be favorable to that society's long-run interests. Informed and rational debate does not guarantee that the United States will pursue a coherent trade and investment strategy, because even if policy is formulated in the context of such a debate there is much scope for disagreement and for special interest brokering. But with respect to NAFTA, when push comes to shove, the debate has been neither particularly well informed nor rational. And while there may be a number of good reasons to reject NAFTA or to modify it substantially, the shame of the current situation is that if NAFTA were to fail, it would be for the wrong reasons.

Notes

1. The president's support is unequivocal if one ignores the fact that he has called for negotiation of three separate "supplemental" agreements. This probably was unwise and seems to have resulted from a campaign pledge apparently made in some haste. As of the time of this writing, it is impossible to tell whether or not NAFTA will be ratified. See, e.g., "Sand in the wheel of trade," *The Economist* 327, no. 7806 (10–16 April 1993): 25.

2. I should note that in making this statement, I do not mean to imply that the U.S. government necessarily achieved its particular objectives at the expense of the objectives of the Canadian or Mexican governments. Often, the objectives of the three nations were sufficiently compatible that treaty language satisfactory to all three parties could be achieved. The Mexican government in particular has significantly unilaterally altered its own policies with respect to direct investment during recent years in ways that accord with established U.S. objectives.

3. For most practical purposes, an investor in the context of chapter 11 of NAFTA means the home nation (headquarters) suborganization of a multinational firm. Investment in this context means the host nation (subsidiary) suborganization of such a firm.

4. However, some insight can be gained from the chapter by Allan Nymark, in this same volume.

5. More generally, there is a lack of consensus on the appropriate and inappropriate use of government subsidies, of which investment incentives are a subset.

6. An examination of the economic effects of performance requirements and a bibliography of the relevant literature is contained in Edward M. Graham and Paul R. Krugman, "Trade Related Investment Measures," in *Completing the Uruguay Round: A Results-Oriented Approach to the GATT Trade Negotiations,* Jeffrey J. Schott, ed. (Washington, D.C.: Institute for International Economics, 1991).

7. As a technical matter, it should be noted that the relevant provisions of the NAFTA pertaining to expropriation of investor property and compensation thereof (article 1110) do not pertain to intellectual property; intellectual property rights are, however, spelled out in chapter 17.

8. For an analysis of Mexican position on these issues and, more generally, the Mexican unilateral reforms, the reader should consult the chapter by Ortiz in this volume.

9. The relevant article (1109) does not apply, however, to transfers associated with issuing, trading, or dealing in securities.

10. See e.g., Michael Gestrin and Alan M. Rugman, "The NAFTA's Impact on the North American Investment Regime," *C. D. Howe Institute Commentary* 42 (Toronto: C. D. Howe Institute, March 1993).

11. This assessment is shared by Gary C. Hufbauer and Jeffrey J. Schott,

NAFTA: An Assessment (Washington, D.C.: Institute for International Economics, 1993), chap. 4. Hufbauer and Schott grade the investment provisions of the NAFTA as "A-" on a scale of A to F, where A is outstanding and F is failing.

12. According to Hufbauer and Schott Canada can use this exemption to discriminate against foreign participants in the cultural industries via denial of national treatment or failure to provide minimum levels of protection as called for in articles 1102–5.

13. Specific extensions are discussed in Hufbauer and Schott.

14. The "pauper labor" argument is more exhaustively discussed in Hufbauer and Schott 1993.

Chapter 6

CANADIAN INVESTMENT AND NAFTA

Alan Nymark and Emmy Verdun

Introduction

Canada has perhaps the most open policy in the world towards foreign investment. This is reflected in the magnitude of the international presence in Canada. By 1988, the most recent year reported, foreign control of assets in all industries stood at 18.9 percent. During the 1980s foreign control in manufacturing remained relatively stable at about 45 percent of the assets of all firms in Canada.

The total stock of foreign investment reached over $540billion at the end of 1992—including $282 billion of portfolio investment and $137 billion of foreign direct investment (FDI).[1] The sources and destination of the stock of FDI diversified in the 1980s from Canada's traditional partner, the U.S., to European and Pacific Rim countries. The U.S. share of the stock of FDI in Canada dropped during the 1980s from 77.8 percent in 1980 to 63.6 percent in 1991. In 1992 the U.S. share rose slightly to 63.9 percent. As will be seen later, there has been a rebound in the flows of FDI from the U.S., especially in manufacturing in Canada, since the U.S.-Canadian Free Trade Agreement in 1989.

For Canada the impact of the North American Free Trade Agreement (NAFTA) on foreign investment must be seen in this broader perspective of a country already open to international capital and doing very well in the competition for new investment. Nevertheless, globalization and the reduction of trade and investment barriers have intensified the efforts in Canada to

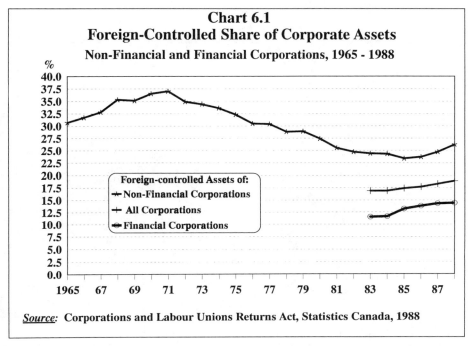

Chart 6.1
Foreign-Controlled Share of Corporate Assets
Non-Financial and Financial Corporations, 1965 - 1988

Foreign-controlled Assets of:
- ✦ Non-Financial Corporations
- + All Corporations
- ● Financial Corporations

Source: Corporations and Labour Unions Returns Act, Statistics Canada, 1988

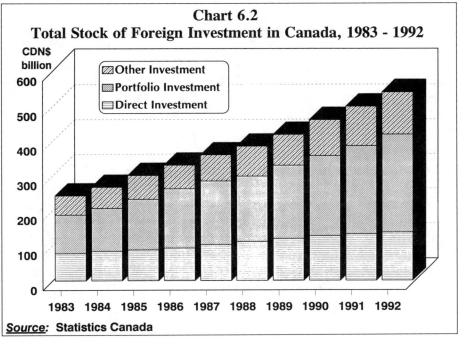

Chart 6.2
Total Stock of Foreign Investment in Canada, 1983 - 1992

- ▨ Other Investment
- ▨ Portfolio Investment
- ▤ Direct Investment

Source: Statistics Canada

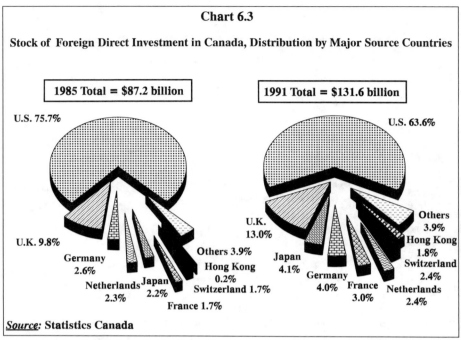

Chart 6.3

Stock of Foreign Direct Investment in Canada, Distribution by Major Source Countries

1985 Total = $87.2 billion

1991 Total = $131.6 billion

U.S. 75.7%

U.K. 9.8%

Germany 2.6%

Netherlands 2.3%

Japan 2.2%

Others 3.9%

Hong Kong 0.2%

Switzerland 1.7%

France 1.7%

U.S. 63.6%

U.K. 13.0%

Others 3.9%

Hong Kong 1.8%

Switzerland 2.4%

Netherlands 2.4%

France 3.0%

Germany 4.0%

Japan 4.1%

Source: **Statistics Canada**

ensure that the Canadian investment climate remains highly competitive.

In this chapter, the investment climate in Canada is evaluated first to set the context for an assessment of the impact of NAFTA and the performance of multinational enterprises (MNEs) in Canada. And finally a number of investment policy issues which are shaping up in the post-NAFTA environment are reviewed from a Canadian perspective.

Investment Climate in Canada

While the size of the market to be served by an investment is a critical factor in the decision to make an investment, the investment climate in general will determine whether the investment is made or not. Reducing trade and investment barriers appears in today's world to be necessary but not sufficient to attract foreign capital.

A host of factors determines the investment climate: a country's overall economic performance, taxation, infrastructure including knowledge networks, proximity to markets, cost of capital, price and currency stability, skills and adaptability of the labor force, the attitude and policies of the government towards investment, and, of course, various firm specific requirements.

Investors contemplating direct investments also make their decisions based on issues of political stability and economic performance over the longer term. In other words the latest quarterly results or even record of one government do not necessarily provide the kind of assurances that investors need to make strategic decisions involving significant fixed capital.

In this regard Canadian economic performance over an extended period of time stacks up well internationally:

1. From 1980 to 1991, the average annual growth in Canada's gross domestic product (GDP) was 2.6 percent, second only to that of Japan among the G-7;

2. In 1991 Canada's standard of living, as measured by GDP per capita, was second only to that of the United States in the G-7;

3. The quality of life in Canada, as measured by the United Nations' Human Development index, is ranked as second (to Japan's) in the world;

4. From 1985 to 1990 employment growth in Canada surpassed that in the other G-7 countries, averaging 2.3 percent annually.

The 1980s has been a difficult decade for all G-7 countries with two major global recessions, rising debt, and a serious productivity problem. In response there has been something close to a revolution in Canadian economic policy. At its core has been a recognition that in order to assure Canadians an increased standard of living, it is essential to resolve the lagging productivity riddle of the 1980s.

Investment in capital, people, technology, and infrastructure is the key. The government is pursuing a concentrated effort on a policy framework aimed at "investing in growth." The results have been, on balance, impressive in creating an environment that favors investment.

The macroeconomic framework has created a stable business environment through the pursuit of low inflation, fiscal prudence, and tax reform:

> 1. Canada now has the lowest inflation rate among all of the OECD countries, less than 2 percent at an annual rate, the lowest in 25 years. This has had a significant impact on the real cost of capital for investment.
> 2. Personal, corporate, and indirect taxation has been reformed. Taxes on corporations in Canada as a percentage of GDP are at a twenty year low (2 percent in 1991), just below that of the United States. Depending on President Clinton's initiatives, Canada's tax advantage may increase over the medium term.
> 3. The federal Spending Control Act has fixed spending limits by law. The goal is to enlarge the existing operating surplus in order to counter the cost of servicing the debt and to reduce significantly the overall deficit by 1998 to 1.7 percent of GDP.

Canada has also pursued an aggressive agenda of structural change over the past decade. In addition to pursuing a more open international trade and investment regime and competitive tax system, Canada has substantially deregulated the transportation, communications, energy, and financial services sectors; updated the competition and business framework including bankruptcy laws; and provided greater protection for intellectual property. This broad microeconomic agenda has also included major initiatives in upgrading human resources and providing one of the most hospitable environments in the world for research and development.

This structural economic agenda has led to the following investment climate results:

1. Canadian investment intensity, as measured by business capital formation as a proportion of GDP, surpasses that of the United States;

2. Canadian investment in machinery and equipment as a percentage of GDP has surpassed that of the United States and is approaching that of Germany;

3. From 1989 to 1992 productivity growth in Canada has improved and there has been a substantial reduction in wage inflation; these two factors have lowered the growth in Canada's unit labor costs. Now, Canadian unit labor costs are fully competitive with those in the United States.

These policies were particularly difficult to undertake because changes of such magnitude create significant transitional adjustment costs for business and labor and the benefits take time to be realized. In addition, much of the agenda was introduced as the global economy went into recession. However, there are a variety of signs that suggest Canada is on the threshold of a period in which its growth will spur economic performance to the forefront of the G-7.

Canadian Trade and Investment Policy

FTA marked a turning point in the hundred year national debate with respect to closer economic relations with the United States. With respect to investment, FTA and NAFTA mark another important shift for Canada—it has moved from a country that was quite skeptical of the benefits of foreign investment to the situation today—Canada, along with the United States, represents the leading edge of commitment to international investment agreements.

Negotiation of NAFTA was a strategic move on Canada's part, more than one based on expectations of immediate gains. One of the principal Canadian objectives in negotiating NAFTA was to ensure that Canada remains an attractive place to invest. This was accomplished by securing Canada's place in the largest trading arrangement in the world. NAFTA ensures that Canada and the United States participate in the North American market on the same terms. Had NAFTA been negotiated without Canada, the United States would have been the main beneficiary, being the only country with privileged access to both Canadian and Mexican markets.

Mexico is moving from a closed economy to an open economy. That is a win-win-win opportunity for all three partners in North America under a trilateral free trade arrangement. With improvements in Mexico's economy, Canadians will also benefit.

For Canada the impact of NAFTA and other pressures of globalization on the location decisions of MNEs will have an important effect on the level, growth, and composition of activity in the country. More specifically, how will regional integration affect

> Current MNE activity and performance in Canada?
> Potential growth in FDI in Canada?
> Offshore FDI interest in Canada? Canadian direct
>   investment abroad?
> Domestic investment?

The European Community's experience with "E.C. 1992" offers some lessons. Foreign investment in the E.C. has increased significantly; however, much of it continues to serve domestic or regional markets within Europe rather than serving the whole of Europe from single plants. This is especially true of Japanese investment which appears to remain politically risk adverse. Of perhaps greater interest, however, is the fact that intra-E.C. investment has grown by a factor of five in recent years. FDI appears to be one of the main vehicles E.C. firms have used to benefit from E.C. integration. This suggests that secondary or restructuring effects may be far more important than the initial trade effects of integration.[2]

In attempting to assess NAFTA, it is worth looking at Canada's performance under FTA.[3] With respect to trade, under FTA Canada's trade surplus with the United States has increased, and Canada's exports did best in those sectors liberalized by FTA, particularly in non-resource-based manufacturing. For example, the sectors in which Canadian exports to the United States grew more than 70 percent were the high-technology sectors of office, telecommunications and precision equipment, and paper (excluding newsprint). Canada has also increased its market share in key sectors of the U.S. economy in comparison to its share in other markets. For example, non-resource-based exports to the United States were up 34 percent between 1989 and 1991 while such exports to non-U.S. markets declined by almost 6 percent.

Canada's general objectives in joining NAFTA negotiations were to retain the benefits of FTA, including secure access to the United States, and to ensure that Canada remained an attractive location for investment. Canada's specific goals regarding investment were to:

1. Ensure further liberalization of the Mexican investment regime;

2. Provide greater certainty and security for Canadian investment in both Mexico and the United States;

3. Improve on FTA provisions in areas which had the potential for protectionist action by the United States;

4. Resist attempts by the United States to tackle its "unfinished business" left over from FTA negotiations; and

5. Retain Canadian policies in particularly sensitive sectors such as culture and social services.

Clearly the first two goals were achieved. Canada was also able to protect its sensitive sectors of culture and social services and to retain its ability to review foreign investments under the Investment Canada Act, despite U.S. opposition. The offensive targets with respect to the United States included: extraterritoriality, national security measures, technology protectionism, and restrictions on maritime transportation. Canada had some success. NAFTA contains a specific provision prohibiting forced repatriation (a form of extraterritoriality) and the exception for national security measures, while broad, is subject to dispute settlement. Maritime transportation is covered, although with a carve-out for national treatment and Most Favored Nation (MFN).[4]

FDI Flows to Canada Since FTA

Gross and net flows of FDI can be volatile, making analysis of trends difficult. Nevertheless, an examination of FDI flows over the four years pre- and post-FTA reveals some interesting results. First, there has been a significant increase in gross and net FDI flows to Canada since FTA. Gross inflows of FDI to Canada in the four years prior to FTA totalled $31.8 billion. In the four years since FTA, gross inflows totalled $41.8 billion. Net FDI inflows to Canada totalled $19.8 billion or on average $5 billion per year in the post-FTA period. In contrast, net FDI flows totalled $7.6 billion or on average $2.0 billion per year in the pre-FTA period.

Second, despite the general downward trend in the United States share of the stock of FDI in Canada, the United States share of net FDI flows to Canada increased significantly in the post-FTA period relative to the pre-FTA period. The opposite pattern emerged for net FDI flows from other countries such as the U.K. and Japan. As a result of American disinvestment in Canada in 1985 and 1986, the United States accounted for − 29 percent of net FDI flows to Canada during 1985 to 1988. In contrast, during 1989 to 1992 the United States accounted for 40 percent of net FDI flows to Canada. The U.K. share of net FDI flows was 46 percent during 1985 to 1988 but only 6 percent during 1989 to 1992. Similarly, Japan's share of net FDI flows decreased from 26 percent during 1985 to 1988 to 14 percent during 1989 to 1992.

Third, U.S. FDI in Canada shifted to manufacturing from other sectors. While the overall share of manufacturing in net FDI inflows remained relatively constant at two-thirds of the total, the U.S. share of net FDI directed to the manufacturing sector increased from 15 percent in the pre-FTA period to 60 percent in the post-FTA period. The U.S. share of net FDI inflows in the finance sector fell from 51 percent in pre-NAFTA period to 38 percent in the post-FTA period. In both periods, the United States accounted for large disinvestments in the natural gas and petroleum and mining sectors (U.S.-controlled firms were sold to Canadians or the take-over of a U.S.-controlled firm was financed within Canada).

The Impact of NAFTA on Investment at the Sectoral Level

At a sectoral level, there is little hard evidence of what one can expect from NAFTA. A recent study by Lorraine Eden and Maureen Appel Molot of Carleton University investigates the rationale for investments in Canada and Mexico. Their analysis indicates that Mexican plants fulfill primarily a cost reduction function (although this is often overstated), based on low unit labor costs, whereas Canadian plants are primarily market-based and resource-seeking. Thus, Canadian and Mexican plants, like their national economies, may be more complementary than competitive.[5]

To address the question of the potential impact of NAFTA on investment at the sectoral level, five studies were examined which provide estimates—formal or informal—of this impact on North American trade and investment flows. The studies were done by: the U.S. International Trade Commission; Hufbauer and Schott; DRI/McGraw-Hill; Industry, Science and Technology Canada; and Investment Canada.[6]

There is considerable variation among the studies respecting the detail and sectors selected for examination. For example, the Investment Canada study examines seventy-five individual products at a five digit classification level. The Hufbauer-Schott study examines seven sectors. The USITC study examines thirteen industrial sectors, four energy sectors, sixteen agricultural sectors, and five service sectors. Sectoral definitions also differ among studies (in other words, include larger or smaller industrial groupings).

TABLE 6.1

Net Flows of FDI to Canada by Major Country & Region of Origin, 1985–1992

U.S.
Million
Dollars

	Total	U.S.	U.K.	Other E.C.	Japan	Other
1985	(2,800)	(2,840)	(105)	(32)	110	67
1986	1,375	(1,464)	1,777	474	296	292
1987	4,600	2,055	710	360	258	1,217
1988	4,450	26	1,131	389	1,318	1,286
1985–88	**7,625**	**(2,223)**	**3,513**	**1,491**	**1,982**	**2,862**
1989	2,400	(261)	(591)	1,891	1,029	332
1990	6,820	1,979	1,436	1,894	713	798
1991	5,890	3,205	445	1,010	411	819
1992	4,717	2,932	(149)	745	520	669
1989–92	**19,827**	**7,855**	**1,141**	**5,540**	**2,673**	**2,618**

Continued on next page

Table 6.1—*Continued*

Percent

	Total	U.S.	U.K.	Other E.C.	Japan	Other
1985	100.0	101.4	3.8	1.1	-3.9	-2
1986	100.0	-106.5	129.2	34.5	21.5	21.2
1987	100.0	44.7	15.4	7.8	5.6	26.5
1988	100.0	0.6	25.4	15.5	29.6	28.9
1985–88	**100.0**	**-29.2**	**46.1**	**19.6**	**26.0**	**37.5**
1989	100.0	-10.9	-24.6	78.8	42.9	13.8
1990	100.0	29.0	21.1	27.8	10.5	11.7
1991	100.0	54.4	7.6	17.1	7.0	13.9
1992	100.0	62.2	-3.2	15.8	11.0	14.2
1989–92	**100.0**	**39.6**	**5.8**	**27.9**	**13.5**	**13.2**

SOURCE: Investment Canada compilations using Statistics Canada data.

TABLE 6.2

Net FDI Flows to Canada by Major Industries, 1985–1992 (U.S. Million Dollars)

	Manufacturing Industries	Petroleum Natural Gas net FDI	Mining & Smelting	Merchandising	Finance	Other	Total
1985	770	(4,006)	42	199	145	50	(2,800)
1986	1,768	(2,261)	348	645	623	252	1,375
1987	927	624	333	47	2,308	361	4,600
1988	1,711	1,160	740	176	240	423	4,450
Total	5,176	(4,483)	1,463	1,067	3,316	1,086	7,625
% of Total	67.9	−58.8	19.2	14.0	43.5	14.2	100.0
1989	3,481	(2,498)	(827)	385	1,069	792	2,402
1990	2,990	1,675	300	185	992	678	6,820
1991	4,199	974	20	52	355	290	5,890
1992	2,391	(261)	792	462	1,060	273	4,717
Total	13,061	(110)	285	1,084	3,476	2,033	19,829
% of Total	65.9	−0.6	1.4	5.5	17.5	10.3	100.0

SOURCE: Investment Canada compilations using Statistics Canada data.

TABLE 6.3

U.S. Direct Investment in Canada: Net Flows by Industry and U.S. Net Flows as a Percent of Total Flows (U.S. million dollars)

	Manufacturing	Petroleum & Natural Gas	Mining & Smelting	Merchandising	Finance	Other Industries	Total FDI
1985	673	(3,773)	(117)	166	116	95	(2,840)
1986	514	(2,574)	(39)	260	70	305	(1,464)
1987	(381)	426	(46)	133	1,834	89	2,055
1988	(46)	167	56	124	(328)	53	26
Total U.S.	760	(5,754)	(146)	683	1,692	542	(2,223)
Total FDI	5,176	(4,483)	1,463	1,067	3,316	1,086	7,625
U.S. as % of Total	14.7	128.4	−10.0	64.0	51.0	49.9	−29.2
1989	3,172	(2,668)	(1,209)	292	101	51	(261)
1990	768	372	103	9	224	504	1,980
1991	2,311	472	(12)	66	176	194	3,207
1992	1,568	(286)	389	278	801	182	2,932
Total U.S.	7,819	(2,110)	(729)	645	1,302	931	7,858
Total FDI	13,061	(110)	285	1,084	3,476	2,033	19,829
U.S. as % of Total	59.9	1,918.2	−255.8	59.5	37.5	45.8	39.6

SOURCE: Investment Canada compilations using Statistics Canada data.

There is no basic disagreement among the studies where coverage overlaps. Large, long-term investment increases are expected to accrue to Mexico in the following sectors: autos and auto parts; computers, computer components and electronics; apparel; and major household appliances. Somewhat lesser long-term increases are also expected in the bearings and pharmaceuticals sectors. In the short-term, significantly increased investment in Mexico is forecast for the computer, computer components, and electronics sectors, and the major home appliance sector.

The USITC cites the pharmaceutical and petrochemical sectors as areas where U.S. investment in Canada is expected to expand.

On the export market side, sectors such as environmental technology, agricultural and mining equipment, oil and gas production equipment, other industrial machinery, urban transit and rail equipment, and engineering and construction services are variously cited as some of the areas of strong Mexican demand. Canada already possesses expertise in such areas. It is these or other product/service areas requiring either capital-intensive or knowledge-intensive inputs in which Canada's relative trade and investment advantages lie.

As with FTA, the real significance of this agreement is that there is no going back to the past—Canada's future prosperity will depend heavily on Canadian business turning an agreement into profits. Indeed, NAFTA puts North America on the leading edge of international investment agreements. Whether Canada's principal competitors are prepared to liberalize and bind themselves similarly is open to question.

Within North America, NAFTA removes most internal barriers to business activity. This puts the focus directly on the economics of each country. That is why Canada has singled out the "investment in growth" policy agenda described above and why it is essential that Canada maintains a highly competitive investment climate.

Performance of MNEs

The available empirical evidence from the United States, Canada, and other countries strongly suggests that the activities of global corporations have a significant positive impact on domestic innovation, investment, productivity, and living standards. For instance, work by Litchenberg in the United States suggests that mergers have significantly improved total factor productivity by eliminating inefficient plants, increasing the utilization of inputs, reducing product and industry diversification, and lowering fixed costs.[7] It appears that almost all of the reduction in unit costs resulting from improvements in productivity was passed on to consumers in the form of lower prices.

John Baldwin's research is in line with the U.S. results, namely that mergers in the 1970s improved the productivity and profit performance of the Canadian firms involved.[8] Moreover, the improved profit performance did not come at the expense of wages.

The Investment Canada research suggests similar positive results.[9] Economic performance of firms after an international takeover between 1983 and 1987—measured in terms of increased profitability and investment and research and development intensities, and lower debt-equity ratio—improved considerably.

Recent Conference Board of Canada survey results are in line with the findings of Baldwin and Investment Canada.[10] Market penetration and market access, geographic expansion and diversification, and economies of scale were mentioned by the respondent firms as the major reasons for mergers and acquisitions (M&A). The survey results also suggest that the M&A activity significantly increases production efficiency and lowers unit costs.

The studies cited above focus on the behavior of firms after a take-over. A joint study by Economic Council of Canada and Investment Canada examined the behavior of foreign-controlled and Canadian-controlled MNEs. The study analyzed the productivity and trade performance of foreign-controlled and Canadian-controlled MNEs in the manufacturing sector. Theories of FDI suggest that MNEs possess firm-specific ownership advantages. The study looked for evidence that such advantages are translated into benefits for Canada, such as technology spillovers and improved productivity. Some of the results of the study confirmed this hypothesis:

1. From 1985 to 1988 value-added per employee was 19 percent higher in the foreign-controlled manufacturing establishments than in the domestic ones;

2. In three of the four largest manufacturing industries (petroleum, paper, and primary metals), foreign firms had higher value-added per employee than the domestic firms while in the fourth (motor vehicles), domestic and foreign firms had roughly similar value-added per employee; and

3. Foreign-controlled MNEs had higher propensities to export and to import than Canadian-controlled MNEs, and also had a very high level of intrafirm trade.

In short, increased global economic integration brought on by the activities and strategies of global firms would appear to enhance the living standards of Canadians, and increase the flexibility and dynamism of the Canadian economy.

Some have argued that there may also be potential negative effects of globalization even though on balance the impact has been positive. For example, the fierce competition among countries and global firms for markets and technology could intensify adjustment pressures. The adjustment difficulties may be more severe for low-wage and low-skilled people, because of the growing competition for these jobs from the Asia Pacific Rim and other newly industrialized countries. These countries are highly cost competitive in labor-intensive and light manufacturing products.

In addition, there are concerns that global corporations could adversely affect Canada by reducing domestic competition, avoiding taxes, and weakening the commitment to consumer interests and social justice. There is little empirical evidence, however, that these fears will be founded in Canada. Moreover, these potential negatives could turn into positives by ensuring that Canada has a flexible, dynamic economy which encourages adjustment, innovation, and competition. It also means one has to ensure that our human resources and adjustment policies are fully in tune with a changing world.

An area of growing importance is the role of Canadian-based MNEs in a global economy. Canadian direct investment abroad grew significantly in the 1980s and totalled $98.9 billion at year-end 1992. There is very little research and analysis on the evolution of Canadian-controlled businesses from domestic to MNE status, on to global status, and finally to stateless corporation status. For example, whether there have been many Canadian firms that have moved research and development outside of Canada to take advantage of the critical mass in another location or whether Canadian firms with operations abroad are more profitable than similar firms that remain solely in Canada is not known. Increasingly, however, it is recognized that it is strategically important for corporations to be in the primary markets where they also trade.[11]

Post-NAFTA—A New International Framework for Investment?

NAFTA investment provisions have been described elsewhere in this book. They mark a significant development in Canada's international investment policy. While they build on FTA, NAFTA is broader and deeper in scope. In fact, NAFTA investment provisions go beyond those in any international investment agreement whether bilateral or multilateral. As such, the question naturally arises—what next?

Currently, Canada is looking at the prospect of actual or potential international negotiations on a variety of investment issues, including the European Energy Charter, Canada's bilateral Foreign Investment Protection Agreements (FIPAs), a possible Wider Investment Instrument (WII) under the auspices of the OECD, various investment issues in the GATT Uruguay Round, and possible accession to NAFTA. In addition, Canada's domestic policy on investment is also under review in certain areas. The government has already announced liberalization of its policy on foreign take-overs in the oil and gas and cultural sectors. Developments in the United States and Europe together with the precarious financial state of the airline industry are leading to public debate about existing restrictions on foreign ownership in airlines.

Emerging issues in other policy areas also have implications for Canadian investment policy. One obvious example is environmental regulation. The debate about whether Mexico would become a "pollution haven" as a result of NAFTA indicates that investment as well as trade issues are linked to environmental policies. Other issues include the linkages between investment and competition, national security, industrial, labor, and technology policies.

No doubt the United States and Mexico are now reviewing their international investment agendas. What follows is a brief survey of issues from a Canadian perspective.

Multilateral Versus Regional Versus Bilateral Investment Negotiations

Japan and the E.C. have expressed concerns that the FTA (and now NAFTA) creates a "Fortress North America." Similarly, Canadian and American business leaders expressed fear that without a European base of operations they would be left outside the "Fortress Europe" created by "E.C. 1992." This concern is one of the manifestations of the debate about whether multilateral, or regional, or bilateral agreements are the best way to attain greater openness in world trade and investment. Some argue that incremental liberalization among like-minded countries serves as a model that will be emulated, in time, in the multilateral forum. Others argue that such agreements, by providing discriminatory preferences to a few countries, hinder the cause of multilateral liberalization generally and undermine the basic principle of MFN specifically. Canada strongly believes that NAFTA is complementary and supports GATT.

Regardless of which side of the debate one takes, it is clear that multilateral agreements will coexist with regional and bilateral agreements for the foreseeable future. In fact, both the GATT (article 24) and the OECD codes (article 10) permit exceptions to the MFN obligation for certain types of bilateral or regional agreements. The GATT contains explicit conditions for the MFN exception: for example, a free trade agreement must eliminate duties on substantially all trade among the parties and must not introduce new barriers to trade for other GATT members. The OECD exception is less explicit, but also includes the notion of no new barriers for other OECD members.

In the mid-1980s the United States decided to use all approaches to varying degrees. The Uruguay Round of GATT negotiations is still viewed as the highest priority, but the United States is also pursuing regional negotiations (FTA, NAFTA, NAFTA accession, Enterprise of the Americas, Energy Charter) and bilateral negotiations (a growing list of BITs—bilateral investment treaties). In addition, the United States has a unilateral approach as well in "Super301," which is intended to pry open markets closed by unfair practices. The United States will likely continue this multifaceted approach to trade and investment policy over the rest of this decade.

Canada's policy on trade and investment has also included multilateral, regional, and bilateral approaches. Although Canada is a strong supporter of the GATT, including the current round of GATT negotiations on the "new" issues, Canada has also signed the FTA, NAFTA, and six bilateral FIPAs. To date, Canada's use of the unilateralism has been largely limited to unilateral liberalization—for example, the replacement of FIRA (Foreign Investment Review Agency) with Investment Canada and the recently announced changes to the policy on foreign take-overs in the oil and gas and cultural sectors. In a few cases, Canada has used unilateral measures defensively, as in the Foreign Extraterritorial Measures Act which prohibits any Canadian-based company from complying with a United States order banning trade with Cuba.

The question increasingly being discussed internationally is whether it is possible to achieve a GATT for investment. If that is the direction in which the international community is moving, the route then becomes an important issue.

The GATT has a long and successful history in liberalizing trade and its membership is more comprehensive than that of the OECD, APEC, or other economic organizations. GATT

recognition of the interrelationship between trade and investment is evident in the Uruguay negotiations on the new issues of
trade in services, trade-related investment measures, and intellectual property. Nevertheless, the negotiations on these "new"
issues have been difficult, particularly because of the pronounced split between the industrialized countries and the less
developed countries (LDCs) on investment policies and the role
of government in the economy. While some LDCs and NICs
have begun the difficult task of liberalizing and modernizing
their investment policies, many are not yet ready to do so. As a
result, the GATT would face many challenges in negotiations on
a broader investment instrument in the foreseeable future, although some argue that a GATT Investment Code among the
industrialized members is feasible.

Level of Investment Obligations: National Treatment and MFN Versus Reciprocity or Effective Access

The most basic obligation in all investment treaties is national
treatment: investments of another party must be treated no less
favorably than those from the party itself, in like circumstances.
The other standard obligation is Most Favored Nation (MFN)
treatment: investments of another party must be treated no less
favorably than those of any other party or nonparty, in like
circumstances.

In principle, these two obligations in an investment agreement
would eliminate all discriminatory treatment of investments
from another party to the Agreement. In practice, however, the
elimination of discrimination is tempered by exceptions (both to
the specific obligation and to the Agreement as a whole) and by
measures or practices (whether government or private) that have
the effect of excluding or discriminating against investment from
another party. For example, banking in Canada is based on a
system of country-wide branches which is effectively prohibited
by U.S. law. Thus, while Canadian banks may receive "national
treatment" in the United States they do not have the same
access to the U.S. market as U.S. banks have to the Canadian

market. Examples of private practices that effectively exclude outsiders are the keiretsu in Japan and the extensive commercial-financial linkages in Germany. Ostensibly these private practices are not under government control; however, without tacit government agreement they would not likely continue. Similarly, a high level of state participation in the economy or of corporate concentration also effectively reduces foreign (and private domestic) participation. Although all countries have sectors with state participation or high corporate concentration, the degree varies considerably among countries. In Canada, basic telecommunications service is provided by regulated monopolies, some of which are government-owned. The United States, on the other hand, has demonopolized its basic telecommunications market—and these companies are keen to expand into Canada. Similarly, Canada's electric utilities are mostly provincial Crown corporations with virtual monopoly power. Again, the United States has much greater private sector participation in the production and distribution of electricity. Yet Canada has the highest level of foreign ownership and control of any industrialized country—clearly not closed to foreign investment.

These examples of government and private actions that have the effect of discouraging or prohibiting FDI clearly indicate that the principles of national treatment and MFN cannot, in themselves, guarantee access for foreign investors. Various responses to the limitations of these principles are being proposed. Reciprocity is one mechanism that has been used extensively in the past and is now being proposed as a new means to gain access. Other concepts are "equivalent competitive access" or "effective access." In some respects, the use of Super 301 by the United States can be viewed as a means to address the failure of national treatment and MFN.

The concept of reciprocity is put forward as one means of addressing the differences in openness to foreign investment in a particular country. The issue here is that national treatment and MFN are meaningless if a whole sector is closed to one party in an agreement but open to another party. The United States has, at various times, advocated reciprocity as a means of ensuring that other countries match the U.S. level (or at least meet a minimum level) of openness. Reciprocity is often used in the context of financial services, especially for the types of financial services a particular institution is permitted to provide. For example, a narrow interpretation of reciprocity would deny U.S. banks in Canada the ability to branch until the United States permitted interstate branching. Obviously a major weakness of reciprocity is the additional distortions it can introduce. Reciprocity can also be used to provide conditional, rather than unilateral, liberalization. In this case, the United States would waive the 25 percent foreign ownership limit in airlines only for those countries which matched the United States. This type of reciprocity also violates the principle of MFN.

The concept of "equivalent competitive opportunity" or "effective access" has been proposed as another means of addressing restrictions on trade and investment in services that cannot be effectively addressed by national treatment or MFN obligations. This concept, unlike national treatment and MFN, does not have a standard wording or meaning. It is an emerging concept which is still being defined. At present, it appears to be as much a relative as an absolute standard of obligation. For example, one meaning in the context of financial services is that a foreign bank must have equivalent opportunity to provide particular financial services (such as underwriting of securities, acting as principal agent for government bond issues, selling insurance, establishing branches) as a domestic bank.

In the telecommunications sector, for example, the United States is unwilling to grant unconditional MFN in the GATT negotiations because there is greater access for foreign firms to the U.S. telecommunications market than for U.S. firms to foreign markets. Thus, the United States argues that it is unfair to expect the United States to grant MFN to a country unless that country provides equivalent access—and countries where government or private monopolies provide most basic services clearly do not meet this test. The meaning of equivalency, however, is problematic. How does one measure the effects of regulations on foreign ownership, standards, and rate settings in terms of access? Does one measure actual market penetration? While foreign firms have access to the giant U.S. market in principle, their share of that market is minuscule. Does one require regulation of the sector on the same basis? This would appear to favor harmonization of regulations—to those of countries with larger economies. In this example, the use of reciprocity or equivalent access results in conditional MFN, which is contrary to the basic premise of GATT.

Similarly, equivalent competition opportunity or effective access attempts to tackle the very real problem that as formal barriers to investment fall, the remaining barriers are less easily identified and removed. The policy issue is how can effective access be defined in a manner that helps to eliminate real barriers to investment without imposing a subjective policy view on other countries. Canada and the United States, for example, may argue that their companies do not have effective access to the Japanese equity market—based on the overall effect of both government and private practices. The Japanese might argue that their economy is open to investors who persevere and learn the differences inherent in the Japanese culture and economy. Many would argue that the determination of which practices amount to real barriers and which are legitimate national differences in economic structure and policies is inherently subjective. On the other hand, there is a growing recognition among business and government leaders that one of the real effects of globalization is the tendency toward policy convergence. For example, the E.C. now has an E.C.-wide law on mergers and acquisitions as well as a bilateral agreement with the United States to foster cooperation in enforcement of cross-border cases. The next step may well go beyond national treatment to address international harmonization of laws and enforcement practices. Similarly, there would be no issue regarding transfer pricing if all countries had the same tax rules. The need for (and benefits of) policy convergence are being recognized; however, the need for national sovereignty (the ability to retain legitimate economic and policy differences) pushes against policy convergence.

Exceptions to the Obligations

No obligation in an investment agreement is ever absolute: negotiating exceptions to specific obligations and exclusions from the whole agreement is the major work of the negotiators. The U.S. concept of "balance of benefits" is partly based on the notion that each party must provide some concessions and must meet a minimum standard of acceptable investment policy. During NAFTA negotiations, for example, vehement opposition by the United States to an exception for the Investment Canada review process stemmed not because it posed any substantive problems for American businesses but because it would set a precedent for Mexico and other potential NAFTA parties. In the final agreement, the Canadian and Mexican review mechanisms were exempted as was the U.S. national security mechanism under Exon-Florio.

In both FTA and NAFTA negotiations, Canada's negotiating mandate was based on "grandfathering" of virtually all existing measures that did not conform with the obligations. Will this pattern continue? If so, the limit of liberalization through the current model of investment agreements may already have been reached. In both agreements, the liberalization by Canada and the United States is largely in the form of prospective commitments.

Yet, a major purpose of investment agreements is to liberalize the treatment of foreign investment, and thus negotiations must be about reducing the number and scope of exceptions and exclusions. The future policy issues for NAFTA partners internally as well as in relation to non-NAFTA countries might be: what exceptions are NAFTA partners willing to discuss further with a view to rollback and what exceptions are NAFTA partners seeking to have non-NAFTA partners concede? These questions should be addressed in terms of sectors (transportation, telecommunications) as well as principles (foreign review mechanisms, national security, taxation, subsidies).

Technology Protectionism and National Security

In the past, concerns about protectionism resulting from industrial policy were focused on government measures such as discriminatory subsidies and government procurement as well as state ownership. The response to the distortions and protectionism caused by these measures can be seen in unilateral action (antidumping and countervailing duties and privatization) and in multilateral action (the GATT government procurement code). An analogous issue in the 1990s relates to technology protectionism and how it affects investment.

The development and diffusion of technology are recognized as critical to the competitiveness of a country's economy. No country proposes to close its borders to technology flows; nevertheless, how a country ranks with respect to technology is one factor in the development of policies which can affect foreign investment. The public debate in the United States about the loss of technology superiority to the Japanese in particular sectors has spawned proposals (some of which have been adopted) that effectively discriminate against foreign participation in certain high technology sectors. For example, the technology consortium Sematech has no foreign-controlled members partly as a result of discriminatory subsidies and government procurement practices. The United States claims that Sematech is merely acting in the interests of its private sector members, but government practices make this possible.

In the case of technology, a related issue is the extent to which measures such as discriminatory subsidies, government procurement, and foreign investment screening are being disguised as national security measures. The current debate in the United States over the link between the competitiveness of the American defence base and that of its industrial base more generally illustrates this point. The questions are: what is a legitimate national security measure and what is unfair protectionism in the high technology sector? The rising cost of research and development and the increasing scope of technology with both defence and commercial applications are increasing the complexity of this issue and blurring the distinctions between national and economic security.

The end of the cold war, the loss of U.S. preeminence in certain technologies, and the lagging competitiveness of certain American manufacturing sectors are fuelling public debate and leading to suggestions that promoting the development of U.S.-controlled technology in the United States is one means of addressing these problems. The pattern of U.S.-controlled firms in technology consortia such as Sematech is one example of concerted private and government action in this area. Similarly, recent changes have made the Exon-Florio regulations more restrictive, and more clearly designed to keep certain technologies and firms under U.S. control. Many in the United States consider that current measures do not go far enough. The difficulty for small, trade-dependent countries like Canada is that such practices can undo some of the liberalization promised in the GATT, FTA, and NAFTA. The real danger for Canada (and other countries) is that U.S. measures based on a very broad concept of national security may become disguised protectionism.

Canada too faces many of the same issues and problems as the United States. Canada is inevitably more dependent on other countries for its defence and technology needs. For Canada, as for other countries, there is a link between technology development and diffusion on the one hand and productivity and competitiveness on the other. Canadian high technology firms also face the dilemma that growth beyond a certain size often entails foreign capital—and the loss of a Canadian "jewel." In addition, Canada is the only G-7 country not to have a review mechanism for foreign investment based on national security concerns. While the United States is moving toward protecting its strategic technology firms from friends and foes alike, Canada does not have a mechanism to review foreign investment on even a narrow definition of national security. There is growing evidence the technology espionage for economic gain is replacing the more traditional cold war espionage of the past.

NAFTA does contain a broad exception for national security measures, but does not directly address the issue of technology protectionism. Questions for future negotiations include: how can a legitimate national security measure be distinguished from technology protectionism and how can technology protectionism be addressed in bilateral, regional, and multilateral agreements?

Linkages Between Investment and Other Policies

In an era of globalization, domestic policies in such areas as competition law, environmental regulation, taxation, labor standards, and social policies all have the potential to significantly and directly affect international investment decisions. The E.C.'s refusal to permit Aerospatiale and Alenia to acquire de Havilland on the grounds that the acquisition would cause adverse effects on competition in the E.C. is a graphic example of how competition policy can affect investment decisions. Similarly, while New York state's decision to withdraw its offer to buy electricity from Hydro Québec was ultimately based on lower projections of electricity demand, public debate also focused on environmental and social considerations (the possible environmental damage in Québec and disputes over land claims with the Cree Indians of James Bay). The current debate in the United States on intrafirm transfer pricing and whether multinationals pay their fair share of corporate income taxes is another example of the linkages between investment and other policies.

The policy questions relate to which other policies have the greatest effect on investment decisions, and how these effects should be addressed. For example, harmonization of competition policies among the G-7 or G-24 would eliminate the differential effects of competition policy on investment decisions. Another means to address this linkage is through bilateral or multilateral agreements (to share information, to take into account the effects on investments in other countries, and to cooperate in enforcement of cases that involve several countries). The inclusion of obligations relating to environmental standards in NAFTA investment chapter sets a precedent; the outcome of the supplemental negotiations on environmental and labor issues may also establish a new model.

Conclusion

There is every reason to expect that economic adjustment to NAFTA will leave all three participating countries better off in both trade and investment terms. For Canada industrial rationalization in the four years since the U.S.-Canadian FTA has witnessed a resurgence of U.S. interest in investing in Canada, especially in the manufacturing sector.

With declining government intervention domestically as well as at the border on a regional and global basis, the pressure to maintain a highly competitive investment climate will be intensified. This will have profound implications for economic policy. There is strong evidence that Canada has recognized this need and has shifted priorities accordingly. The competitiveness agenda is shifting from a trade orientation to dealing with the implications of integration of production across borders.

Looking ahead, international negotiations on investment matters will intensify as all countries seek to establish more transparent and hospitable rules in the process of facilitating cross-border activities of MNEs. Canada, the United States, and Mexico are now in the lead in establishing modern international investment frameworks. Whether one will see the equivalent of the GATT for investment in this century will in large part depend on the Europeans and Japanese opening effective access to their capital markets in equivalent terms to what North America has done with NAFTA.

Notes

1. Foreign direct investment (FDI) refers to investment that is made to acquire a lasting interest in an enterprise in a country other than that of the investor. Flows of FDI refer to the movement of investment funds across the border; this includes outgoing as well as incoming investment. Investments that do not involve the cross-border flow of funds are not counted. Thus, if a foreign-controlled firm finances an expansion by borrowing funds in Canada there is no cross-border flow. Flows of FDI are reported in both gross and net terms. A gross inflow of FDI includes equity and long-term debt investments by foreign investors while a gross outflow of FDI includes the repayment of a long-term loan and sale of equity to domestic residents. The net flow of FDI is the difference between gross inflows and outflows of FDI. The stock of FDI represents the net book value of long-term capital owned by foreign investors in businesses in Canada in which foreign investors have an effective voice in management. The stock of FDI increases (or decreases) by the combined

changes in net FDI flows, in retained earnings, assessed book value of assets, and reclassifications of ownership (foreign versus domestic). Foreign portfolio investment refers to foreign investment in equity and debt instruments where the investor does not have an effective voice in management. For practical purposes, a foreign investment is classified as direct (rather than portfolio) if the foreign interest holds at least 10 percent of the voting equity.

2. John H. Dunning, *Multinational Enterprises and the Global Economy* (Reading: Addison-Wesley, 1993) and John H. Dunning, "Global Economy, Domestic Governance Statistics and Transnational Corporations: Interactions and policy Implications," *Transnational Corporations* 1, no. 3 (1993).

3. Michael Gestrin and Alan M. Rugman, "The NAFTA's Impact on the North American Investment Regime," *C. D. Howe Institute Commentary* (Toronto: C. D. Howe Institute, 1993); Ranga Chand, *NAFTA: The Economic Implications for Canada,* Conference Board of Canada, International Business Research Centre, 1993; Steven Globerman and Michael Walker, *Assessing NAFTA: A Trinational Analysis* (Vancouver: The Fraser Institute, 1993).

4. Article 1138 states that a decision about whether to permit or reject an investment on the basis of the Article 2102 National Security exception is not subject to the dispute settlement provisions of NAFTA. However, there is no general exclusion from dispute settlement for Article 2102, and the Canadian view is that the dispute settlement provisions therefore apply to Article 2102. The United States would not likely agree with this interpretation.

5. Lorraine Eden and Maureen Appel Molot, "Comparative and Competitive Advantage in the North American Trade Bloc," *Canadian Business Economics* 1, no. 1 (Fall 1992).

6. U.S. International Trade Commission, *Potential Impact on the U.S. Economy and Selected Industries of the North American Free-Trade Agreement* (January 1993); Gary C. Hufbauer and Jeffrey J. Schott, *NAFTA—An Assessment* (Washington, D.C.: Institute for International Economics, 1993); Investment Canada, *The Opportunities and Challenges of the Impact of the North-America Free Trade Agreement on Mexican Industrial Trade with the United States* (Ottawa: DRI/McGraw-Hill, November 1991); Industry, Science, and Technology Canada, *North American Trade Liberalization—Sector Impact Analysis* (September 1990).

7. Frank R. Lichtenberg, *Corporate Takeovers and Productivity* (Boston: The MIT Press, 1992). 8. John Baldwin, *The Dynamics of the Competitive Process,* Statistics Canada (1991).

8. John Baldwin, *The Dynamics of the Competitive Process,* Statistics Canada (1991).

9. Investment Canada, *Business Performance Following a Takeover,* Working Paper No. 11, 1992.

10. Steven J. Reitsma and R. Shyam Khemani, *The Canadian Corporate Response to Globalization,* Conference Board of Canada, mimeo (June 1992); Ronald Corvari and Robert Wisner, *Foreign Multinationals and Canada's*

International Competitiveness, Economic Council of Canada and Investment Canada, draft, 1992; John Baldwin, *The Dynamics of the Competitive Process,* Statistics Canada (1991); Investment Canada, *Canadian Direct Investment Abroad,* Steven Globerman, ed., University of Calgary Press, Research Series, vol. 4, February 1994.

11. Alan M. Rugman, *Multinationals and Canada-United States Free Trade* (Columbia: University of South Carolina Press, 1989).

Chapter 7

NAFTA AND FOREIGN INVESTMENT IN MEXICO

Edgar Ortiz

Introduction

The North American Free Trade Agreement (NAFTA) between Canada, the United States, and Mexico has been subject to close analysis by scholars, business persons, and politicians around the world. Several reasons account for this interest in NAFTA. First, a great deal of the interest in NAFTA arises since the North American bloc will constitute the largest in the world which could give its member countries a competitive edge in global competition. Second, NAFTA confirms world trends toward the formation of strong economic blocs. Although this might bring greater stability to trade flows among nations, it will also increase competition, which could even lead to unprecedented trade wars. Third, NAFTA constitutes an unparalleled association between two developed nations and one developing nation.

NAFTA is seen by many as the key for Mexico's economic development, with a large volume of investment expected to be attracted by low labor costs. Through job creation, technology transfers, and linkages with other sectors it is believed that foreign direct investment (FDI) will induce high rates of growth.[1] NAFTA is supposed to launch a take-off in the Mexican economy, transforming it into a developed country.[2] Finally, Mexico's daring policies of the last few years, including integration with its northern neighbors, are seen as a model to be followed both by other developing countries, and also by all those nations transforming their economies into a market system.

In sharp contrast with those expectations, some see the benefits from NAFTA accruing to the United States due to existing asymmetries. Higher technological development, the presence of skilled labor and management, and advanced infrastructure are seen as the reasons which would lead to U.S. benefits.[3] Moreover, it is argued that FDI distorts Mexico's economic growth.

In sum, two questions that need answering are whether or not NAFTA will bring about important changes in Mexico's FDI, and whether or not FDI from Canada and the United States can be related to Mexico's future economic growth. Contributing to the settlement of this controversy, this chapter analyzes current trends in FDI in Mexico, especially sectoral activity. Because the financial sector has the potential to become the link in trade and investment activity carried out by Canadian and U.S. firms, possible trends in this sector are also discussed.

The chapter has been organized in seven sections. Following this introduction, sections two and three establish a framework for analysis. Section two identifies current Mexican views on FDI and economic integration with the United States and Canada. Section three examines briefly Mexico's trade liberalization policies and their relationship with NAFTA. Section four deals with NAFTA and emerging FDI patterns in Mexico, stressing the role of North American investment, and sectoral impacts. Section five assesses the importance of Mexico's financial sector on NAFTA integration efforts, emphasizing the case of banking and securities brokerage institutions. The chapter ends with a brief conclusion which examines expected trends toward investment in Mexico resulting from its association with Canada and the United States.

A Mexican Perspective on NAFTA

The idea of establishing a North American common market among Mexico, Canada, and the United States dates back to the end of the 1970s. Although Mexico and the United States have always maintained complex relations, prior to the 1973 oil crisis

U.S.-Mexico relations were somewhat friendly but distant. They could be characterized as a "benign neglect" by the United States and as a "cautious and defensive" stance by Mexico. Similarly, while economic integration between the United States and Canada increased recently, relations between Mexico and Canada were warm but insignificant. Sharing borders with the United States as well as deep economic, political, and cultural impacts from such a large nation contributed little to strengthen Canadian-Mexican ties.[4]

Such attitudes changed in the 1970s, especially due to the oil crises. Authorities in the United States became aware not only of their dependency on unreliable and politically explosive foreign sources for primary goods inputs, but also of the great potential that their neighboring countries had to supply needed imports, and to spur regional economic growth via increased trade and foreign investment. Thus, stronger economic relations between the United States and Mexico, and the United States and Canada were promoted. Propositions to create a North American market were made while simultaneously stressing potential mutual benefits.[5]

In Mexico and Canada such alternatives were also analyzed. Indeed, following several years of debate in the political, business, and academic worlds, Canadians approved a bilateral free trade agreement with the United States in 1987, which was confirmed by reelecting Prime Minister Brian Mulroney on this issue in November 1988.[6] However, establishing closer ties with Mexico was largely ignored in the United States.

In Mexico the notion of a North American free trade or common market agreement was usually rejected. Critics stressed the fact that the United States viewed economic integration unilaterally, as a function of its own economic needs and national security. Consequently, they emphasized the dangers to autonomous economic development, and national identity and sovereignty of prevailing "silent integration" trends, as well as those that would take place from any formal integration scheme.[7]

Mexico also restricted FDI as multinational corporations (MNCs) were seen as arms of U.S. domination. It was argued that MNCs caused disarticulation in the economy and stratified the world in a structure of core-periphery relations. Responding to social pressures, the Mexican government enforced tough foreign investment control laws, restricting entry to many sectors and limiting capital to 49 percent. However, the government followed a pragmatic approach, aware of the need of foreign capital. Throughout the years, many firms were allowed to operate in Mexico beyond the limits established by the law. Capital ownership of up to 100 percent was allowed in some cases, as in the pharmaceutical industry.

These protectionist views began to change in the 1980s. However, only partial agreements were proposed, which would not disrupt the Mexican economy, and would respect national identity.[8] With regard to FDI, the debt crisis made Mexicans aware of the importance that foreign investment has on economic development. However, steps were taken to promote it only selectively. Mexico's 1984–1988 Trade and Industrialization Plan stated that FDI participation in Mexico would be selective and strictly complementary to domestic efforts carried out in areas with export potential.[9]

A more positive attitude has emerged in the last few years. Indeed, economic policy has taken a healthy about-face in Mexico, amazing the world. Following a severe crisis caused by excessive borrowing in a protected economy, Mexico shows signs of a strong economic recovery. These signs are: a successful renegotiation of its foreign debt, which has ended negative capital transfers; daring liberalization policies to enhance market forces and open the economy to foreign trade and investment, as well as to promote an outward oriented highly competitive industrial sector; a strong privatization program of state enterprises, which includes reprivatization of the banking sector nationalized in 1982; innovative "social solidarity" program of development projects in the communities; and unprecedented negotiations to build a trading block with Canada and the United States. In addition, the government has also promoted political reforms to strengthen political processes, reform the public sector, and fight corruption—particularly from union leaders.

The basis for all these changes was set up under the government of President de la Madrid, 1982 to 1988, but it is President Salinas, who during the last few years has astonished leaders around the world with his economic, social, and political policies to modernize Mexico and promote sustained development.[10] Indeed, his policies have been regarded as a model for both developing countries and Eastern European countries which are now seeking to transform to market economies. Former Secretary of State James Baker, for instance, once stated that "President Salinas's bold economic reform and modernization program is a model for countries both from this hemisphere and other countries around the world."[11] In short, Mexico's economic policies are now regarded as a model for nation building and economic transformation.

NAFTA is the key to Mexico's long-term economic reforms. Mexico has undergone a "silent integration" with the United States for many years as a result of increasing trade, investment, and labor flows among both nations.[12] Now most people, from scholars to business persons and politicians, support President Salinas's efforts for integration with its neighboring northern countries. Mexico's strong nationalism and zealotry for its sovereignty, particularly in its relations with the United States, has been left behind. It is believed that NAFTA will induce major investment in Mexico and large exports to the U.S. (and Canadian) markets, leading to important efficiency and employment gains, increased exports, rapid growth, and increased welfare.[13]

Foreign direct investment is the moving force behind Mexico's new era of economic growth. New regulations were passed 15 May 1989. These acknowledge the importance of FDI for economic growth and for promoting technological development and international competitiveness. Among the new regulations, ownership requirements were eliminated for maquiladora plants. For other productive sectors, the new FDI regulations specify with greater clarity the types of investment and limitations allowed to foreigners, and specifies branches where investment is reserved for either Mexican nationals or the state.

However, doubts still remain among some people. Some have lost their original enthusiasm about NAFTA and are reassessing it in the light of political changes in the United States. It is believed that NAFTA has a rather low priority with President Clinton; gone is the vigor with which President Bush promoted NAFTA. The parallel agreements on labor and environmental issues, proposed by President Clinton, are also seen as a problem for NAFTA.

This plays into the hands of the Mexican opponents. Some groups feel that the Salinas reforms and particularly NAFTA are desperate efforts to maintain the political elite in power. In their view, NAFTA gives the ruling party, Partido Revolucionario Institucional (PRI), the political and strategic support it needs to remain in power.[14] Finally, some even feel that Salinas has given excessive importance to NAFTA and that trade and FDI would rather weaken the economy in the long run. It is maintained that NAFTA, in addition to negative results due to existing asymmetries with the United States, will lead to a loss of sovereignty.

NAFTA and other policies implemented by the Salinas government are seen as a fundamental break with the principles and objectives of the Mexican Revolution of 1910. NAFTA is seen as an institutional arrangement whose ultimate (U.S.) policy goal is to obtain Mexican laws that allow FDI into Mexico without restrictions. The U.S. motives for a trade agreement with Mexico are also seen as part of a strategy to use Mexico as a strategic source of inputs (mainly oil) and a greater market for investment and exports.[15] Rigidities in the political system, which repress transformation towards a full fledged plural democracy are also pointed out.[16] Indeed, there remain doubts about the compatibility of markets and democracy, as well as in the relevance of the Salinas model for other countries.

Trade Liberalization Policies in Mexico

Before the Salinas measures, Mexican markets remained highly protected both by tariffs and licensing requirements. Mexico considered joining the General Agreement on Trade and Tariffs (GATT) but the decision, in 1980, was negative. Mexico withdrew its application to join the GATT due to political reasons, to hold down pressures from groups opposed to this measure. In the early 1980s production continued to be inward oriented, and firms remained protected from outside competitors. Moreover, the peso was overvalued. In general, imports increased more rapidly than exports so that the economy showed high trade deficits during the 1977 to 1981 oil boom period. Indeed, by 1982, Mexico imported $23,929.6 billion and exported $19,419.6 billion, which resulted in a trade deficit of − $4,510.0 billion.[17]

As a result of the debt crisis, imports were repressed and some efforts began to promote manufacturing exports. The authorities concentrated their efforts in obtaining surpluses, but to meet debt payments, rather than for economic development, as would have been desirable. During 1982 exports increased to $21 billion and imports decreased sharply to $14 billion, which amounted to a surplus of $7 billion. These policies and trends continued during the following years. Indeed, during 1983 imports decreased to $8.5 billion. The following four years, 1984 to 1987, imports increased slightly, varying around $13 billion. In 1988 trade liberalization led to a sharp increase in imports, amounting to $20 billion. But the trade deficit for 1989 was $2.6 billion. In 1991 the deficit was $11 billion. Preliminary figures for 1992 show an all time trade deficit of $19 billion. For 1993 the trade deficit could be near $27 billion.[18]

In spite of restrictions due to the debt crisis, the current liberalization process started in 1983 and 1984.[19] It proceeded at a rather slow pace, but important measures were taken.[20] First, the exchange rate was adjusted. An over adjustment took place to take care of high inflation rates and as a means to promote exports.[21] From 1985 to 1987 trade liberalization was used as an important mechanism to induce industrial restructuring (and control inflation). Other liberalization policies began to be pursued, namely, restructuring and privatization of the state enterprises sector, and negotiations to join GATT were started again. In 1986 they ended successfully, accelerating the liberalization process by eliminating quantitative restrictions, controls, and official prices; and by reducing import tariffs and the dispersion rate of tariffs.[22] In addition to these policies, the exchange rate was depreciated and local demand was further repressed—to control inflation. These policies initiated during the government of President Miguel de la Madrid, 1982 to 1988, have been vigorously continued by President Salinas De Gortari.

Today Mexico has a more liberalized trade regime. Tariffs average 13.1 percent (compared to 27 percent in 1982) and licensing for imports, a real bureaucratic drawback in the past, has been eliminated for most goods. The dispersion on trade tariffs has also been reduced from 24.8 percent to 4.3 percent in 1989.[23] Trade liberalization has contributed to the control of inflation and the increase of productive imports repressed by the debt crisis.[24] A structural change in the composition of exports also appears to be taking place.

In the context of NAFTA this means that the impact of trade liberalization agreements among the North American countries would be rather small. Trade between Canada and the United States has been already liberalized with their agreement reached in 1987. Further, the United States economy has long been the most open of the three economies, with tariff rates averaging 5 percent. Now, as previously pointed out, Mexico has carried out unilaterally important steps to open its economy to foreign goods. Licensing for imports has been eliminated for over 80 percent of all goods, and the mean tariff is now 13.5 percent. The number of tariff rates has been reduced from sixteen existing in 1982 to five in 1990.[25] Moreover, during the last few years trade among the North American countries has grown significantly, particularly between Mexico and the United States. But this growth has been caused by sharp imports from Mexico and might be reaching a limit.[26]

Foreign Direct Investment in Mexico

U.S. Investment in Mexico

In 1991 U.S. investment abroad amounted to approximately $225 billion of which three-fourths was concentrated in developed nations. The remaining one-fourth went to developing countries, with 11 percent of the total U.S. investment going to Latin America. In North America U.S. investment in Mexico accounts for only 3 percent of total foreign investment while Canada has 35 percent.[27] United States' investment in Canada and Mexico is quite similar, 62 percent. However, there is an asymmetry between Canada and Mexico. Canada has important investments abroad with 61 percent concentrated in the United States. Mexico's investment beyond its borders is limited to a few multinational corporations,[28] although some are prominent—such as CEMEX, a cement company, and Televisa whose television programs have penetrated markets internationally.

Aggregate Trends of FDI in Mexico

The 1973 Law for the Promotion of Mexican Investments and Regulation of Foreign Investment (which was intended to regulate FDI) did not completely discourage FDI.[29] Mexico is the major recipient of U.S. FDI to developing countries with a 12 percent share. However, growth has taken place essentially during the last few years. As shown in table 7.1, cumulative foreign investments amounted to $3.8 billion by 1971.[30] FDI grew moderately the following seven years, averaging $300 million per year. By 1978 foreign investments increased to a total of $5.6 billion.

Foreign direct investment has always been tied to Mexico's economic cycles. Thus, during 1979 to 1981, corresponding to the oil boom period FDI increased rapidly by $4.1 billion, raising the total stock of foreign investments to $10 billion. Initially, the debt crisis negatively affected the patterns of investment in Mexico. FDI increased the following two years by half the amounts of previous years. Total FDI increased to $11.4 billion by 1983. Vigorous increases began to take place the following years so that by 1988, total foreign investment reached $24 billion.

During the six year presidential term of President de la Madrid, FDI increased by $13 billion—a 146 percent change over total investment obtained by President López Portillo ($5.5

TABLE 7.1

FDI in Mexico (U.S. million dollars)

Year	Annual changes	Cumulative presidential term	Historical
1971	168.0	168.0	3,882.4
1972	189.8	357.8	4,072.2
1973	287.3	645.1	4,359.5
1974	362.2	1,007.3	4,721.7
1975	295.0	1,302.3	5,016.7
1976	299.1	1,601.4	5,316.8
1977	327.1	327.1	5,642.9
1978	383.3	710.4	6,026.2
1979	810.0	1,520.4	6,836.2
1980	1,622.6	3,143.0	8,458.8
1981	1,701.1	4,844.4	10,159.9
1982	826.5	6,470.6	10,786.1
1983	683.7	683.7	11,470.1
1984	1,442.2	2,125.9	12,899.9
1985	1,871.0	3,996.9	14,628.9
1986	2,424.2	6,421.1	17,053.1
1987	3,877.2	10,298.3	20,930.3
1988	3,157.1	13,455.4	24,087.4
1989*	2,913.7	2,913.7	27,001.1
1990	4,978.4	7,892.1	31,979.5
1991	9,897.0	17,789.1	41,876.5
1992p	8,334.8	26,123.9	50,211.3

* From 1989 on investments in the securities market is included.
p Preliminary figures.

SOURCE: *Secofi, General Direction For Foreign Direct Investments.*

billion).[31] However, it must be pointed out that during de la Madrid's regime debt-equity swaps were responsible for nearly a $3 billion dollar increase in FDI. Debt-equity swaps were initiated in April 1986 and interrupted in November 1987, reportedly due to its inflationary impacts.[32]

Growth of FDI during the first four years of President Salinas's term has been spectacular. The stock of foreign investment has increased to $50 billion by December 1992. Foreign direct investment has increased during the 1989 to 1992 period by over $23 billion.

FDI by Country of Origin

Looking at FDI patterns by country of origin in table 7.2, firms from the United States are the main participants in Mexico. However, in the long run, investment from this nation has tended to decrease from 70.1 percent of total FDI in 1975 to 60.7 percent in 1992. FDI from Canada is extremely small at 1.5 percent. Nevertheless, it is worth noting that investment from Canada and the United States has grown considerably during the last few years. During the first four years of President Salinas, U.S. investment has increased by $8 billion which is almost equivalent to total U.S. investment accumulated from 1946 to 1984.

One important by-product of NAFTA has been a heightened awareness among Canadians of their role on the Western Hemisphere, and the role that Mexican-Canadian relationships can play in furthering Canadian goals. Interest in Mexico and Latin America has always been present in Canada. This has manifested itself in the past in Canadian lending, and in the friendly approach of its government and institutions to solve the Mexican foreign debt problem. Canadian firms are now showing increased interest in Mexico. FDI from Canada should increase significantly, possibly surpassing the importance that investment from non-North American countries now play in Mexico.

Following U.S. investment patterns are those made by the

TABLE 7.2

Foreign Direct Investments by Country (%)

Year	United States	United Kingdom	Germany	Japan	Switzer-land	France	Spain	Sweden	Canada	Holland	Italy	Others
1975	70.1	5.5	6.2	2.0	4.3	1.8	0.9	1.0	2.9	0.0	0.9	4.4
1976	72.2	3.9	6.5	2.0	4.2	1.4	1.1	1.0	2.0	0.0	1.5	4.2
1977	70.2	3.7	7.3	4.2	5.3	1.3	1.0	0.9	2.1	0.0	0.6	3.4
1978	69.8	3.6	7.3	4.8	5.5	1.3	1.4	1.5	1.8	0.0	0.6	2.4
1979	69.6	3.0	7.4	5.5	5.3	1.2	1.8	1.7	1.6	0.0	0.8	2.1
1980	69.0	3.0	8.0	5.9	5.6	1.2	2.4	1.5	1.5	0.0	0.3	1.6
1981	68.0	2.9	8.1	7.0	5.4	1.1	3.0	1.4	1.3	0.0	0.3	1.5
1982	68.0	2.8	8.0	7.2	5.3	1.1	3.2	1.3	1.3	0.0	0.3	1.5
1983	66.3	3.1	8.5	6.8	5.1	2.0	3.1	1.5	1.4	0.0	0.3	2.0
1984	66.0	3.1	8.7	6.3	5.0	1.8	2.9	1.8	1.5	0.0	0.3	2.6
1985	67.3	3.1	8.1	6.1	5.4	1.7	2.6	1.6	1.6	0.0	0.2	2.3
1986	64.8	3.3	8.2	6.1	4.8	3.3	2.8	1.5	1.6	0.0	0.2	3.4
1987	65.5	4.7	6.9	5.6	4.4	2.8	2.9	1.4	1.4	0.0	0.2	4.1
1988	62.1	7.3	6.6	5.5	4.2	3.1	2.6	1.4	1.3	0.9	0.2	4.9
1989	63.1	6.8	6.3	5.0	4.5	2.9	2.6	1.3	1.4	1.0	0.2	5.1
1990	62.9	6.3	6.5	4.8	4.4	3.1	2.3	1.2	1.4	1.3	0.2	5.6
1991	63.4	5.9	6.0	4.5	4.2	4.3	2.2	1.1	1.5	1.5	0.2	5.4
1992p	61.7	6.4	5.7	4.3	4.6	4.0	2.1	1.0	1.5	1.6	0.2	6.9

NOTE: Does not include investments in the securities markets nor the amount of foreign capital authorizations given by ncfdi.

p Preliminary figures.

SOURCE: Secofi, *General Direction For Foreign Direct Investments*.

United Kingdom (6.4 percent), Germany (5.7 percent), Japan (4.3 percent), Switzerland (4.6 percent), Spain (2.1 percent), Holland (1.6 percent), and Canada (1.5 percent). NAFTA will lead to some readjustments in these patterns within Mexico. Previously, before the 1982 debt crisis, firms from these countries invested in Mexico to overcome protectionism and serve the local market. Sharp falls in domestic demand and liberalization policies induced many firms to invest in Mexico to take advantage of low labor costs and penetrate U.S. markets. This has been the case of Japanese and Korean firms.

Indeed, Japanese firms apparently already took a strategic position from the onset of the oil boom period. As shown in table 7.2, the relative importance of Japanese investment in Mexico increased from 2 percent of the total in 1975 to 4.2 percent in 1977 and 7.2 percent in 1982. During the last ten years investment from Japan has increased at a slower pace. In absolute terms it now reaches $1,616.0 billion, which is 4.3 percent of total foreign investment in Mexico. Further relative reductions are most likely to occur as a result of NAFTA.

Although massive moves of U.S. and Canadian firms to Mexico should not be expected, investment from the partner nations should increase in the next few years to take advantage of favorable conditions created by NAFTA for the aggregate North American market. However, tight rules of origin, like the 62.5 percent national content negotiated for the automobile industry, will likely discourage investment from Japanese firms.

Mexico's role as a stepping stone to enter U.S. markets has been limited. Firms from the region are locating in the three countries according to their strategic needs. Basically, this means that MNCs from the area will decide to invest in Mexico if low labor costs gives them a competitive edge without adversely affecting quality standards and technological development. On the other hand, firms will decide to invest in Canada if their regional and global strategies call for key resource inputs which are easily accessible through existing infrastructure, and are close to markets, like the United States. Firms will also choose to invest in Canada if competitive advantages can be derived from medium size plants that require high-technology, skilled labor and management, and if demand for goods or services in question is limited and therefore can only be served with this type of investment. Investment for U.S.-Canadian adjacent markets could fall in this category. Finally, MNCs from the North American countries will decide to invest in the United States when economies of scale and scope, skilled labor and management, and high technology are involved.[33]

FDI by Sector

Long-term patterns of growth of FDI by sector also reveal some important changes. The largest share corresponds to investments made in the industrial sector. The stock of investments in the sector is $21.8 billion. However, its importance has tended to decrease from 75 percent in 1975 and a peak of 79.2 percent in 1984 to 50.6 percent in 1992. Investment in commerce, mining, and the agricultural sector have remained relatively stable. The big change has taken place in services. Investment in this sector has had explosive growth since 1987 (17.2 percent vis-à-vis averages around 10 percent in previous years), and rapid growth has continued. By 1992 investment in this sector accounted for 40.1 percent of total foreign investment in Mexico. In absolute terms, FDI in services now accounts for $17,242.1 billion.

This has important implications for Mexico and NAFTA. First, it means that fears of job losses in the United States and Canada are unfounded. Most foreign investment is carried out in the service sector, which by no means denotes foreclosure of business in the United States or Canada. Many are a simple extension to the Mexican market of service chains established in those nations. Second, this also means that FDI is not promoting a significant transformation of the industrial sector. From this also follows that Mexico's increase in international competitiveness is rather limited. Similarly, these patterns of investment foretell only moderate increases in exports in the upcoming years in manufacturing, mining, and the primary sector which have the potential to generate exchange surpluses.

TABLE 7.3

Trends in Sectoral Foreign Direct Investment
(U.S. million dollars)

Year	Total	Industry	%	Services	%	Commerce	%	Mining	%	Agriculture & Cattle	%
1975	5,016.7	3,769.0	75.1	350.2	7.0	571.9	11.4	317.6	6.3	8.0	0.2
1976	5,315.8	4,079.9	76.8	414.1	7.8	580.0	10.9	234.4	4.4	7.4	0.1
1977	5,642.9	4,292.0	76.1	412.5	7.3	667.0	11.8	262.9	4.7	8.5	0.2
1978	6,026.2	4,682.4	77.7	473.7	7.9	598.4	9.9	263.9	4.4	7.8	0.1
1979	6,836.2	5,274.1	77.1	585.2	8.6	636.5	9.3	332.9	4.9	7.5	0.1
1980	8,458.8	6,559.8	77.6	716.5	8.5	754.5	8.9	419.6	5.0	8.4	0.1
1981	10,159.9	7,965.4	78.4	1,036.3	10.2	924.6	9.1	230.6	2.3	3.0	0.0
1982	10,786.4	8,346.7	77.4	1,271.8	11.8	925.8	8.6	237.3	2.2	4.8	0.0
1983	11,470.1	8,943.7	78.0	1,284.7	11.2	984.4	8.6	252.3	2.2	5.0	0.0
1984	12,899.9	10,213.3	79.2	1,406.9	10.9	1,015.9	7.9	258.0	2.0	5.8	0.0
1985	14,628.9	11,379.1	77.8	1,842.2	12.6	1,125.4	7.7	276.0	1.9	6.2	0.0
1986	17,053.1	13,298.0	78.0	2,165.3	12.7	1,276.6	7.5	306.8	1.8	6.4	0.0
1987	20,930.3	15,698.5	75.0	3,599.2	17.2	1,255.4	6.0	355.6	1.7	21.6	0.1
1988	24,087.4	16,718.5	69.4	5,476.6	22.7	1,502.2	6.2	380.5	1.6	9.6	0.0
1989	26,587.1	17,700.8	66.6	6,578.9	24.7	1,888.5	7.1	390.0	1.5	28.9	0.1
1990	30,309.5	18,893.8	62.3	8,781.9	29.0	2,059.8	6.8	484.0	1.6	90.0	0.3
1991	37,324.7	20,220.1	54.2	13,958.5	37.4	2,496.1	6.7	515.0	1.4	135.0	0.4
1992p	43,029.8	21,782.8	50.6	17,242.1	40.1	3,307.0	7.7	523.6	1.2	174.3	0.4

p Preliminary figures.

SOURCE: Secofi, *General Direction for Foreign Direct Investments.*

A closer look into the sectoral distribution of FDI (table 7.4) supports this. The increase of FDI during Salinas's administration is concentrated in four sectors: manufacturing (26 percent), transportation and communications (27.7 percent), financial services (17.2 percent), and community services (15.2 percent). In agriculture and cattle, FDI is negligible at 0.9 percent, signifying that reforms to property rights implemented since 1991 to promote large-scale projects in agriculture, and to end minifundism and uncertainty on property rights, have not yet induced FDI into this sector. A similar situation characterizes the mining sector, which undoubtedly needs further liberalization policies to attract foreign capital.

Regarding the manufacturing sector, in the past, industrial FDI in manufacturing differed in importance, growth, and impact. Cycles were led by fixed investment in sectors that had significant import substitution. During the 1970s MNC penetration concentrated in manufacturing industries which led import substitution (in transport equipment, electrical and nonelectrical

TABLE 7.4

Recent Foreign Direct Investment by Sectors*
(U.S. million dollars)

Sector	Cumulative 1989–1992	%	1993**	%
Total	18,942.50	100.00	322.24	100.00
Agriculture & Cattle	164.70	0.90	0.02	0.01
Mining	143.00	0.80	0.10	0.00
Manufacturing	5,064.30	26.70	219.14	68.01
Construction	394.70	2.10	10.96	3.40
Commerce	1,805.00	9.50	13.95	4.33
Transportation & Communication	5,229.60	27.60	0.09	0.03
Financial Services	3,267.30	17.20	1.04	0.32
Community Services	2,873.90	15.20	77.03	23.90

*Does Not Include Investments In The Securities Market.

**Preliminary figures.

SOURCE: *Secofi, General Direction For Foreign Direct Investments.*

machinery, chemicals, and rubber products). The market portions of MNCs in manufacturing production were concentrated in a small number of sectors. State-owned enterprises were able to capture market share in tobacco, chemicals, oil by-products, and basic metal industries. Patterns of competition and industry leadership were in concentrated and differentiated oligopolies. These market forms were associated with the presence of MNCs and state-owned enterprises and only marginally with large private national firms.[34]

Mexico's 1982 crisis triggered structural changes in the industrial sector. The industrial projects undertaken by foreign enterprises during the debt crisis period were in autos, electronics, and rubber products. This pattern of authorized investment indicates that foreign firms tended to concentrate on manufacturing activities that started in the 1970s. However, since 1987 growth in FDI began to lose its dynamism. An exceptionally large share of FDI flows in services (mainly tourism, consulting, engineering firms and financial nonbanking firms) have signaled a change in the structure of FDI.

The Financial Sector and Economic Integration

Table 7.4 also reveals the importance of FDI in financial services in Mexico. From 1989 to 1993 investment in financial services has risen by $3 billion, which amounts to 17.2 percent of FDI for the period. Similarly, FDI made through the stock market amounts to $7 billion. Moreover, FDI carried out in this manner has always exceeded 25 percent in the last few years. In 1992 venture capitalists invested $2.6 billion in Mexican firms which amounted to 31.5 percent of total FDI made during the year. A possibility that NAFTA brings forth is increased investment in the financial sector and through it increased investment to Mexican firms.

Negotiations in this sector were difficult and complex. As in the case of trade and investment, their objective was to create a freer flow of financial services among the three countries which also means freer access of financial institutions of one nation to the markets of the other three nations. However, negotiations were tangled by sharp differences in goals and financial systems and institutions, and differences in currencies. The most important differences concerning financial institutions and their regulation derive from U.S. McFadden and Stell-Glass laws which inhibit banking to state activity and clearly separate investment banking from commercial banking. Canada and Mexico, on the other hand, have national banking systems and are moving towards universal banking. On the second issue, the U.S. dollar is the dominant currency in the region and Canada and Mexico want to retain control on monetary policymaking. In addition to these issues, differences existed because Mexico's financial system is beginning a process toward change, resulting from privatization and the emergence of large "financial groups." The financial system and its institutions have not taken full shape yet. Thus, the Mexican government looked for favorable conditions to allow growth of domestic financial institutions. These problems were solved with an agreement that contemplates national treatment, a programmed period of transition, and safeguard clauses.

NAFTA agreements on the financial sector built significantly upon the U.S.-Canadian FTA. Chapter 17 of the Agreement reached between these two nations is based on the principle of national treatment. In chapter 14 NAFTA extends this principle to the three nations, contemplating a programmed period of transition and limits to investment and market shares, similar to those enforced in the U.S.-Canadian FTA to protect local financial institutions, and provides reviewing mechanisms. Principles developed in this section apply to financial services in banking, insurance, securities, and "other" financial services. Each country defines its specific liberalization commitments to the other countries, specifications of a transition period, and some safeguard provisions to the principles that should applied.

Mexico's commitments to Canada and U.S. financial institutions and investors from these sector can be summed up as follows:

1. Canadian and U.S. financial institutions will be granted immediate, but limited access to Mexico upon

the implementation of the Agreement. Most limits will be removed by the year 2000.

2. Canadian and U.S. banking institutions will initially face an individual ceiling of 1.5 percent and on the aggregate of 8 percent of domestic capital. The aggregate limit will be increased gradually to 15 percent by the year 2000. Concerning securities services, the aggregate initial cap is 10 percent and will be increased to 20 percent during the same period. Security brokerage firms can have an initial participation of 4 percent of the market. After the year 2000 most limits will be relaxed, but Mexico has the right to extend them if aggregates of Canadian and U.S. banks move above 25 percent of domestic capital.

3. The individual cap of 1.5 percent will be removed by the year 2000 for banking institutions growing through internal funds, including allocations from the parent. However a 4 percent limit will be put in place. If a Canadian or U.S. bank has interests of .5 percent in a Mexican bank, through a subsidiary, the foreign institution will be allowed to buy a domestic bank that comprises 3.5 percent of the market, which would total the maximum 4 percent share allowed.

4. In the annexes, a 30 percent limit on common capital is fixed for joint investment carried out by Canadian and U.S. investors in the commercial banking sector. This limit does not apply to investment made in foreign subsidiaries. Similarly, foreign investment in brokerage houses is also limited to 30 percent; individual investment should not exceed 10 percent. Individual Mexican investors, however, can own up to 15 percent of these types of institutions with authorization of the Ministry of Finance. The above limits do not apply to investment made by foreign subsidiaries.

5. Finally, an informal agreement was reached to ensure that Mexico fairly reviews entry applications of Canadian and U.S. parties. No preferences should be given to either party.

NAFTA also includes a mechanism to settle disputes, which also applies to the financial sector. When financial matters are involved, dispute resolution panels will be composed of five members selected from a trinational roster of financial and legal experts. The panel should submit its resolution, confidentially, within ninety days, unless the disputing countries decide otherwise. The disputing parties will have fourteen days to provide comments. The final report from the panel should be presented within thirty days of the presentation of the initial report. Countries should then agree to solve the dispute based on the panel's recommendations. If a panel determines that the responding country has acted inconsistently with NAFTA obligations, and the disputing countries do not reach an agreement within a month (or some other agreed period), the complaining country has the right to suspend the specific benefits granted to the other country involved until the dispute is finally resolved.

In short, the financial sector remains highly protected in Mexico, although this is also true for Canadian and U.S. institutions. Beyond capital and market participation limits, also enforced by Canada and United States, in consistency with their own laws and the U.S.-Canadian agreement, the most significant drawbacks are U.S. laws regarding the scope of investment and commercial banking, and the limited reach of commercial banking to state activities. Unfortunately, changes are likely to come slowly concerning those regulations.

At any rate, for Mexico the need for further real investment and the dynamics of its growth will most likely outgrow the limitations placed on financial investment. In the last few years financial markets and institutions have been responsible for a significant mobilization of foreign capital to Mexican firms. Moreover equity and nonequity international capital movements will continue to grow in importance in a globalized economy. Thus, in the context of NAFTA, financial linkages should be strengthened to allow a more efficient allocation of resources to the region. Restraining financial growth and financial integration in the area could lead to investment diversions to other regions.

This strategy is not beyond reach for the North American countries. Although Mexico is the junior partner in this venture,

Mexico has the characteristics needed to carry out this type of program. Its capital market has grown substantially during the last few years. Similarly, banking experience has a long standing in Mexico and banks have been recently privatized. Finally, Mexico has a rather large industrial base and significant FDI from the other two countries in NAFTA.

Conclusion

Mexico has undergone unparalleled changes during the last few years. Positive attitudes towards NAFTA tend to prevail, contrasting to earlier opposition to any sort of economic association with the United States. Strong liberalization programs have paved the way for significant increases in FDI. The manufacturing sector is undergoing important changes. Recent increases in FDI have been concentrated in the services sector. NAFTA opens multiple opportunities for investment in Mexico. However, massive shifts of plants to Mexico from the United States and Canada to take advantage of low labor costs should not be expected. Adjustment by multinational corporations to NAFTA is based on plans already underway. Overall, FDI should increase significantly in Mexico as a result of NAFTA and continued sound domestic policymaking. Further analysis is needed to determine if FDI is creating specialization niches that achieve Mexico's goal for a competitive manufacturing sector. Finally, the financial sector can play an important role in promoting economic integration among the North American countries, despite the protectionist biases found in NAFTA concerning financial services. Further deepening of NAFTA with financial opening and financial integration will be needed to promote greater investment flows in North America.

Notes

1. A view close to the one identified here can be found in Luis Rubio et al., *El Acuerdo de Libre Comercio México-Estados Unidos. Camino para Fortalecer la Soberanía* (Mexico City: Diana, 1991).

2. Politicians have tended to exaggerate the benefits of NAFTA for populist reasons. Their analysis lacks rigor, but influences public perceptions.

3. Points of view critical of NAFTA (from a Mexican viewpoint) can be found in John W. Warnock, *Free Trade and the New Right Agenda* (Vancouver: New Star Books, 1988) and Robert J. Kreklewich and Viviana Petroni, "Critical Perspectives of North American Integration," in Benito Rey Romay, ed., *La Integración Comercial de México a Estados Unidas y Canadá* (Mexico City: Siglo XXI, 1992). See also mimeo, Centre for Research on Latin American and the Caribbean, York University, 1992.

4. For a detailed analysis on the evolution of Mexican perceptions and points of view regarding economic integration with the United States, see Edgar Ortiz, "North American Union: The Mexican Point of View." Mimeo, FCPyS (Universidad Nacional Autónoma de México, 1984) and Edgar Ortiz, "Mercado Común Norteamericano: ¿Integración Silenciosa o Negociada?," *Relaciones Internacionales* 12, no. 47 (Mexico City : UNAM, January–April 1990).

5. President Carter made some statements in this direction as early as 1978. Later, in 1979, the U.S. Commerce Department studied a trade agreement for North America. A presidential report was presented in August 1981. Ronald Reagan, former California Governor Jerry Brown, and President George Bush made different proposals throughout the years. For a summary of earlier proposals, see Carlos Rico, "The Future of Mexican-U.S. Relations and the Limits of Rhetoric of 'Interdependency,' " in C. Vazquez and M. Garcia, eds., *Mexican-U.S. Relations: Conflict and Convergence* (Los Angeles: University of California at Los Angeles, 1983).

6. For a Canadian perspective, see R. Stern, Phillip H. Trezise, and J. Whalley, *Perspectives on a U.S.-Canadian Free Trade Agreement* (Washington, D.C.: Brookings Institutions, 1988) and Khosrow Fatemi, *International Trade and Finance: A North American Perspective* (New York: Praeger, 1988).

7. Magdalena Galindo, "Perspectivas de las Relaciones entre México y America Latina: Un Enfoque al Partir del Concepto de Hegemonia," in Raúl Benítez et al., eds., *Viejos Desafíos, Nuevas Perspectivas. México-Estados Unidos y America Latina* (Mexico City: UNAM/Porrúa, 1988) and Luis González Souza, "Recolonización 'Belitrónica' o Soberanía Latina Americana," in Raul Benítez et al., ed., *Viejos Desafíos, Nuevas Perspectivas. Mexico-Estados Unidos y America Latin* (Mexico City : UNAM/Porrúa, 1988).

8. Jorge Castañeda and Robert A. Pastor, *Límites en la Amistad. México y Estados Unidos* (Mexico City: Joaquín Mortiz/Planeta, 1989).

9. For an interesting study on U.S. FDI in Mexico, see Paulino Arellanes, "Crisis Capitalista e Inversiones Extranjeras en México," Ph.D. Dissertation, FCPyS, Universidad Nacional Autónoma de México (1992), and Raúl Ornelas Bernal, *Inversión Extranjera Directa y Restructuración Industrial* (Mexico City: UNAM, 1991).

10. Gary C. Hufbauer and Jeffrey J. Schott, *North American Free Trade: Issues and Recommendations* (Washington, D.C.: Institute for International Economics, 1992).

11. "Baker Praises Mexico as an Economic Model," *New York Times,* 10 September 1991, A6.

12. Ortiz, "Mercado Común Norteamericano" and Sidney Weintraub, *Free Trade between Mexico and the United States* (Washington, D.C.: Brookings Institute, 1984).

13. Herminio Blanco, "Naturaleza y Alcance del Tratado de Libre Comercio," in H. Blanco et al., *Hacia un Tratado de Libre Comercio en América del Norte* (Mexico: Porrúa, 1991) and Adalberto García Rocha, "Naturaleza y Alcance del Tratado de Libre Comercio," in Blanco et al., *Hacia un Tratado.*

14. This view was expressed even before any trade talks were started. It was given in the context to the debate on silent versus negotiated integration. See Adolfo Aguilar Zimzer, "México y Estados Unidos hacia el año 2000. Integración silenciosa o alianza concertada," in P. González Casanova, ed., *México Hacia el Año 2000. Desafíos y Opciones* (Caracas: Nueva Sociedad, 1989).

15. John Saxe-Fernández, "Aspectos Estratégicos. Militares Inmersos en el Proyecto de Integración de América del Norte," in Benito Rey Romay, ed., *La Integración Commercial de México a Estados Unidos y Canadá.*

16. Strong criticism is not limited to left partisans. For a thorough criticism from a conservative, nationalistic perspective, see José Angel Conchelo, TLC: Un Callejón sin Salida (Mexico City: 1992).

17. Sources for the statistical data analyzed in this work are: Banco de México, *Indicadores Económicos,* and *Informe Anual,* various issues (1970–1988).

18. For an earlier evaluation on this problem, see Edgar Ortiz, "Reconversión Industrial y Comercio Exterior: Limitaciones y Perspectivas," *Empresa Pública: Problemas y Desarrollo* 1, no. 5 (July–December 1987).

19. For a detailed, critical analysis of industrialization and trade policies during the government of President Miguel de la Madrid, see Joon Cheol Choi Kim, "Crisis Económica y las Nuevas Estrategias de Industrialización y de Comercio Exterior de México (Durante el Regimen de Miguel de la Madrid)," Ph.D. dissertation, Universidad Nacional Autónoma de México (1990).

20. The foundations for Mexico's structural changes and current liberalization policies were laid down in President de la Madrid's development and trade and industrialization plans. See Ejecutivo Federal, Plan Nacional de Desarrollo, 1983–1988 (Mexico City: Ejecutivo Federal, 1983) and Secretaria de Comercio y Fomento Industrial, Programa Nacional de Fomento Industrial y Comercio Exterior, 1984–1988 (Mexico City: SECOFI, 1984).

21. See Edgar Ortiz, "Crisis y Dueda Externa: Limitaciones de las Políticas de Estabilización y Alternativas para el Desarrollo y la Renegociación del Endeudamiento," *Cuadernos de Administración Pública,* FCPyS/UNAM 2 (1988).

22. See Joaquín Tapia Maruri, "Liberalization, Its Impact on Trade Balance, Economic Activity and Inflation: The Mexican Experience, 1971–1988," Pa-

per, North American Economics and Finance Association, New York, December 1989.

23. Jaime Zabludosky, "Trade Liberalization and Macroeconomic Adjustment," in Dwight S. Brothers and Adele E. Wick, eds., *Mexico's Search for a New Development Strategy* (Boulder: Westview, 1990).

24. For empirical results on this matter, see Tapia Maruri, "Liberalization."

25. Zabludosky.

26. It is worth mentioning that some people now oppose NAFTA arguing that the economy has been liberalized and should continue opening up to world trends in trade and finance, rather than limiting itself to a regional agreement.

27. Arellanes (1992) and Alan M. Rugman, "Prospects for a North American Free Trade Agreement," Working Paper, Ontario Centre for International Business, University of Toronto (1991).

28. Rugman.

29. Wilson Peres-Núñez, *Foreign Direct Investment and Industrial Development in Mexico* (Paris: OECD, 1990).

30. FDI data in this work corresponds to that reported by Dirección General de Inversión Extranjera. Three sets of data are gathered by this government agency: (1) FDI which needs approval by the Comisión Nacional de Inversión Extranjera; (2) FDI which does not need approval and is registered by Registro Nacional de Inversiones Extranjeras; and, (3) direct investment made through the Mexican Stock Market (additions to capital of Mexican enterprises intended for new corporate projects). International portfolio investment made in the secondary capital markets is, correctly, not included in FDI statistics. However, all these data cover intended investment, not investment actually carried out during the year. Intended investment is a useful proxy for actual investment for several reasons. First, surveys reveal that most of the stated FDI is actually carried out; less than 5 percent of the projects might not be carried out, but even in these cases they are often later incorporated in new projects. Second, during the first year around 50 to 70 percent of each stated FDI project is carried out; the remainder is carried out within the following two years. The types of FDI requiring approval has decreased. Also, the time for approval has been shortened to forty-five days. Any investment not approved within that period is automatically approved. All these changes have expedited FDI in Mexico so that the reported data closely approximates investment actually carried out during the year. Fourth, the Banco de Mexico also reports FDI made during the year. It reports investments actually made, but its figures are based on a survey of multinational corporations. Finally, FDI made through the stock market has increased sharply during the last few years. It accounted for 31 percent of total FDI in 1992. Investment (mainly corporate and institutional) made through this market mechanism is very important because it is being channeled to the most dynamic firms. Some local mutual funds also channel venture capital to emerging dynamic firms. In short,

the figures reported by Dirección General de Inversión Extranjera are comprehensive and give a clear picture of FDI trends.

31. Six year terms are known as sexenio.

32. David Felix, ed., *Debt and Transfiguration? Prospects for Latin America's Economic Revival* (Armonk, N.Y.: M. E. Sharpe, 1990) and Manuel Lasaga, "How to Assess the Market Value of Developing Country Loans: The Case of Latin America," in Antonio Jorge and Jorge Salazar-Carrillo, eds., *The Latin American Debt* (New York: St. Martin's Press, 1992).

33. Alan Rugman presents a sophisticated theoretical model to explain FDI within North America along the lines here expressed. See Rugman.

34. Peres-Núñez.

PART 3

INDUSTRY STUDIES

Chapter 8

THE STRATEGIC RESPONSE OF MNEs TO NAFTA

Michael Gestrin and Alan M. Rugman

Introduction

The North American Free Trade Agreement (NAFTA) will have
a significant impact upon the North American investment regime. For example, the Agreement will open up the Mexican
economy to Canadian and U.S. investors, it will provide en-
hanced security for all foreign direct investment (FDI) in the
NAFTA area, and it will make the discriminatory measures
which each of the signatories has chosen to maintain more
transparent.[1] This chapter considers how changes to the North
American investment regime resulting from NAFTA will affect
actual investment patterns. The conclusions are based upon an
analysis of NAFTA's treatment of a group of key industries
using a theoretical model of multinational enterprise (MNE)
behavior which has been developed from internalization theory.

The main conclusion of this research is that NAFTA will have
a negligible impact upon the inward and outward FDI positions
of Canada and the United States. In addition, the Agreement
will give rise to strong increases in inward FDI for Mexico.

The Strategic Behavior of MNEs and NAFTA

Economic relations among NAFTA signatories are dominated
by the activities of MNEs. As strategic actors MNEs both react
to changes in their environment and act to shape this environ-

ment to their advantage. Conventional (neoclassical) economic analysis tends to characterize environmental change as exogenous to the decision-making processes of firms. This type of analysis, however, overlooks two advantages particular to MNEs.

The first relates to their ability to internalize portions of their value-added chains. Through internalization the MNE maximizes the strategic benefits of the combination of Firm Specific Advantages (FSAs) held by the firm and Country Specific Advantages (CSAs) characterizing the national economies in which the firm operates. FSAs are defined as the competitive strengths of the company. These can be either production-based (cost or innovation advantages) or marketing-based (customization advantages). CSAs are initially defined as the natural factor endowments of a nation—basically the variables in its aggregate production function. However, CSAs can be influenced, indeed changed, by government policies.

The second advantage enjoyed by most MNEs is the capacity to change the environment in which they operate. More specifically, through the lobbying efforts of various industries NAFTA has come to reflect the interests of MNEs in North America. The Agreement therefore establishes NAFTA-based CSAs (advantages with respect to competitors based in the other NAFTA signatories) and NAFTA-based Region Specific Advantages (RSAs)(advantages with respect to competitors based outside NAFTA area). The implications of these two characteristics of MNEs, namely their ability to internalize and their capacity to change the environment in which they operate, are considered in turn.

The Organizational Responses of MNEs to NAFTA

The process of strategic planning follows a pattern in which the competitive strengths of the corporation are constantly reassessed in light of new information about the domestic and international environments within which the firm operates. Such environmental changes include trade liberalization measures such as NAFTA. Internalization theory serves to explain and predict how MNEs will react to environmental change. At the heart of the theory is the idea that markets and hierarchical structures (firms) are alternatives. Internalization allows a multinational enterprise to establish and maintain better proprietary control over its FSAs so that the economic rents associated with these do not accrue to other firms.[2]

Profitability, growth, market share, and any other goals pursued by MNEs may also depend upon the ability of an MNE to internalize CSAs. CSAs, as mentioned above, are generally viewed as the variables of the aggregate production function, and their value to particular firms will depend upon their quality, quantity, and cost relative to substitute factors in other countries.[3] However, they also include tariffs, nontariff barriers, and other government barriers to trade, including regulations on foreign direct investment (factors which are not commonly included in the neoclassical aggregate production function). To the extent that such measures favor domestic firms, these firms can be said to benefit from shelter-based CSAs.[4]

Internalization theory therefore predicts that the overall welfare impact of bilateral trade liberalization will be positive. Its main effects will be to reduce transaction costs associated with trade and to create more certainty for investment decisions. In cases where foreign direct investment and exports are complements, bilateral trade liberalization should increase the level of both.[5] The substitution of exports for foreign direct investment can be expected in cases where tariffs and regulations on trade are the main rationale for engaging in foreign direct investment and where exit barriers are low; under these conditions adjustment costs of relocating production activities will also be low. A largely neutral response in terms of FDI flows results when the activities of MNEs are strongly motivated by strategic considerations other than the desire to obviate tariff barriers. Documented examples of such common MNE behavior include the "exchange of threats" strategy identified by Graham[6] and the "window on Research and Development" behavior identified in the technology literature.[7]

Two important points have been raised in the above analysis.

First, the theory of the MNE and a large body of empirical work has shown that the organizational structures of MNEs are shaped by a multitude of factors reflecting the complexity and high degree of imperfection (oligopolistic market structures, lack of information, and the partially excludable and nonrival nature of knowledge and technological know-how) of international markets. Put differently, the liberalizing measures of NAFTA (many of which are phased-in over ten years) will only have an impact upon the investment patterns of MNEs where the activities of particular firms were originally and primarily motivated by high transaction costs in trade associated with the protectionist measures now being liberalized. In this regard, since the Agreement leaves the investment and trade regimes of Canada and the United States more or less the same and liberalizes many sectors of the Mexican economy, internalization theory predicts that MNEs will not be motivated, as a group, to react strongly to NAFTA in Canada or the United States, but may shift some resources from other low-cost economies to Mexico. This investment diversion is due to the fact that, under NAFTA, Mexico will enjoy the freest access to the U.S. economy of any developing country.

Second, since MNEs are strategic actors, it can be assumed that all MNEs likely to be affected by NAFTA will already have gauged the likelihood of the Agreement coming into effect and will have anticipated this possibility in their strategic decision-making.[8] Furthermore, it must be remembered that Mexico undertook to liberalize its economy unilaterally beginning in the mid-1980s and that the U.S.-Canadian trade and investment relationship is already, under the terms of the U.S.-Canadian Free Trade Agreement (FTA) of 1989, the largest between any two countries in the world. In many respects, NAFTA is a reflection and a continuation of the process of economic liberalization which has characterized relations between the three NAFTA signatories since the mid-1980s and which has been driven by the activities of MNEs. It is therefore wrong to characterize MNEs as reactive entities which will suddenly and dramatically respond to the political and legislative act of ratifying the Agreement—rather, MNEs have been basing their long-term strategies upon the underlying forces and processes which will have been underway for a decade by the time the Agreement comes into effect and which ultimately will make NAFTA politically viable.

The theory of MNEs suggests that NAFTA will not bring about substantial movements of capital either in or out of the United States and Canada but will likely bring about some investment and trade diversion from some less developed countries (LDCs) to Mexico. Previous experience in the case of FTA provides support for the view that most MNEs are motivated by a complex "basket" of factors such that the mild (and gradual) liberalization measures of agreements like FTA and NAFTA are not sufficient to warrant large-scale organizational readjustments.

The Impact of MNEs Upon NAFTA

Conceptually, any industry can be analyzed in terms of whether or not it benefits from strong CSAs and whether or not the industry itself has strong or weak FSAs. A strong CSA or FSA is defined here as an advantage sufficient to ensure competitiveness with respect to foreign rivals.

Figure 8.1 presents a way of classifying industries in terms of the strengths of their CSAs and FSAs. International competitiveness is assured whenever FSAS and CSAs are strong simultaneously (quadrant 1). If CSAs are weak, however, FSAs will have to compensate if the industry in question is to compete with global rivals (quadrant 2). A similar situation arises when an industry suffers from weak FSAs; then only through strong CSAs can an internationally competitive position be maintained (quadrant 3). Finally, for industries where both CSAs and FSAs are lacking, competing internationally with efficient foreign rivals becomes virtually impossible (quadrant 4).

An example may make this clearer: the Canadian forest products industry is not particularly strong in terms of its FSAs, but it does enjoy a compensating CSA in terms of an abundance of trees. More generally, well-endowed natural resource sectors

Figure 8.1

The Competitive Strategies Matrix

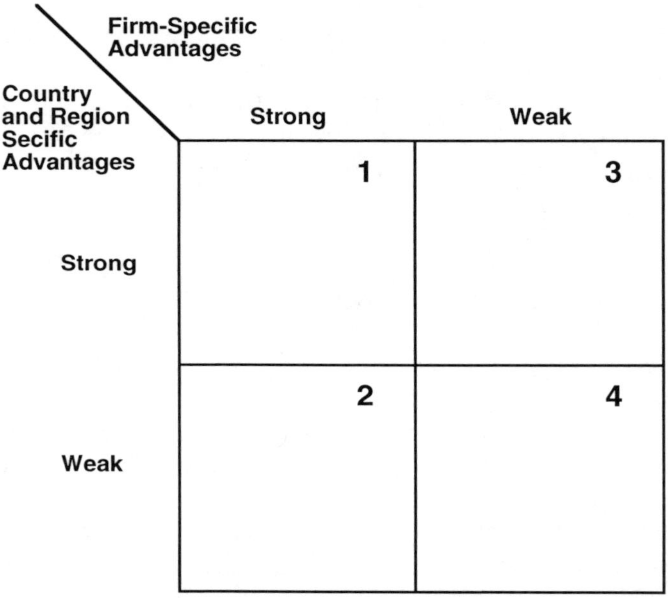

are often located in quadrant 3 because an overwhelming CSA can limit international competition and hence reduce the main impetus for developing strong FSAs. This dynamic constitutes the flip side of Porter's observation that, within the context of the diamond framework, a weak area of the economy can turn into a competitive advantage if this weakness impels other segments of the economy to continuously strive for competitive advantage.[9] Another group of industries which commonly locate in quadrant 3 are those whose strong CSAs derive from government protection or favoritism of one form or another. Among the industries often included in this quadrant are sunset and sunrise industries (which vary from economy to economy).

Trade and investment liberalizing agreements such as NAFTA can affect both CSAs and FSAs. Trade liberalization has an impact upon FSAs through its dynamic effects—by encouraging a more open and competitive economic environment, NAFTA will force firms to develop strong FSAs. NAFTA, however, has a more immediate (and usually protectionist) impact upon CSAs. This is due to such factors as the Agreement's effect upon tariffs, rules of origin, and dispute settlement mechanisms.

Four possibilities arise with regards to NAFTA's impact upon CSAs:

1. That the Agreement weakens an industry's CSAs by removing protective measures vis-à-vis competitors in other NAFTA signatories

2. The Agreement weakens an industry's CSAs by removing protective measures vis-à-vis competitors based outside NAFTA region—in this case a reduction of Region Specific Advantages (RSAs)

3. The Agreement strengthens an industry's CSAs with respect to competitors based in other NAFTA signatories; and

4. The Agreement strengthens an industry's RSAs with respect to competitors based outside NAFTA region.

The reader should note that, conceptually, CSAs and RSAs are the same thing. The distinction is useful, however, insofar as it highlights some of the dynamics behind the negotiation of trade and investment agreements such as NAFTA. First of all, depending upon the size and extent to which an MNE has internalized operations across borders in North America, it will have a preference for NAFTA-based RSAs over NAFTA-based CSAs. The reason for this is that NAFTA-based CSAs do not confer any particular advantage to the regional firm and, in fact, are likely to raise transaction costs for the MNE. National firms (or champions), on the other hand, have not internalized aspects of their operations across borders, and thus prefer CSAs to RSAs. The generalization which emerges from these observations is that firms will always seek to enhance their competitive position by establishing CSAs (or RSAs) which offer the closest fit (in a geographic sense) to match the scope of their operations.

Another reason for drawing the distinction between CSAs and RSAs is that, to the extent that an agreement such as NAFTA affects one or the other, one can roughly gauge to what extent the Agreement will affect investment patterns among NAFTA signatories versus the extent to which it will affect investment patterns between NAFTA region and the rest of the world. What this subsequent analysis will reveal is that, in terms of evaluating the impact of NAFTA, the areas in which investment patterns are most likely to experience considerable change are those in which firms or industries have weak FSAs and NAFTA does not supply these with either the CSAs or RSAs necessary for their continued commercial viability. These concepts (CSAs, RSAs, and FSAs) are extremely useful in analyzing both the structure of the operations of various industries in North America as well as the extent to which the interests of MNEs are reflected in NAFTA.

To summarize, the theory of the MNE outlined above allows one to make the following two predictions: MNEs (with strong FSAs) which have already adapted to an integrated North American market will seek, through lobbying efforts, to further liberalize trade and strengthen their RSAs and MNEs (and domestic or noninternationalized firms in each of the markets) which have not internalized their operations across the three markets will seek protectionism through NAFTA to strengthen their CSAs with respect to competitors based in the other NAFTA markets.

Using figure 8.1, one can now analyze the impact of NAFTA upon the key industries in each of NAFTA signatories. This analysis will focus upon the Agreement's impact along the vertical axis—the axis which pertains to CSAs and RSAs. Recall that quadrant 4 of the matrix, reflecting weak CSAs, RSAs, and FSAs, is the one quadrant which foreshadows drastic change (which can take the form of either restructuring or exit). The other three quadrants, on the other hand, represent situations in which the investments of MNEs are financially viable and, while in isolated cases drastic changes based upon strategic considerations are possible, in the aggregate these three quadrants will be relatively passive in terms of investment flows.

NAFTA's Impact Upon CSAs and RSAs

By applying figure 8.1 to the main industrial sectors of each NAFTA signatory, one is able to identify areas in each of the three economies likely to be dramatically affected by the implementation of NAFTA.[10] The analysis begins with a consideration of NAFTA's impact upon the CSA position of key industries in each of NAFTA signatories. Subsequently, NAFTA's impact upon RSAs is considered.

NAFTA and CSAs

Figure 8.2 places various industries from the three NAFTA signatories in the CSA-based competitive advantage matrix. Since this analysis is only concerned with the specific impact of NAFTA upon various economic sectors, the vertical axis specifies CSAs which have been either strengthened or weakened by the Agreement. In other words, only industries whose CSAs have changed as a result of NAFTA have been included in the figure.

Quadrant 1 includes industries which are both strong in terms of their FSAs and their NAFTA-based CSAs. This combination is somewhat counterintuitive since the literature on CSAs and FSAs unambiguously identifies artificial CSAs (the type of CSAs generated by government) as a threat to the long-term potential for maintaining strong FSAs.[11] The reason for this is that artificial, shelter-based CSAs shield domestic producers from international competition which is ultimately an essential ingredient for developing strong FSAs. Not surprisingly, then, the industries which find themselves in quadrant 1 are generally charac-

Figure 8.2

The Impact of NAFTA on Country Specific Advantages

Country Specific Advantages ＼	**Firm Specific Advantages**	
	Strong	Weak
Strengthened by NAFTA	**1** <u>United States</u> high technology related to defense; some energy <u>Canada</u> some energy <u>Mexico</u> none	**3** <u>United States</u> maritime; cabotage; steel; agriculture; textiles <u>Mexico</u> energy; telecommunications services; national resources <u>Canada</u> culture; agriculture
Weakened by NAFTA	**2** <u>United States</u> none <u>Canada</u> apparel <u>Mexico</u> none	**4** <u>United States</u> apparel; citrus products; roses; household appliances <u>Canada</u> textiles; household appliances; steel; beer <u>Mexico</u> most manufacturing

terized by political features which have motivated government to establish barriers to foreign competition even though, at least from a business perspective, this protection is not needed.

The most significant sectors included in quadrant 1 are the high technology sectors related to defense in the United States and some areas of the energy sectors in the United States and Canada (especially uranium, again for security reasons). Mexico also has security concerns, and has placed severe restrictions upon foreign investment in its energy and natural resource sectors in NAFTA, however, these industries are not characterized by strong FSAs, and therefore do not appear in quadrant 1.

Indeed, Mexico has no industries listed in quadrant 1. While, as discussed previously, quadrant 1 does not imply potentially disruptive changes in investment patterns, of concern is the likely effect of continued (and potentially expanded) protection for the U.S. high technology sector upon FSAs.[12]

Quadrant 3 contains the industries which are popularly known as the "sacred cows" of each of the signatories. These industries or sectors are generally characterized by some form of strong leverage or clout in domestic political circles. The sacred cows of the United States and Canada are not affected by NAFTA. In the United States the maritime sector, cabotage in all forms of transportation, steel, and many agricultural products benefit from protection under the terms of NAFTA. In Canada the best known sector receiving protection under NAFTA is the cultural sector. As in the United States, several subsectors of the agricultural sector are also protected, namely diary, poultry, and eggs. The areas in Mexico which are characterized by weak FSAs and protection under NAFTA are those found in Mexico's annex 3 constitutional reservations.[13] The most significant of these cover most of the energy sector (coal being one of the few areas liberalized), telecommunications services (which in many respects mirrors Canada's cultural reservations), and control over natural resources. It is expected, given the extent to which Mexico's FSAs are weak in some of these sectors, especially in energy, that strong NAFTA-based CSAs could have the effect of retarding Mexico's economic progress due to the creation of bottlenecks in critical areas.

Quadrant 2 is almost empty reflecting, interestingly, the fact that NAFTA, on the whole, has not made North America a more dynamic and competitive environment for firms which already enjoy strong FSAs. One notable exception consists of the Canadian apparel industry. The reason that this sector has had its NAFTA-based CSAs reduced pertains to the effect of the Agreement upon this sector's main input—textiles. By tightening considerably the content rules for textiles and apparel, Canadian apparel producers, which have enjoyed strong design-based FSAs, will have a harder time sourcing high quality, inexpensive textiles outside of NAFTA area.

Finally, quadrant 4 lists sectors which will experience the most significant change as a result of NAFTA. In the United States these include the apparel sector, various agricultural products in which Mexico enjoys a comparative advantage, and household appliances. In Canada the sectors which will have to undergo considerable adjustments to NAFTA include household appliances, steel, and beer (these sectors were also affected by FTA). The latter two sectors have weak CSAs by omission since FTA and NAFTA could not address the problems associated with the abuse by U.S. firms of American trade law. The household appliances sectors of the United States and Canada will both suffer from increased competition from Mexico.

The most striking feature of quadrant 4 is the inclusion, for Mexico, of its entire manufacturing sector. After decades of import substitution policies and protectionism, Mexican manufacturing, in the aggregate, suffers from extremely weak FSAs. Under the terms of NAFTA, however, all tariff protection for the manufacturing sector will be eliminated during the Agreement's ten year phase-out period. Most tariff protection, in fact, will disappear during the first five years of the Agreement coming into effect.

Compared with the quadrant 4 lists of Canada and the United States, Mexico will clearly bear the brunt of adjustment costs (and consequent efficiency-based opportunities) associated with NAFTA. Indeed, while adjustment to increased international competition has been focussed in a few sunset industries in the United States and Canada, the Mexican economy is currently pursuing a wholesale restructuring of at a pace which has not been matched in the history of economic reform.

A final comment on figure 8.2 serves as a starting point for consideration of NAFTA's impact on RSAs. Figure 8.2 does not include several key sectors of the North American economy, especially autos and auto parts. The reason for this is that during the 1980s and early 1990s most MNEs have been pursuing regionalization strategies aimed at rationalizing, through strategic internalization, the organization of their value-added chains across national boundaries. Indeed, as argued earlier, these large firms have explicitly sought to avoid the development of

NAFTA-based CSAs since these can only lead to higher transaction costs for both the internalized as well as the international
market transactions of these firms.

NAFTA AND RSAs

Figure 8.3 is the same as figure 8.2 except that the vertical
axis now concerns the strengthening or weakening of RSAs by
NAFTA. Conceptually, the main difference between the industries placed in figures 8.2 and 8.3 is that those located in the
former are characterized (predominantly) by uninational corporate structures while those in the latter have adopted a regional
outlook. Put differently, the industries listed in figure 8.3 per-
ceive a North American border in their strategic planning and
largely ignore the national boundaries which separate the three
NAFTA signatories.

The interpretation of figure 8.3 is the same as that for figure
8.2. Quadrants 1–3 are largely neutral in terms of their implications for investment patterns, while quadrant 4 implies that
considerable readjustment for the sectors listed is essential. The
only difference in this regard is that the investment flows under
consideration in figure 8.3 are those between NAFTA area and
the rest of the world.

The first striking feature of figure 8.3 is the fact that, on the
vertical axis, quadrants 2 and 4, representing weak NAFTA-
based RSAs, are empty. This reflects a profound feature of
MNE activity—international production by large MNEs is undergoing a process of regionalization along triad lines, not a
process of globalization. If particular industries had achieved a
high level of integration of value-added activities at the global
level, they would view RSAs in the same negative light as
regionally integrated firms view CSAs. No industries, however,
have sought, either in the main text of NAFTA, or in the lists of
reservations, to eliminate or phase-out NAFTA-based RSAs in
order to lower transaction costs between NAFTA-based and
non-NAFTA-based operations.

Quadrant 1 lists industries which enjoy both strong FSAs and

Figure 8.3

The Impact of NAFTA on Region Specific Advantages

Firm Specific Advantages		
Region Specific Advantages	Strong	Weak
Strengthened by NAFTA	United States 1 chemicals; computers; trucking petrochemicals; energy; agriculture; electronics Canada chemicals; energy; some forest products Mexico electronics; apparel	United States 3 autos; auto parts Canada autos, auto parts Mexico T.V. tables
Weakened by NAFTA	2 United States none Canada none Mexico none	4 United States none Canada none Mexico none

strong NAFTA-based RSAs. Unlike the list of industries in quadrant 1 of figure 8.2, however, the list in quadrant 1 of figure 8.3 is much more mainstream in its composition. Recall that strong NAFTA-based CSAs are generally only conferred upon industries which are characterized by some sort of political attributes which are independent of their competitiveness. Sectors related to national security therefore dominated quadrant 1 of NAFTA-based CSA matrix.

A subtle difference between NAFTA-based CSAs and RSAs underlies this apparent discrepancy. As discussed, a strong NAFTA-based CSA usually takes the form of discriminatory measures which favor domestic over foreign producers. RSAs are based upon similar preferential treatment being offered at a regional level. RSAs, however, usually involve the opening of a particular sector in one NAFTA signatory in which RSAs are strong. RSAs have been strengthened under these conditions since the MNEs with strong FSAs now have better access to a larger basket of productive resources, relative to non-NAFTA competitors.

In theory, the same dynamic can take place at the national level. For example, if NAFTA had served to lower interprovincial trade barriers in Canada, then quadrant 1 of figure 8.2 would contain some Canadian industries unrelated to national security issues. Their NAFTA-based CSAs would have become stronger not through extra protection but through a NAFTA-induced rationalization of production at the national level which in turn would give rise to efficiency gains relative to foreign competitors. What quadrant 1 indicates, therefore, is that the chemicals (including pharmaceuticals), computer, trucking, petrochemicals, energy, and several agricultural sectors in the United States stand to gain strong RSAs as a result of NAFTA through an opening of these sectors in Mexico to American investment.

Non-NAFTA based investors will also enjoy better access to these areas, but in many ways U.S. investors will still enjoy preferential treatment relative to outsiders. Furthermore, even if U.S. investors did not get preferential treatment relative to outsiders, their RSAs would still be made stronger since Mexico represents an improvement of the organization of the regional operations of U.S. MNEs. Outsiders making investments in Mexico with a view to serving the North American market will remain at a disadvantage in terms of having to deal with the higher transaction costs associated with NAFTA's tight rules of origin.

Canada also stands to gain from the preferential opening of the Mexican market in the areas of chemicals, energy, and some forest products. The two industries in which Mexico is expected to enjoy substantial gains are textiles and apparel. In this case, substantial investment diversion from low cost producers in Asia is expected.[14]

Quadrant 3 contains the single most important sector in the North American economy—the automotive sector. Relative to Japanese and some European producers, this sector in North America suffers from weak FSAs. Under the terms of NAFTA, however, automotive and automotive parts producers will enjoy strong RSAs. These will primarily be based upon the continued protection offered to domestic producers in the auto pact, as well as to the increased domestic content requirements imposed by the Agreement.

Conclusion

This chapter has considered the likely impact of NAFTA upon the investment decisions of MNEs operating in North America. The focus on MNEs as the largest fifty North American MNEs accounts for approximately 70 percent of Canadian-U.S. trade (the Big Three automakers account for 30 percent). An understanding of the relationship between MNEs and the institutional environment in which they operate is essential to an understanding of what the impact of NAFTA will be upon North American investment patterns. By applying internalization theory and by extending the concept of CSAs to a regional level of analysis (RSAs), one concludes that the impact of NAFTA upon investment patterns in Canada and the United States will be mainly neutral, while Mexico will benefit from considerable investment diversion away from other LDCs.

Notes

1. For a more detailed discussion, see Michael Gestrin and Alan M. Rugman, "The NAFTA's Impact on the North American Investment Regime" in *C. D. Howe Institute Commentary,* No. 42 (Toronto: C. D. Howe Institute, March 1993), and Alan M. Rugman and Michael Gestrin, "The Investment Provisions of MAFTA" in Steven Globerman and Michael Walder, eds. *Assessing NAFTA: A Trinational Analysis* (Vancouver: The Fraser Institute, 1993), 271–92.

2. Alan M. Rugman, *Inside the Multinationals: The Economics of Internal Markets* (New York: Columbia University Press, 1981).

3. Alan M. Rugman, Donald Lecraw, and Laurence Booth, *International Business: Firm and Environment* (New York: McGraw-Hill, 1985).

4. Alan M. Rugman and Alain Verbeke, *Global Corporate Strategy and Trade Policy* (London and New York: Routledge, 1990).

5. A. E. Safarian, "The Relationship Between Trade Agreements and International Direct Investment," in David W. Conklin and Thomas A. Courchene, eds., *Canadian Trade at a Crossroads: Options for New International Agreements* (Toronto: Ontario Economic Council, 1985) and A. E. Safarian, *Multinational Enterprise and Public Policy* (Aldershot, U.K. and Brookfield, Vt.: Edward Elgar, 1993).

6. Edward M. Graham, "Oligopolistic Imitation and European Direct Investment in the United States," D.B.A. Dissertation, Harvard University (1975).

7. Organization for Economic Cooperation and Development, The Technology/Economy Programme, *Technology and the Economy: the Key Relationships* (Paris: OECD, 1992) and John H. Dunning, *Multinational Enterprises and the Global Economy* (Reading: Addison-Wesley, 1993) chaps. 11–12.

8. A similar point was made in Alan M. Rugman, *Multinationals and Canada-United States Free Trade* (Columbia: University of South Carolina Press, 1990).

9. Michael E. Porter, *The Competitive Advantage of Nations* (New York: The Free Press, 1990).

10. A similar analysis, using a related framework, was done with respect to FTA by Rugman, *Multinationals;* Alan M. Rugman and Alain Verbeke, "Multinational Corporate Strategy and the Canada-U.S. Free Trade Agreement" *Management International Review* 30, no. 3 (1990): 253–66; and Alan M. Rugman, Alain Verbeke, and Stephen Luxmore, "Corporate Strategy and the Free Trade Agreement: Adjustment by Canadian Multinational Enterprises" *Canadian Journal of Regional Science* (Summer-Autumn, 1990): 307–30.

11. Alan M. Rugman and Michael Gestrin, "U.S. Trade Laws as Barriers to Globalization," *World Economy* 14, no. 3 (1991): 335–52.

12. For a more detailed discussion of these issues, see Edward M. Graham, "Foreign Direct Investment in the United States and U.S. Interests," *Science* 254 (20 December 1991): 1740–45 and Edward M. Graham and Michael E. Ebert, "Foreign Direct Investment and U.S. National Security: Fixing Exon-Florio," *World Economy* 14 (1991): 245–68.

13. See Gestrin and Rugman (1993) for more details on the organization of the reservations.

14. United States, *Potential Impact on the U.S. Economy and Selected Industries of the North American Free-Trade Agreement* (Washington D.C.: United States International Trade Commission, Publication 2596, January 1993).

Chapter 9

IMPACT OF NAFTA ON THE FOREST PRODUCTS INDUSTRY

Don G. Roberts and Ilan Vertinsky

Introduction

Canada, the United States, and Mexico concluded the negotiation of the North American Free Trade Agreement (NAFTA) on 12 August 1992. The details of the Agreement were completed and published on 8 September 1992. If the Agreement is ratified by all three countries it will go into effect on 1 January 1994. There are many provisions to the Agreement which may affect trade flows in forest products among the three countries and consequently lead in the long-run to some modifications in the structure of their forest products industries.

In this chapter, the potential consequences of NAFTA from the perspective of the North American forest products sector are explored. Examination of table 9.1 shows that in relative terms the size of the forest products sector in Mexico and trade in forest products with Mexico are small. This fact, and the fact that under the Free Trade Agreement (FTA) between Canada and the United States all tariffs (excluding countervailing duties on softwood lumber) are being eliminated by 1993, suggest that NAFTA will have little structural impact on the U.S. and Canadian sectors while having a significant impact on the Mexican sector. Thus this chapter focusses on changes in the Mexican forest products sector and relates them to changes in the trade patterns between Canada, the United States, and Mexico. In addition, the chapter examines potential developments in the

Mexican forest products sector and the Mexican economy in general that may affect the volume and mix of forest products imports by Mexico. These may affect Canada and the United States both directly and indirectly.

The analysis begins by exploring those features of NAFTA that are of particular importance to the forest products industry. Then the current state of the forest products industry in Mexico, current trade patterns in the sector, and the regulatory regimes that govern production and trade in forest products in Mexico are described. Some of the key changes that have already taken place in the regulatory regime governing the sector and the changes which are scheduled to occur either in anticipation of NAFTA or as a consequence of it are identified. Next, alternative scenarios of the possible impacts of these changes on the structure of the forest products sector and the mix and volume of imports and exports to and from Mexico are analyzed. Then the competitive position of North American producers and their potential rivals in the continental market is evaluated. In particular, the opportunities for and threats to Canadian and American manufacturers are identified. The chapter concludes with observations about the possible strategies that North American forest products producers may employ to benefit from NAFTA.

Provisions of NAFTA That May Affect the Forest Products Sector

Reductions in Tariff and Nontariff Barriers

The most direct impact of NAFTA on trade in forest products will result from the gradual elimination of all tariffs on goods originating or deemed to originate in North America. Some tariffs on forest products (newsprint and framing lumber) will be eliminated as soon as NAFTA is implemented. Another group of products (pallets and doors) will see tariffs phased out over five years in equal annual decrements. A third group of products (mechanical wood pulp and waferboard) will see tariffs eliminated gradually over ten years in equal annual decrements. Table

9.2 presents Mexico's nominal tariffs, estimated effective rates of protection and tariff phase-out periods for key forest products.

The three countries are also required to eliminate other non-tariff barriers such as import licenses on quotas on the importation of specific goods. Countries may impose border restrictions to protect the life and health of humans, animals and plants, and the environment. To reduce the chance that such restrictions will be used to erect nontariff barriers, a section of NAFTA regulates the development, adoption, and enforcement of sanitary and phytosanitary measures, requiring that such regulations (1) be based on scientific principles and risk assessment, (2) be applied only to the extent necessary to provide a specified level of protection, and (3) not result in unfair discrimination or be disguised as barriers to trade. NAFTA requires each country to ensure that such measures be those that are the ''least restrictive to trade, taking into account technical and economic feasibility.''

NAFTA calls for the establishment of a committee on sanitary and phytosanitary measures to promote the harmonization of regulations and facilitate cooperation. The provisions concerning environmentally motivated restrictions on trade allow greater discretion and may leave more latitude for using them as mechanisms to erect protective barriers to trade. NAFTA specifies that environmental provisions preempt other trade provi-

TABLE 9.1

Value of Production, Exports, and Imports of Forest Products, 1988 (U.S. billion dollars)

	Canada	United States	Mexico
Production	33.8	170.1	2.3
Exports	17.2	8.3	0.01
Imports	1.7	14.2	0.4

SOURCE: Food and Agriculture Organization of the United Nations (FAO) *Forest Products Yearbook*, 1990; United Nations, *Industrial Statistics Yearbook*, 1989.

TABLE 9.2

Nominal Tariffs, Effective Rates of Protection, and Phase-Out Period for Selected Forest Products, 1992

	Tariff (%)	ERP (%)	Phase-out Period
Softwood Lumber, Rough or Dressed:			
SFP for timber frame housing	10	18	1994
Other species (44.0710.01)	15	27	1994–2003
Softwood Plywood (44.12.19.01)	15	31	1994–2003
Particle Board/Waferboard (4410.10.01)	20	66	1994–2003
Mechanical Wood Pulp (4701.00.01)	5	8	1994–2003
Unbleached Coniferous Sulfate Pulp:			
(4703.11.02) for use in newsprint/some kraft paperboard	5	9	1994
Chemical Wood Pulp, Dissolving Grades (4702.00.00)	0	0	N/A
Bleached Coniferous Sulfate Pulp (4703.21.03)	0	0	N/A
Newsprint (4801.00.00.99)	15	32	1994
Other Paper and Paperboard (all of Chapter 48, except 4801.00)	10	N/C	varies

SOURCE: Schedule of Mexican Customs Tariffs; Lévesque, Beaubien, Geoffrion, Inc.; Department of External Affairs.

sions in the Agreement. Thus, for example, recycled content requirements may preempt other provisions of NAFTA and serve to improve the terms of trade of both Mexico and the United States at the expense of Canada.

Investment Provisions

The second major aspect of NAFTA which may lead to some restructuring in the North American forest products industry is the set of provisions concerning investment. These provisions, which free the flows of capital among the three countries and significantly increase the safety of foreign investment, are likely to result in a greater flow of capital to Mexico and over time increase the productivity of Mexican forest product producers.

Trade Dispute Settlement Mechanisms

Since the forest product industry is very volatile and some of its sectors are characterized by high fixed costs, trade disputes concerning unfair trade practices are likely to arise periodically. The provision for safeguarding domestic sectors and those dealing with disputes concerning subsidies and trade remedies are of particularly great importance to the forest products sector. During a transitional period, NAFTA permits a country to temporarily suspend the agreed duty elimination or reestablish a pre-NAFTA rate of duty to deal with import surges from another country. This type of measure can be taken only once and its duration should not exceed three years. Perhaps more threatening to dominant exporters is the global safeguard feature in NAFTA. If a NAFTA partner undertakes a safeguard action on a multilateral basis, a NAFTA partner will not be excluded from the safeguard measure (which may contain quotas and higher tariffs) if the partner is one of the top five suppliers or the rate of growth for imports is appreciably higher than that of total imports of those goods.

In the matter of trade disputes, NAFTA provides a marginal improvement on the U.S.-Canadian FTA as it deepens the institutional structure of the dispute settlement mechanism. NAFTA establishes a mechanism for independent binational panels to review final antidumping and countervailing duty determinations by the authorities in each country. A panel must apply the importing country's domestic law in reviewing a determination. Panel decisions are binding.

In addition to the binational panels, NAFTA will establish a Trilateral Trade Commission designed to review trade relations and disputes among the parties involving the interpretation and implementation of the Agreement. NAFTA also establishes a secretariat to provide administrative and technical support to the binational panels.

Parallel Environmental Accord

Perhaps the most contentious provisions in NAFTA had not been finalized by June 1993; they deal with the "parallel" environmental and labor accords. The Clinton administration and U.S. Congress have made it clear that their support for NAFTA is conditional on the completion of such side agreements. Of the two parallel accords, it is the one on the environment which has the greatest potential implications for the forest products sector.

NAFTA is the first major trade agreement to focus considerable attention on the interface between trade and the environment. It may well be through the parallel accords that NAFTA will be breaking its newest ground. However, it should be noted that even without a parallel accord on the environment, NAFTA already has environmental provisions. In the original negotiated text, each country:

> 1. Has the right to determine the level of protection required to protect their environmental and their human, animal, or plant life or health;
> 2. Has the right to maintain environmental standards that are higher than those recommended by international organizations; and
> 3. Recognizes that no country can lower health, safety, or environmental standards to attract investment.

NAFTA also calls for the establishment of a North American Commission on the Environment (NACE). Given that the parallel accords are still being negotiated, it is difficult to clearly define the objective and role of NACE. From the perspective of Canada and Mexico, it is preferable that NACE's objective would be quite general (to promote sustainable development and foster cooperation on environmental issues), and its role relatively unobtrusive (to support, coordinate, and review recommendations on environmental laws, regulations, and stewardship). The U.S. negotiators appear to be arguing for a

NACE with stronger enforcement powers which would play a more activist role in dealing with environmental issues across all three countries. In particular, the United States wants strong assurances that Mexico will not use lax regulations and/or enforcement to attract and retain investment. The large assimilative capacity of Canada's environment coupled with its relatively small manufacturing sector suggests that Canada should be less vulnerable to environmental disputes dealing with industrial pollution. However, Canada's forest products sector may be vulnerable to environmental disputes because it is affected by policies on both pollution (pulp and paper effluent) and harvesting (cut-block design).

It is logical that Canada and Mexico will vigorously oppose any enforcement measures which include trade sanctions. The primary reason for this is that trade sanctions are asymmetric in their effects. While they would be highly effective when used by the United States, they would be relatively ineffective when applied by Canada or Mexico. The asymmetry arises from the relative size of the three national economies and differing degrees of dependence on exports. At the aggregate level, exports to the United States account for over 20 percent of Canadian gross domestic product (GDP) and about 15 percent of Mexican GDP. In contrast, exports from the United States to Canada and Mexico account for only about 2 percent and 0.5 percent, respectively, of U.S. GDP.

Aside from the contentious issue of enforcement powers, NAFTA negotiators will have to determine whether the parallel environmental accord is limited to transboundary environmental problems, and which specific environmental regulations will be covered. Again, from the Canadian and Mexican position, it is likely they will be arguing that NAFTA should only consider pollution regulations which are at the federal level, and which are already being met. Given that regulations on resource harvesting and extraction are a provincial responsibility, it would be politically infeasible for the Canadian federal government to agree to a NACE which has influence over forest management practices.

In the context of the forest products industry, it should be noted that even in the absence of any environmental side agreement, it is unlikely that Mexico will turn into a "pollution haven," and thus divert investment from the United States and Canada. This is unlikely to happen for a number of reasons:

1. Given Mexico's tariff reductions and falling effective rates of protection, the attractiveness of forest product investment in Mexico is significantly reduced;

2. It is less expensive to build clean technologies in new pulp and paper mills than to modify polluting technologies in older mills (the latter is the focus of much of the investment in Canada, while the former is associated with the investment diversion argument);

3. Pulp and paper mills are large facilities, and are relatively easy and inexpensive to monitor for pollution;

4. Given increasing consumer awareness and activism, it is becoming difficult for developing countries to export if "clean" technologies are not used; and,

5. Concern over the environment is a "luxury good" which is becoming increasingly affordable in countries which can provide an attractive business climate for capital intensive industries.

To conclude, NAFTA will gradually free the flows of trade in forest products between the three countries, will free investment flows and increase the safety of North American investors when investing in a NAFTA partner and reduce somewhat the likelihood of successful protectionist measures such as antidumping and countervailing duties. Opening market access and barrier removal is likely to result ceteris paribus, in increases in exports of forest products from the United States and Canada to Mexico, while the freeing of capital flows and the increase in foreign investor safety is likely to result in higher flows of capital to Mexico and lead to some restructuring of its industrial base, thus potentially affecting domestic supplies of forest products. Before providing a detailed analysis of how patterns of trade and production in forest product sector may change in the three countries, it is necessary to examine the status and prospects for the forest products sector in Mexico—the Mexican sector is the one most vulnerable to increased foreign competition, and is likely to undergo the greatest change.

The Mexican Forest Products Sector

Land Ownership

Mexico's total forest area is 18.7 million hectares (compared to 453.3 and 298 million hectares in Canada and the United States, respectively). Some 9.9 million hectares of its forest land is covered by softwood trees. The dominant species in Mexico's temperate forests are pine, fir, oak, and alder. Some of the more important species in the tropical forests include mahogany, red cedar, and chicazapote. Mexico has the potential to increase its wood supply significantly by expanding its plantations since it has appropriate commercial sites with climate suitable for rapid-growth tree species.

Historically, productivity in the forestry sector has been inhibited by a land tenure system which has discouraged investment and led to high transportation costs. The Mexican constitution of 1917 embraces the principle of promoting equality and distributing resources more equally. It instructs the executive branch to distribute land to any newly formed town or group of peasants without land to form ejidos, which are community-held lands. To comply with this instruction the constitution empowered the executive branch to expropriate land from private owners. In order to protect these land holdings from reverting back to private ownership, those with a stake in the community land holding were not permitted to sell, rent, or mortgage the land. Inheritance rights were tightly regulated. Ejidos land could be utilized either by individuals and their families on subdivided plots or by the group of owners collectively. The hiring of labor was forbidden. As a consequence of these stipulations, roughly 70 percent of the forest areas of Mexico are controlled by over five thousand ejidos. Approximately 23 percent of the land is privately owned and distributed among two hundred thousand proprietors. The government owns the remaining 7 percent. There are less than three hundred thousand hectares of forest plantations in Mexico and incentives for intensive forest management elsewhere are absent.

As a result, forests in Mexico have been deprived of the capital investment in management and infrastructure that has been so successful in other regions of the world. Despite generally favorable growing conditions, it is estimated that the productivity of the country's forests averages only 1.5 cubic meters per hectare per year. By far the largest demands put on the forests of Mexico are from a somewhat antiquated sawmill industry. The pulp and board industries generally rely upon wastepaper, thinnings, tops, and sawmill residuals for their raw material supply.

The Forest Products Industry

Production.   In 1990 Mexico had almost 1,400 sawmills, 37 panel mills and 15 pulp mills (8 sulphate, 2 mechanical, and 5 nonwood), and 67 paper and board mills. The development of the forest products sector in Mexico was propelled by a policy of import substitution that was dominant until 1986. This policy involved protection of the industry with tariff barriers as high as 40 percent. In the newsprint industry the state-owned agency Pipsa had a monopoly on all newsprint imports. Consumption of forest products was restricted to a large extent by production capabilities.

The major constraint on Mexico's solid wood products industry is the limited supply of economic logs, which forces most sawmills to operate at about 30 to 40 percent of capacity. Most of the forests near the mills have already been harvested and the remaining forested areas are located at higher elevations where the costs of road building are high. To increase utilization of forests closer to mills the minimum butt diameter allowed for harvesting has decreased significantly. Thus, for example, in the southern parts of Mexico mahogany butt diameter limits were reduced from 105 centimeters in 1984 to 60 centimeters in 1992.[1] This has resulted in significant increases in average processing costs. Production of solid wood has focused mainly on furniture (hardwood and softwood) packaging, fencing and railroad ties, and moldings and other interior finishing items.[2] The high level of protection and the scarcity of capital provided few incentives for technological innovation in the wood processing industry. Some wood processing capacity was developed in the duty-free zones (maquiladoras) established along the U.S. border. The forest products mills in these zones are involved in production of wood parquet flooring, wooden doors and moldings, wooden kitchen cabinets, wood fencing, and railroad ties.

Tables 9.3 to 9.5 provide production figures for the Mexican forest products industry and consumption and trade volumes.

Consumption.   Generally per capita consumption of most forest products increased over the past decade. The increase in consumption, however was volatile, reflecting the swings in imports triggered largely by changes in oil exports and the consequent changes in availability of foreign exchange. Growth reflected both increases in per capita consumption and rapid growth in population (the annual growth of population in Mexico was 2.55 percent, compared to 1.08 percent in Canada and 0.96 percent in the United States). The average consumption per capita in Mexico is still relatively low, however, compared with consumption in developed countries. For example in 1987 consumption per capita of paper and board reached 306.7 kilograms in the United States, 213.3 kilograms in Canada, 142.3 kilograms in the United Kingdom, 69.6 kilograms in Korea, but only 33.2 kilograms in Mexico. Table 9.3 provides apparent consumption and per capita consumption figures for forest products for 1989 to 1991.

Trade Regime

Since Mexico's accession to the GATT in 1986 and its subsequent economic reforms many of the barriers on forest products imports to Mexico have been lowered. Since December 1987 the maximum ad valorem import tariff rate has been set at 20 percent of the free on board (f.o.b.) invoice value of the goods. Current tariff rates range from zero percent (chemical wood pulp and bleached coniferous pulp) to 20 percent (waferboard and joinery). Mexico uses the Harmonized System of Tariff Nomenclature and applies its tariffs on a nondiscriminatory basis with the exception of preferential duty rates offered to members of the Latin American Integration Association (and the elimination of tariffs sanctioned by its recently signed free trade agreement with Chile).

Though the nominal rates on forest products were relatively low, the effective rates of protection were high on most products except pulps (see table 9.2). Thus, for example, the effective rate of protection on softwood lumber was 18 percent for fir (compared to a nominal rate of 10 percent) and 27 percent on other species (compared to a nominal rate of 15 percent). The effective rate on soft plywood was 31 percent while for particle board it was a prohibitive 66 percent. Newsprint was protected by an effective rate of 32 percent. Generally, nominal tariffs tend to be higher for products with a higher degree of processing. The high effective rates of protection are largely a result of this "cascading" tariff structure and the importance of the intermediate goods in producing the final product.

The paper industry in Mexico was also constrained by a lack of inexpensive fiber sources and capital. Until recently, lack of competition stifled any attempt to seek improved efficiency. A major source of fiber for the industry has been non-wood-based pulps. Bagasse/straw-based pulps accounted for over 30 percent of Mexico's total production of virgin pulp (pulp not containing recycled materials) in 1989. These non-wood-based pulps are of significantly lower quality than the wood pulps produced in Canada and the United States. Their suitability as an input for printing and writing paper is particularly limited. In the newsprint market, however, bagasse-based newsprint is relatively inexpensive and meets the quality requirements of Mexican newspaper publishers. Mexico relies to a significant degree on recycled fiber for its pulp and paper industry. According to a study by Mexican Pulp and Paper Association (CNICP), recy-

TABLE 9.3

Mexican Apparent Consumption and Per Capita Consumption of Forest Products, 1989–1991

Commodity	Apparent Consumption			Per Capita Consumption		
	1989	1990	1991	1989	1990	1991
Solid Wood (hundred m³)				(m³ per million persons)		
Wood based panels	674	579	N/A	7,977	6,721	N/A
Softwood	2,582	2,506	N/A	30,560	29,089	N/A
Industrial roundwood	7,091	6,694	N/A	83,927	77,702	N/A
Paper and Board (hundred tons)				(kg per person)		
Newsprint	347	425	401	4.1	4.9	4.6
Woodfree printing, writing	468	535	596	5.5	6.2	6.8
Casemaking materials	880	929	975	10.4	10.8	11.1
Kraftliner	596	614	628	—	—	—

				(kg per person)		
Other wrapping papers	258	332	362	3.1	3.9	4.1
Tissue	274	327	371	3.2	3.8	4.2
Other paper	96	90	158	1.1	1.0	1.8
Board	323	295	334	3.8	3.4	3.8
Total	2,710	2,982	3,240	32.1	34.6	36.9
Wood Pulp (hundred tons)			(kg per person)			
Bleached sulfate	445	468	436	5.3	5.4	5.0
Unbleached sulfate	176	172	184	2.1	2.0	2.1
Bleached sulfate	1	2	0	0.0	0.0	0.0
Bagasse/straw	259	254	237	3.1	2.9	2.7
Mechanical	173	183	167	2.0	2.1	1.9
Total	1,054	1,079	1,025	12.5	12.5	11.7
				(kg per person)		
Wastepaper (hundred tons)	1,966	2,155	2,176	23.3	25.0	24.8

NOTE: Mexican population (millions): 1989—84.49; 1990—86.15; 1991—87.84.

SOURCE: *Pulp and Paper International*, 1991.

TABLE 9.4

Production of Forest Products in Mexico, 1989–1991

Commodity	Production		
	1989	1990	1991
Solid Wood (hundred m³)			
Wood based panels	645	550	N/A
Softwood lumber	1,929	1,853	N/A
Industrial roundwood	7,077	6,680	N/A
Paper and Board (hundred tons)			
Newsprint	327	355	346
Woodfree printing, writing	479	523	503
Casemaking materials	881	928	968
Kraftliner	584	595	610
Other wrapping papers	271	311	324
Tissue	352	385	388
Other paper	49	38	35
Board	312	284	289
Total	2,737	2,871	2,896
Wood Pulp (hundred tons)			
Bleached sulfate	238	227	181
Unbleached sulfate	176	165	178
Bleached sulfate	0	0	0
Bagasse/straw	259	254	237
Mechanical	126	126	108
Total	799	772	705
	Recovery		
Wastepaper (hundred tons)	1,008	1,267	1,237

SOURCES: FAO *Yearbook of Forest Products*, 1990; *Pulp and Paper International*, 1991; IMF *International Financial Statistics*.

cled fibers are expected to constitute almost 65 percent of Mexico's production of paper by the year 2001. The industry relies on significant imports of wastepaper from the U.S. as a source of fiber. It is forecasted that pulp made from imported wastepaper will account for roughly 20 percent of Mexico's total consumption in the year 2001 (given the trend in the United States to legislate recycling content in newsprint, this supply of wastepaper may involve prohibitive costs in the next decade). Another factor which may reduce the competitiveness of the industry in the near future is new requirements to install pollution abatement equipment. The majority of the mills are located in the vicinity of Mexico City where the protection of the supply of water is a major concern. The requirement for stringent environmental protection (of both air and water) may force many mills to relocate or close down. To conclude, the forest products industry in Mexico is highly vulnerable to increased market access by U.S. and Canadian companies and without an infusion of capital and restructuring is not likely to maintain its share of rising domestic consumption.

Elimination of tariffs may have its greatest effect on those producers that enjoyed the highest effective rates of protection. In particular Mexico's newsprint, plywood, and particle board industries are likely to be adversely affected by NAFTA. In addition to the ad valorem tariff, a customs processing fee of 0.8 percent is assessed on the f.o.b. invoice value. A 15 percent value added tax is the levy on the total of the f.o.b. invoice value and the ad valorem tariffs on most products (including forest products). Other nontariff barriers included requirements for phytosanitary certificates and various types of import licenses. Import license requirements were largely eliminated and by 1990 less than one-fifth of total imports to Mexico required prior import authorization: the import of paper board and newsprint, for example, was freed from license requirements although importation of some types of solid wood products still requires a license.

Trade Patterns in Forest Products

Mexico remains a net importer of forest products. Indeed the share of imports in domestic consumption has increased as market access for foreign imports has improved. Table 9.5 provides import and export volumes for 1986 to 1991. Chemical

TABLE 9.5

Mexican Trade in Forest Products, 1989–1991

Commodity	Exports			Imports		
	1989	1990	1991	1989	1990	1991
Solid Wood (hundred m³)						
Wood based panels	15	15	n/a	44	44	n/a
Softwood lumber	25	25	n/a	678	678	n/a
Industrial roundwood	0	0	n/a	14	14	n/a
Paper and Board (hundred tons)						
Newsprint	8	0	6	28	70	61
Woodfree printing, writing	46	37	25	35	49	118
Casemaking materials	13	18	11	12	19	18

Kraftliner	n/a	n/a	n/a	12	19	18
Other wrapping papers	37	37	39	24	58	77
Tissue	83	62	26	5	4	9
Other paper	0	1	1	47	53	124
Board	13	13	11	24	24	56
Total	201	168	120	174	279	464
Wood Pulp (hundred tons)						
Bleached sulfate	31	31	0	238	272	255
Unbleached sulfate	0	0	0	0	7	6
Bleached sulfate	0	0	0	1	2	0
Bagasse/straw	0	0	0	0	0	0
Mechanical	0	0	0	47	57	59
Total	31	31	0	286	338	320
Wastepaper (hundred tons)	0	0	0	958	888	939

SOURCES: FAO Yearbook of Forest Products, 1990; Pulp and Paper International, 1991; IMF International Financial Statistics.

pulp remains the dominant import among the forest products, accounting for about 40 percent of the value of all forest product imports to Mexico in 1988. Printing and writing papers and softwood lumber follow each representing about 20 percent of imports, with newsprint's share remaining relatively low at less than 5 percent.

United States' producers dominate Mexico's forest products imports, providing about 80 percent of its imported pulp, 90 percent of its imported softwood, and almost 100 percent of its imported wastepaper. Total exports from Canada to Mexico were $87.7 million in 1991, but fell to $53.8 million in 1992. In 1992 forest sector exports to Mexico constituted only 7 percent of Canada's total exports to Mexico. The composition of exports from Canada is unstable reflecting Canada's historic position as a marginal supplier of forest products to Mexico. Canada imported about $111.2 million worth of furniture from Mexico in 1992, a sharp increase from $21.4 million in 1991.

CNICP has forecasted the supply/demand balance for selected pulp and paper products (excluding newsprint) to the year 2001. Their forecast foresees demand for paper and board growing at an annual rate of at least 5 to 6 percent. By the year 2001 imports are forecasted to account for roughly one-third of Mexico's consumption of writing, printing, and packaging papers and almost one-half of its consumption of tissue papers. Table 9.6 provides CNICP's specific forecasts for production, consumption, and export and import balances.

The CNICP's forecasts do not anticipate an additional expansion of capacity of paper and board production in Mexico. If such investments take place, imports of paper and board would decline while imports of pulp would increase significantly since the domestic fiber supply is limited.

The critical variable in forecasting the future capacity and structure of the Mexican forest product industry is the flow of foreign capital to it. Indeed if one expects the trend toward liberalization in the economy to continue, capital will flow to those sectors where Mexico now has a comparative advantage. This will mean a shift to higher value-added products.

TABLE 9.6

Demand/Supply Balance for Selected Pulp and Paper Products, 2001 (One thousand tons)

	Production	Consumption	Surplus/Shortage
Printing/writings	475	725	−250
Packaging papers	1,433	2,222	−789
Tissue	347	634	−287
Pulp:			
Bagasse	178	176	+2
Unbleached chemical plup	223	225	−2
Bleached chemical plup	258	420	−162
Recycled fibers	1,188	1,670	−482
Total (no investment in P&B production)	1,847	2,491	−644
Total (if investments in P&B to satisfy domestic demand)	1,847	3,960	−2,113

SOURCE: Camara Nacional des las Industrias de la Celulosa y del Papel (CNICP), 1989. The CNICP-sponsored study does not include forecasts for newsprint or any of the solid wood products.

Investment Barriers

In May 1985 the Mexican government liberalized the 1973 foreign investment law. Regulations now permit foreign investors to own 100 percent of projects in sectors designated as unclassified. All cellulose industries are now included in the unclassified sector. In contrast, forestry and forest nursery businesses were classified as activities reserved exclusively for Mexican nationals. Companies in this category can have foreign investment only to the extent that is authorized by the National Commission for Foreign Investment. Timber and other forest product harvesting belongs to a class of activities which requires prior authorization if majority foreign ownership is desired. Though formal barriers on foreign investment had been removed to a large extent, there was still concern for the security of foreign capital. The changes anticipated with the implementation of NAFTA will increase protection of foreign investors' rights. In addition, the overall stabilizing impact of NAFTA on the Mexican policy environment is likely to reduce the "political risks" stemming from erratic government policies and unstable macroeconomic environment and encourage further foreign investment in Mexico.

Anticipated Changes in the Policy Environment in Mexico— Pre- and Post-NAFTA

The year 1987 presented a watershed in the recent economic life of Mexico. An anti-inflationary program, the Pacto de Solidaridad Económica, agreement between government, labor, and business organizations was introduced in December 1987. It froze wages and prices and significantly reduced tariffs. It also reduced the high level of nontariff barriers which protected a relatively inefficient industry. In 1989 a new pact was introduced, the Pacto Para la Estabilidad y el Crecimiento Económico. It modified the original pact by allowing more flexibility in prices and wages. Later in the same year a national development plan for 1989 to 1994 was introduced. The plan set national sectoral growth targets but saw private investment as the principal vehicle of growth. The emphasis on private investment was in line with other moves to privatize state companies, deregulate some sectors and encourage foreign investment. Construction was the sector targeted for the most rapid growth in line with government concern for housing. Forestry was one of the priority sectors identified in the plan. The government also adopted macroeconomic policies aimed at reducing inflation and encouraging savings. These policies included vigorous moves to reduce government spending lowering the relative burden of taxation on earned income and targeting subsidies more selectively.[3]

The reflection of government plans was most visible in the paper sector. Until April 1990 Productora e Importadora de Papel (Pipsa) was the country's only producer and importer of newsprint. Up to 1988 the state absorbed corporate losses resulting mainly from poor productivity and the low prices imposed by the government. In 1988 the company was restructured and subsidies were eliminated. In 1989 an 18 percent share in the company was ceded to the publishers of newspapers. In April 1990 the newsprint market was opened and any publisher can now import newsprint directly from any country paying an import duty of 15 percent. Imports, however, were constrained by lack of infrastructure and warehousing necessary to establish effective distribution networks.[4]

The economic growth and the prospects of a stable macroeconomic environment have led to plans for investment and expanded production in the pulp and paper sector. The opening of Mexico to foreign investors and the prospects of NAFTA have particularly encouraged international paper companies to invest in Mexico. Those with plants in Mexico (for example, Scott Paper) will focus initially on increasing productivity of their plants to ensure that they can compete with newcomers and imports. Plans for expansion, however, are severely constrained by the fiber supply. The option of improving wood supply by setting up plantations near the mills was not feasible until very recently due to the old Mexican Agrarian law.[5]

On 7 November 1991 the president sent a bill to Congress reforming article 27 of the Constitution. While the core of article 27 is to be kept (in other words, affirming the nation's right to expropriate land for the public benefit and impose restrictions on land ownership), it was modified to "spur greater participation by producers in rural areas, to reverse the trend toward small holdings, and to offer mechanisms for association stimulating investment and capitalization".[6] The new law provides the necessary security in land tenancy for ejidos, communities, and private landholders to encourage investment and productivity. The land distribution provision was eliminated—the new rights of landholders include the liberty to buy, sell, or rent the land, to hire labor to cultivate it; and to associate with other producers and third parties in joint ventures to exploit the land. It also establishes a secure framework within which renewable contracts of up to thirty years can take place. These contracts may involve joint venture schemes with private foreign investors.

Individuals and corporations are still subject to limits on landholding. Corporations (domestic and foreign) will now be able to acquire land, but the holding is limited to no more than twenty thousand hectares. Thus, the constitutional reform provides a basis for the establishment of plantations and general restructuring of the forestry sector to improve productivity. In the long run (around the year 2010) one can expect the supply of wood to increase. The extent of this increase will depend on the ability of Mexico to increase its harvest levels without aggravating the current problems of deforestation and possible moves within NAFTA framework to prevent further deforestation. In the short run, any expansion of the paper industry will depend on greater imports of fiber.

The trend in the forest sector that evolved as a result of recent government reform policies was reinforced by the expectation of NAFTA ratification, the market opening it will bring about, the further stabilization of the economy, and the investment flows which are expected as a result of it. As previously indicated, demand for forest products is likely to increase significantly in the next decade as a result of the economic growth brought about by NAFTA and the liberalization of the Mexican economy. The extent to which the demand created will be supplied by local production or by imports will depend on the rate of investment in the domestic sector. In the pulp, paper and board sectors, a scenario of self-sufficiency is inconsistent with the current growth strategy of Mexico. Thus the current state where pulp imports dominate will change to one where higher valued products will assume a major share of imports. This shift may benefit exporters in the United States and reduce the opportunities for Canadian exports to Mexico.

In the solid wood sector change is likely to be slow, though the demographic structure of Mexico is offering some promise for the construction sector. A young population (approximately 70 percent of the population is under the age of 30) and rapid population growth (the annual growth rate in the past year was about 2.25 percent) will increase the demand for housing and commercial construction. This will aggravate the housing shortage that, by government estimates, reached a deficit of over two million units in 1992 (some estimates put the number closer to six million units).

Mexico will need to construct roughly one million new housing units a year just to maintain the status quo.[7] Economic growth will further intensify the demand for housing. This demand, however, may not be translated into significant demand for wood products if Mexican traditional patterns of construction do not change. The Mexicans traditionally built houses with inexpensive brick and masonry. These building materials are associated with a sense of security, an important value in Mexican culture. Given the dry climate of the country Mexicans also worry about flammability of wood. Thus uses of wood were limited in Mexico to furniture construction, packaging, and concrete forming.

A significant increase in building starts may increase the use of timber for scaffolding planks and plywood for concrete forms. These uses are very price sensitive. It is expected that in the next decade wood supply will shrink in North America and lumber prices will increase, hence, the prospects for significant lumber exports to Mexico may not be high. If construction patterns change in Mexico through diffusion, as is happening along the Texas border in the maquiladora zones, the demand for solid wood products may especially increase in commercial construction.[8] This will be the case for wood grades which are within the competitive price ranges of other substitute building materials. However, such a process of "innovation" is typically slow and the likelihood of its spreading from commercial construction to housing is low.

The analysis so far indicates a scenario of significant opportunities opening as a consequence of NAFTA in the pulp, paper, and board sectors for exports to Mexico, and somewhat more constrained opportunities in the solid wood product sector. The exploitation of these opportunities by U.S. and Canadian exporters however will depend on their competitive position in the Mexican market.

Competitiveness of North American Forest Products Producers and Their Rivals

As noted in the introduction, NAFTA is expected to have a relatively small impact on the Canadian and U.S. forest products sectors, but a significant impact on the Mexican sector. Given Mexico's limited forest products industry, falling import barriers, and rising standard of living, the central questions is: which countries will likely supply the bulk of Mexico's future imports of forest products?

Table 9.7 provides some insight into this question for two of the major forest products—bleached kraft pulp and newsprint. The table summarizes the relative cost position of the major producing regions of the world. Producers in the U.S. South, Chile, and Brazil have a clear cost advantage with respect to bleached kraft pulp, and the U.S. South and Pacific Northwest enjoy the lowest average costs of producing newsprint. The average Canadian producer of both of these products is at a clear cost disadvantage in serving the Mexican market, although there are examples of Canadian firms which are near the bottom of the "international cost curve" (for instance, Donohue Inc.).

The countries with the greatest chance to satisfy Mexico's imports of higher value-added paper products are those whose companies are already established in Mexico. Such companies enjoy "first mover advantages" in terms of: (1) established sales/distribution systems; (2) name recognition/brand loyalty; and, (3) alliances with domestic firms. The foreign firms with the greatest presence in Mexico include: Stone-Container (United States) and Jefferson Smurfit (Ireland) in the packaging industry; Scott Paper (United States) in the tissue industry; and Kimberly-Clark (United States) in almost all aspect of the paper industry. Canadian firms have lagged behind their American competitors in establishing a Mexican presence, with Cascades Paperboard International being one of the few to actually undertake foreign direct investment.

In terms of solid wood products, lumber producers in the B.C. interior appear to enjoy a cost advantage over their competitors in the U.S. South. However, the U.S. southern pine producers have mounted a concerted effort to develop the Mexican market, and are expected to be extremely competitive—the same is true for Chilean producers of radiata pine.

TABLE 9.7

Total Production Costs for Pulp and Newsprint in Selected Regions, 1992 (U.S. $/ton delivered to the U.S.)*

Region	Bleached Kraft Pulp**	Newsprint
Eastern Canada	545	556
B.C. Interior	547	N/A
B.C. Coast	605	569
U.S. Pacific Northwest	522	485
U.S. South	468	489
Chile	466	N/A
Brazil	453	N/A
Sweden	677***	N/A

*The cost of producing bleached softwood kraft (BSK) pulp is greater than the cost of producing newsprint in the PNW and the B.C. coast because newsprint producers in these regions primarily use thermo-mechanical pulp (TMP) or groundwood pulp. TMP and groundwood pulp cost less to produce than BSK pulp.

**All pulp data refer to softwood pulp, except for Brazil which is hardwood.

***The pulp figures obtained from RISI for Chile, Brazil, and Sweden have been adjusted to reflect the cost of transportation to the U.S.

SOURCE: Adapted from *Pulp and Paper Review,* RISI, October 1990.

Conclusion

NAFTA will leave little impact on the U.S. and Canadian forest products sectors, but a major one on Mexico's. With respect to the lumber and panel products sector, despite increasing market access associated with the reduction of tariffs, the prospects for significant changes are modest. Competition from U.S. southern pine and Chilean radiata pine lumber is likely to restrict Canadian access to the new Mexican market. However, indirectly the increase in Mexican demand for lumber expected as incomes rise will benefit Canadian producers. In the long run, a change in consumer preferences from masonry to wood housing may create significant demand which is not likely to be met by exports from Chile or the U.S. South.

In the pulp and paper sector the picture is more complex. Demand for paper and board is expected to increase significantly, leading to increased imports. The extent of the increase and the mix of imports will depend on the rate by which Mexican paper and board capacity expands. One expects that NAFTA will lead to an increase in capital flows to Mexico, and result in significant improvements in productivity in the paper and board sectors. This will mean an opportunity for the lower cost Canadian market pulp producers. If, however, the rate of expansion in the paper and board sector fails to meet rising demand, Canadian producers of newsprint and groundwood specialties are likely to benefit. A problem which is looming, especially in the newsprint sector, is the possibility that Mexico will adopt more stringent recycled content regulations for newsprint. Current proposals for "by the roll" recycled content requirements may indeed be vehicles for erecting trade barriers against Canadian suppliers.

Notes

1. Chris Gaston and David Cohen, "The Mexican Opportunity—A Strategic Plan for the B.C. Solid Wood Industry," Faculty of Forestry, University of British Columbia, Working Paper, Vancouver, B.C., 1993.

2. Phil Gilbert, "Mexico—Update on Trade Opportunities for Solid Wood Products from British Columbia," Council of Forest Industries, Vancouver, B.C., December 1990.

3. The Economist Intelligence Unit, "Latin America—Economic Structure and Analysis: Mexico," *EIU Regional Reference Series* (February 1990): 197–224.

4. Rita Pappens, "Pipsa Gets Ready for Free Market," *Pulp and Paper International* 32, no. 12 (December 1990): 48.

5. See, for example, Rita Pappens, "Ponderosa Gears Up for a New Bonanza," *Pulp and Paper International* 32, no. 10 (October 1990): 42.

6. Banco Nacional de Mexico, "New Horizons for Agriculture," *Review of the Economic Situation in Mexico* 68, no. 794 (January 1992).

7. Gaston and Cohen.

8. Gilbert.

Chapter 10

IMPACT OF NAFTA ON ENERGY MARKETS

Daniel A. Hagen, Steven E. Henson, and
David E. Merrifield

Introduction

Prior to its final negotiation, much of the promise of the North American Free Trade Agreement (NAFTA) was thought to reside with liberalization in the large and strategically important Mexican energy sector. While the Mexican Constitution restricts foreign participation in the energy sector, it was hoped that significant liberalization might be possible. The results of the negotiations, however, have left this hope largely unfulfilled. As explained below, the Agreement recognizes (and grants preeminence to) the Mexican state's exclusive right to a wide range of energy-related activities, including investment and the provision of services in these activities. This severely limits opportunities for foreign direct investment in the Mexican energy sector.

While NAFTA-induced trade and investment in the energy sector will likely fall far short of their free trade potential, there is reason to believe that NAFTA will lead to some new opportunities in energy, though perhaps not through the routes originally envisioned. First, in the basic principles of the energy chapter the parties explicitly recognize the desirability of continuing liberalization, which may foretell of more significant liberalization in the future. Secondly, NAFTA establishes opportunities in the area of electricity generation, energy-related government procurement contracts, the extraction of coal, and the production of some basic petrochemicals. Finally, NAFTA is expected to add substantially to Mexico's growth, which will create strong incentives for additional liberalization in the energy sector.

This analysis begins with a review of the NAFTA chapter on energy and basic petrochemicals. This section discusses the extensive manner in which Mexico has been excluded from various commitments to liberalization. The next section examines the potential for increased foreign investment in independently generated electricity, which is an area where, in contrast to the bulk of the energy chapter, significant foreign investment opportunities are provided for. This section contains a discussion of the issue of environmental subsidies, including their potential impact on the location of generating facilities. The third section outlines some additional areas of liberalization, and discusses their significance. The fourth section analyzes the implications for the energy sector of NAFTA-induced growth in Mexican gross domestic product (GDP). This is potentially the most important effect of NAFTA on energy markets. Finally, the last section discusses the overall conclusions regarding the effects of NAFTA on trade and investment in energy.

Overview and Analysis of NAFTA Energy Chapter

Chapter 6 of NAFTA, "Energy and Basic Petrochemicals," contains a number of broad principles and specific provisions affecting both trade and investment. The scope of the chapter (as laid out in article 602) goes beyond that of the U.S.-Canadian Free Trade Agreement (FTA) in two respects. First, it includes basic petrochemicals (which were not included in FTA). Basic petrochemicals are defined to include only five of the twenty products usually classified by Mexico as basic petrochemicals. Secondly, it includes both investment and trade in services, although the chapter's specific provisions in this area are primarily in the form of extensive exclusions and special provisions which apply to Mexico. Most of chapter 6 deals with trade in goods, and parallels closely chapter 9 of FTA. In the case of the United States and Canada, there are relatively few changes vis-à-vis FTA beyond the general improvements (such as dispute settlement) identified elsewhere in this volume.

Reservations and Special Provisions

The preeminent paragraph of the chapter (as specified in the agreement) is contained in annex 602.3, "Reservations and Special Provisions." Paragraph 1 of annex 602.3 reserves for the Mexican state a wide range of "strategic" activities, including investment and the provision of services in such activities. The language of the paragraph acknowledges that this may be seen as inconsistent with other, more liberal parts of the Agreement, but leaves no doubt as to which section is preeminent. Indeed, the final sentence of the paragraph states: "In the event of an inconsistency between this paragraph and another provision of this Agreement, this paragraph shall prevail to the extent of that inconsistency."

The activities reserved for the Mexican state are far-reaching. With respect to crude oil and natural gas, the reserved activities include exploration, refining, processing, foreign trade, transportation, storage, and distribution. Other reserved activities include the production of artificial gas and some basic petrochemicals (including their feedstocks and pipelines); virtually all activities associated with nuclear energy; and the generation, transmission, transformation, distribution, and sale of electricity (with the potentially important exception of independently generated electricity). As noted above, for the purposes of this Agreement basic petrochemicals include only five of the twenty on which Mexico currently places restrictions. It is only for these five (ethane, butanes, pentanes, hexanes, and heptanes) that the reservations apply.

Paragraph 2 of annex 602.3 provides additional clarification regarding private investment and cross-border trade in services. Paragraph 2 makes explicit that private investment is not permitted in the activities listed above. In addition, this paragraph stipulates that cross-border trade in services relating to these activities is conditional upon the granting of special permission by Mexico, which is done on a contract-by-contract basis. The inclusion of provisions relating to cross-border trade in services may signal an intention by Mexico to approve such contracts in some cases; however, such approval remains discretionary. Clarification is also provided (in paragraph 3) regarding cross-border trade in natural gas and basic petrochemicals. This paragraph stipulates that each country shall allow supply contracts to be negotiated between end-users and suppliers. These contracts, however, are subject to regulatory approval. Moreover, as explained above, paragraph 1 makes it clear that the Mexican state reserves the right to block foreign trade of these goods into or out of Mexico.

These reservations and special provisions are particularly unsettling given the size of the Mexican energy sector. Tables 10.1 and 10.2, which show North American production and reserve levels of various primary energy sources, suggest the magnitude of Mexico's potential supply contribution. Mexico currently accounts for about 63 percent of North American petroleum reserves but only 24 percent of production. There is potential for even more rapid growth in Mexico's share of natural gas production: its reserves, at about 21 percent of the total for the three countries, are comparable to Canada's; yet Mexico's production is only about 4 percent of the total.

Other Trade and Investment Provisions

There are several other parts of chapter 6 in which Mexico is granted special treatment. An important example of this is found in article 603, which deals with import and export restrictions and largely parallels FTA. Article 603 begins by incorporating the major provisions of the GATT with regard to prohibiting general restrictions on trade. Minimum or maximum price requirements for imports and exports are explicitly prohibited, except in the cases permitted under enforcement of countervailing and/or antidumping directives. Article 603 also allows for restrictions on the other countries in the Agreement if a party bans imports from or exports to outside countries. For example,

TABLE 10.1

Primary Energy Production by Country, 1991 (Quadrillion BTU's)

	Canada	Mexico	United States	North America
All Sources	13.66	7.88	67.49	89.03
	(15.3%)	(8.9%)	(75.8%)	(100%)
Crude Oil*	3.28**	5.87	15.70	24.85
	(13.2%)	(23.6%)	(63.2%)	(100%)
Natural Gas Plant Liquids	0.64	0.60	2.31	3.55
	(18.0%)	(16.9%)	(65.1%)	(100%)
Dry Natural Gas	3.95	0.91	18.49	23.35
	(16.9%)	(3.9%)	(79.2%)	(100%)
Coal***	1.67	0.21	21.56	23.44
	(7.1%)	(0.9%)	(92.0%)	(100%)
Net Hydro Power****	3.16	0.25	2.88	6.29
	(50.2%)	(4.0%)	(45.8%)	(100%)
Net Nuclear Power****	0.95	0.04	6.54	7.53
	(12.6%)	(0.5%)	(86.9%)	(100%)

*Crude oil includes condensate.

**Includes petroleum processed from Athabasca Tar Sands.

***Coal includes anthracite, subanthracite, subbituminous, bituminous, lignite, and brown coal.

****Generation data consist of both utility and nonutility sources. Net generation excludes energy consumed by the generating unit.

SOURCE: *International Energy Annual 1991,* Energy Information Administration, Office of Energy Markets and End Use, U.S. Department of Energy, DOE/EIA-0219(91), December 1992.

TABLE 10.2

North American Energy Reserves, January 1992

	Canada	Mexico	United States	North America
Crude Oil	5.6	51.3	24.7	81.6
(billion barrels)*	(6.9%)	(62.9%)	(30.3%)	(100%)
Natural Gas	96.7	71.5	167.1	335.3
(trillion cu. feet)	(28.8%)	(21.3%)	(49.8%)	(100%)
Coal**	9,503.0	1,895.0	265,173.0	276,571
(million short tons)	(3.4%)	(0.7%)	(95.9%)	(100%)

Oil and Gas Journal estimates.

**Recoverable coal; uses British Petroleum definition of "proven reserves."

SOURCE: *International Energy Annual 1991*, Energy Information Administration, Office of Energy Markets and End Use, U.S. Department of Energy, DOE/EIA-0219(91), December 1992.

if the United States, Canada, or Mexico were to decide independently to restrict imports of energy-related products from an outside country, the Agreement would not preclude the initiating country from restricting imports (of the outside country's products) that pass through the other member countries. (In the case of such restrictions, the parties are encouraged to avoid undue interference with existing pricing, marketing, and distribution arrangements in each other's energy markets.)

Article 603 also allows any country to institute its own import and export licensing policies, but requires that the implementation of these polices be consistent with the other provisions of the Agreement. Annex 603.6, however, grants Mexico a special provision in this regard. This annex specifically allows the Mexican government the right to limit the number of licenses for the import and export of specific goods for the purpose of reserving trade in these commodities to itself. The list of specific commodities is quite broad and includes crude petroleum oils and oils obtained from bituminous minerals, many types of motor fuels, petroleum gases, and a long list of petroleum-based products.

Article 604 deals with export taxes. A party may impose an export tax or duty on the export of products to the territory of the other countries in the Agreement only if the tax or duty is also applied to the good when used for domestic consumption (which again is consistent with FTA). The taxes must also be nondiscriminatory as regards all parties to the Agreement. This is a rare example of an article for which Mexico is not granted special treatment.

Article 605 contains other export-related provisions, but does not apply to Mexico. Under article 605, any export restrictions implemented under GATT allowances (based on national security, supply shortages, price stabilization, and conservation of resources) must follow specific guidelines. Export restrictions imposed by Canada or the United States on an energy-related product are not to change the proportion of the exporter's shipments of that product made available to the other country, relative proportions being determined by the most recent thirty-six month history of shipments. This is the concept of "proportionality" which has been carried over from the U.S.-Canadian FTA, and does not guarantee that the actual proportion of shipments will be maintained. The article also prohibits the exporting country from charging the other country a higher price for exports of energy or petrochemical goods than the price that is to be charged for local consumption, where such price differentials occur as the result of licenses, taxes, or minimum price requirements. Finally, any such export restrictions should not disrupt normal channels of supply to the other party nor should they alter the proportions of specific products made available (such as between grade of crude oil or different categories of refined products). Annex 605 specifically exempts Mexico from *all* of the provisions of this article.

Article 606 affirms that the principle of national treatment (as provided in article 301) applies to energy regulatory measures. Moreover, it commits the parties to "seek to ensure" that any regulations—federal or subfederal—are applied in a manner which avoids disruptions of contractual relationships "to the maximum extent practicable.'' Both the extension of coverage to subfederal agencies and the Agreement to honor contracts go beyond the provisions contained in the U.S.-Canadian FTA, and appear to have been at least partially motivated by a dispute between Canada's National Energy Board and the California Public Utilities Commission.[1] The ability of the parties to enforce these provisions on subfederal entities is open to question.

While chapter 6 contains no special provisions for Mexico regarding national treatment, annex 301.3 describes exclusions to the national treatment clause. Of particular interest is section B of annex 301.3, in which Mexico is granted special provisions. For the first ten years of the Agreement, Mexico may prohibit the entry of a wide variety of used commodities. The list of used equipment on which Mexico may impose import restrictions includes many items (cranes, bulldozers, and other earth-moving equipment and machinery) that may be of use in energy or mineral extraction. Such restrictions have the potential to impede some energy-related exploration and development in Mexico.

Article 607 deals with issues of national security. It sets out the instances in which any country in the Agreement may implement export or import restrictions on energy or basic petrochemicals under GATT or NAFTA national security provisions. These provisions make it more difficult to invoke national security-based restrictions for energy-related products than would be the case for other goods. Annex 607, however, excludes Mexico from these provisions. Mexico's energy sector will instead be subject to the general national security provisions of NAFTA article 2102, which will make it easier for Mexico to invoke such restrictions for energy-related goods.

Finally, article 608 and annex 608.2 reassert the obligations of the United States and Canada regarding other agreements, most notably annexes from FTA pertaining to unique U.S.-Canadian issues. These include such things as exemptions for Canada regarding the U.S. ban of exports of Alaskan oil and the provision of nondiscriminatory treatment to British Columbia Hydro in the Bonneville Power Administration Intertie Access Policy.

This article completes the process of extending the principles of the FTA energy chapter to NAFTA.

Assessment of the Reservations

On the surface, it is difficult to reconcile the restrictions and special exemptions granted to Mexico with the basic principle of liberalization contained in the first article of the energy chapter. Article 601.2 states that all of the parties to the Agreement "recognize that it is desirable to strengthen the important role that trade in energy and basic petrochemical goods have to play in the free trade area and to enhance this role through sustained and gradual liberalization." While this conflict results in part from the recognition of constitutional restrictions, the special treatment afforded Mexico in such areas as the national security provisions and the proportionality clause goes beyond what is required by the Mexican Constitution.[2]

Perhaps the resolution of the conflict between the principle of liberalization and the general thrust of chapter 6 lies in the expectation that as the Agreement evolves, further liberalization will be forthcoming. Additionally, it may be that the Mexican government intends to permit an expansion of foreign trade and investment in energy which goes beyond that required by the Agreement. In either case, NAFTA makes it clear that the destiny of such liberalization lies firmly in the hands of the Mexican government, which with few exceptions has yet to demonstrate a willingness to commit itself to such a path.

Independent Electrical Generation

One exception to the general protectionist thrust of the energy chapter (as regards Mexico) is in the area of independent generation of electricity. Paragraph 5 of annex 602.3 contains special provisions for Canadian and U.S. investment in electrical generation facilities in Mexico. Canadian and U.S. enterprises are allowed to acquire, establish, and/or operate facilities involving three forms of independently generated electricity: (1) production for own use; (2) cogeneration (in which electricity is generated from heat or other energy by-products resulting from industrial production); and (3) independent power production (which involves the production of electricity by an independent supplier for the primary purpose of sale to other users).

Such provisions are consistent with the Mexican Constitution, which does not restrict the generation of electricity for private use. While independent generation of electricity was previously legal, NAFTA's explicit provision of foreign investment opportunities in this area helps to foster an environment conducive to such investments. Moreover, paragraph 5 stipulates that any surplus electricity from these activities shall be purchased by the Mexican state monopoly (Federal Electricity Commission, or CFE) which guarantees a market to foreign investors. On the down side, however, the CFE is the only buyer (the electricity cannot be sold directly to end-users), and there are no pricing guidelines other than the stipulation that "CFE shall purchase such electricity under terms and conditions agreed to by CFE and the enterprise" (annex 602.3.5). The potential significance of these provisions is examined below in light of the rather considerable U.S. experience with investment in independent electrical generation.

Pricing and Investment: The U.S. Experience

Within the United States, independently generated electricity is one of the most rapidly growing sources of supply. This growth has resulted from the implementation of section 210 of the Public Utility Regulatory Policies Act of 1978 (PURPA) which established a framework for the sale of electricity from independent sources to electric utilities. The Federal Energy Regulatory Commission (FERC) promulgated rules implementing PURPA, including rules regarding the establishment of prices at which the electricity is purchased. The perceived need for such rules derives in part from the fact that electric utilities are not subject to the discipline of a competitive marketplace. These rules require that the prices paid to independent suppliers be based on the utility's "full avoided cost," in other words, the operating and capital costs which the utility avoids as the result of the provision of independently generated electricity.[3] Recent interpretations of the avoided-cost standard allow for the establishment of prices based on competitive bidding between potential independent suppliers. Individual states, through their public utility commissions, adopt specific pricing rules based on these general principles.

Based on the U.S. experience, there is a wide range of possibilities regarding the potential level of investment in Mexico, largely as the result of uncertainty regarding the prices that will be acceptable to CFE. Paragraph 5 of annex 602.3 implies that CFE must purchase independently generated electricity, but the extent to which such supply is forthcoming will be a function of the prices to which CFE agrees. NAFTA itself provides no pricing guidelines. Even if general guidelines were provided (or were understood to exist) the specific implementation of those guidelines can vary dramatically. For example, while all U.S. states are guided by the same general principles in the pricing of independently generated electricity, the actual prices vary considerably by state. This is in part the result of differing cost conditions across states, but it is also a function of differing interpretations regarding what constitutes avoided-cost pricing. Given that electricity is (for all practical purposes) nonstorable, and that its value varies by time of use, the establishment of such rates is exceedingly complex.[4] The differing approaches have led to very substantial differences across states in the level of investment which has occurred. In states in which there are relatively favorable price conditions (from the standpoint of the independent producers) very substantial investment has occurred, with very little investment in states with unfavorable pricing.

The objective, of course, is not to maximize the quantity of independent supply, but to obtain the efficient level. There is little reason to believe, however, that the appropriate prices will be arrived at either from a process of open and free negotiations (given the market failure caused by the CFE's monopsony power) or from a process of administrative price setting (given the inevitable regulatory failure associated with such attempts). Given this uncertainty regarding prices, it is difficult to foretell the extent of future foreign investment in independent generating capacity. With the correct prices, however, the U.S. experience suggests that such investment could be substantial.

Environmental Considerations

In addition to the generation of electricity for sale within Mexico, there is the possibility of U.S. or Canadian firms generating electricity in Mexico for purposes of sale (through CFE) to electric utilities in the United States. Electric utilities in the United States are under increasing pressure to invest in pollution abatement. It has been estimated that compliance with the acid rain provisions of the most recent amendments to the Clean Air Act will cost U.S. utilities approximately $4 billion annually.[5] This raises the issue as to whether an incentive will exist to move electrical generation to Mexico, where environmental laws are not currently enforced as vigorously as in the United States or Canada.

Several factors militate against this possibility. First, paragraph 5(c) of annex 602.3 (which provides for cross-border trade of independently generated electricity) makes it explicit that each party has the right to determine whether such contracts are subject to regulatory approval. Purchases of independently generated electricity by U.S. utilities are in most cases subject to the oversight of state regulatory commissions, which are likely to block such trades if they are perceived as being rooted in a desire to escape environmental regulation. Secondly, the parties agree in article 1114 not to weaken environmental measures for the purpose of attracting or retaining investment, which should discourage the parties from bidding for investment through the relaxation of environmental standards. Finally, the pending side agreement on the environment may go further than this and mandate more stringent enforcement of environmental laws in Mexico. For these reasons, it seems unlikely that NAFTA will induce a significant shift of generating capacity from the United States to Mexico for purposes of avoiding U.S. environmental regulation. This does not mean, however, that such investment would not occur for other reasons.

The above analysis is not meant to be dismissive of all concerns regarding the environmental implications of NAFTA. If environmental costs in some industries are not internalized to the same extent in Mexico as in the United States or Canada (either through regulation or other measures), a differential subsidy will exist in these industries favoring production in Mexico. While such subsidies are implicit, from the standpoint of economic efficiency they are no different from explicit subsidies, in that part of the costs of production are borne by the public at large. (The possibility of cross-border pollution suggests that some of these subsidies may be borne by residents in a neighboring country.) To the extent that the rate of subsidization is not uniform across all sectors in all countries, a tendency will exist to over allocate resources to the more heavily subsidized activities.

The above does not necessarily argue for the adoption of harmonized environmental standards, since for a given activity external costs may be different in the three countries (or, for that matter, in different regions of the same country). It does argue, however, for a more complete approach to accounting whenever the issue of protection is addressed. Failure to do so opens up the possibility that the distortions associated with traditional trade barriers will simply be replaced by a new set of distortions, which may themselves have implications for trade. As Bond and Guisinger have demonstrated, for a given set of tariffs there exists a structure of production subsidies which will yield the same effective rate of protection.[6] To focus on traditional trade barriers alone while ignoring subsidies (environmental or otherwise) is inconsistent with the larger objective of establishing free and fair trade.

Additional Areas of Liberalization

Two additional areas of liberalization affecting energy markets are government procurement and the production of coal. Chapter 10 of NAFTA, "Government Procurement," opens up the procurement contracts of CFE and the Mexican national oil company (PEMEX) to U.S. and Canadian bidders. This applies to both goods and services. The current annual value of these contracts is approximately $8.5 billion.[7] The liberalization of Pemex and CFE procurement is to be phased in over a ten year period. Initially, the proportion of Pemex and CFE procurement open to foreign participation is 50 percent, rising to 100 percent after ten years (annex 1001.2a).

Conspicuous in its absence from the energy chapter's reservations is the production of coal. The existing 10 percent Mexican tariff on coal will be eliminated immediately. The percentage of coal mines and facilities that can be owned by Canadian and U.S. firms will increase to 100 percent from the current restriction of 49 percent. As shown in table 10.2, however, Mexico's coal reserves are less than 1 percent of total North American reserves. The practical significance of this liberalization is thus quite limited.

Implications of NAFTA-Induced Growth

The most important implications of NAFTA for investment in the energy sector most likely will *not* arise directly from the energy chapter itself. Rather, the largest effects will probably result indirectly from the impact of NAFTA on growth in other sectors. In this section the investment implications are discussed by analyzing the likely effects of NAFTA on energy demand and supply. These effects are due largely to NAFTA-induced growth in overall economic activity. In order to analyze these effects, one must first understand the implications of NAFTA for growth in GDP.

Over the last two years there has been an impressive outpouring of studies on the possible economic effects of NAFTA. These vary both in level of aggregation and in methodology. The most common approach uses computable general equilibrium models. Many of these studies are surveyed in Brown; Brown, Deardorff, and Stern; Globerman; Hufbauer and Schott; and

Weintraub.[8] Despite the differences among these models, the bulk of the evidence suggests that the effects of NAFTA on real income and employment are likely to be small for the United States and Canada, both absolutely and in percentage terms, but potentially much larger for Mexico. For example, in most of the static models surveyed by Brown and by Globerman, the effects of various trade and investment liberalization scenarios range from zero to 2.6 percent of GDP for the United States. The corresponding estimates for Mexico are generally several times larger, ranging from 3 to 7 percent of GDP. Some dynamic models, in which investment is endogenous and responds to improved expectations, predict even larger impacts for Mexico, in the 8 to 11 percent range.[9]

The large NAFTA-induced growth in Mexican GDP will affect Mexican demand for marketable energy. Total energy use includes both market sources (petroleum products, natural gas and electricity) and nonmarket sources (gathered wood, animal dung, and other forms of biomass). Total use of market energy sources is the product of marketable energy's share of total energy (ME/E), the energy intensity of the economy (E/GDP), and the level of economic activity (GDP). It is likely that growth in Mexico will cause both ME/E and E/GDP to rise, which implies that total usage of marketable energy will rise more rapidly than GDP.

On both empirical and theoretical grounds it is believed that energy intensity (E/GDP) is an increasing function of GDP at low levels of GDP and a decreasing function of GDP at high levels of GDP.[10] Mexico's comparatively low level of per-capita income (roughly 10 percent of the U.S. level) suggests that Mexico is on the increasing portion of the function. Substitution from nonmarket to market fuels also traditionally accompanies economic development. In order to investigate the likely extent of these effects one must first consider the factors affecting energy use at the microlevel.

Sectoral Analysis

The key consideration in analyzing the demand for energy is that it is a derived demand. Firms use energy along with labor, capital, raw materials, and other inputs to produce various goods and services; households use energy as an input in the production of household services such as space conditioning, laundering, and cooking. Patterns of energy use therefore differ markedly across different categories of end-users. The factors affecting demand for various energy sources are thus different in the industrial, agricultural, transportation, and residential sectors, each of which is considered below.

Predicting the effects on energy demand in the industrial sector is complicated by uncertainty regarding the interindustry effects of NAFTA, and by uncertainty regarding the energy coefficients in each industry's production function. Some of the sectors for which Brown, Deardorff, and Stern predict the largest output gains in Mexico (such as glass, nonferrous metals, and electrical machinery) tend to be relatively energy intensive.[11] Sterner has argued that the high energy intensity of many Mexican manufacturing industries is due in large part to past subsidies to domestic oil consumption, which led firms to adopt energy-inefficient technologies.[12] In 1980, for example, the price of bunker oil was $2.60 per barrel in Mexico, which was approximately 10 percent of the world price; the price of kerosene was approximately 25 percent of the border price.[13] These subsidies, together with low wage rates, slowed the replacement of older equipment by more modern energy-efficient and labor-saving capital. In 1990, however, Mexico adopted the National Energy Modernization Program (NEMP), which has initiated an ongoing process of reducing subsidies and allowing prices to rise to world levels.[14] This will tend to mitigate somewhat the expected growth of energy intensity in the industrial sector.

The effects in the agricultural sector will be very complex. In general, developing countries have experienced rapidly rising energy intensity in agriculture due to two factors: mechanization and increased use of fossil fuels as feedstocks in the production of fertilizer and other agricultural chemicals.[15] In addition, the share of marketable energy has risen as a percentage of total energy as farmers substitute commercial fuels for nonmarket sources of energy. In Mexico, analysis of the effects of NAFTA on agriculture is complicated by internal policy changes underway subsequent to Mexico's joining of the GATT. These reforms will significantly reduce tariffs, domestic subsidies, import controls and licenses, and place restrictions on land tenure in maize farming.[16] It has been estimated that the reform policies could result in rural-urban migration of up to 700,000 workers in the first year, and up to 1.9 million cumulatively.[17]

The energy demand implications of this migration are dramatic. Urbanization has effects on energy use that are separate from the effects of higher income. The impacts include changes in daily personal transportation patterns, which in rural areas may involve little or no commercial fuel use; substitution of commercial for "traditional" energy; and increased transportation distances for agricultural products.[18] The exact magnitude of these effects remains an unanswered empirical question, but it is expected to be substantial.

Of all the sectors considered here, transportation displays the heaviest reliance on liquid fuels and the most limited possibilities for substitution. The demand for transportation is very sensitive to income, both at the aggregate and individual levels. Rail and truck freight transport are both sensitive to industrial production, and hence will be stimulated by NAFTA. Moreover, as income rises the demand for truck transport rises relative to rail, due to its greater convenience; this raises energy intensity due to the higher energy requirements per ton-mile for trucks.[19]

The demand for personal transportation is highly income elastic, mainly due to the increased opportunity cost of time with rising income. This affects both mode choice and the demand for trips. Mode switching is reflected in the replacement of animals by motorized transportation in poor rural areas, and by substitution of more energy-intensive but more convenient modes at higher income levels (automobiles for mopeds for intraurban travel, and air travel for autos or buses for intercity trips.) It is clear that the effects of rising incomes on the demand for faster, more convenient, and more personalized transportation will have potentially large impacts on the use and production of automobiles, and hence on the energy intensity of transportation.

Rising personal income is likely to result in dramatic growth in energy intensity in the household sector. The income elasticity of demand for energy is quite high for two reasons: as incomes rise, there is an increased demand for goods and services, such as travel and comfort, that are relatively energy-intensive; and there is an increased demand for energy sources that are cleaner and more convenient, which tend to be more energy- and capital-intensive. In poor rural areas of developing countries, there is heavy reliance on traditional nonmarket fuels. As incomes rise, there is a shift from labor-intensive solid fuels to more convenient liquid fuels such as kerosene; and at higher income levels there is further substitution to heating oil, natural gas, and electricity. In Mexico, the former effect may not be very large, because only about 14 percent of household energy use is from traditional sources.[20] But the effect will certainly be noticeable, and implies an increase in the share of marketable energy (ME/E).

The demands for natural gas and electricity are especially income elastic, being closely tied to the purchase of durable appliances.[21] Bhatia reports that this result is confirmed by Berndt and Samaniego in the case of Mexican electricity demand.[22] They find that rising income increases both the number of households connected to the transmission system and consumption by households already connected.

Implications for Production and Investment

All of this points to growth in demand for petroleum products, natural gas, and especially electricity, in excess of the rate of growth in real GDP. The growth in electricity demand has, in turn, considerable implications for fuels used to generate electricity, such as natural gas. This will create additional incentives for foreign investment in independent electrical generating capacity, opportunities for which are created by chapter 6 of NAFTA, as was discussed above.

Whether this rapidly growing demand for energy is fully met by increased production (as opposed to reductions in exports) will depend on Mexico's energy and investment policies. In the important petroleum sector, this poses significant challenges for Mexican policymakers. Mexico's oil supply constraints are well documented.[23] A fundamental goal of the National Energy Modernization Plan is to maintain oil exports at approximately their current level of about 1.4 million barrels per day while increasing production to cover growth in domestic demand. This will require extensive expansion and modernization.[24] The ability of Pemex to meet this goal is questionable. It faces a number of competing investment demands, including insufficient refinery and storage capacity, inadequate and outdated retail outlets, and insufficient capacity in petrochemical production. United States' oil companies are reluctant to supply their funds and technical expertise for oil exploration and development in Mexico on a contract basis, without some share in equity or output, particularly when other Latin American and former centrally planned economies are beginning to offer such opportunities at comparatively favorable terms.[25] Given this, fulfillment of Pemex's objectives will likely require significant liberalization with respect to opportunities for foreign direct investment in the oil industry.

The restrictions on foreign direct investment in the energy sector apply equally to natural gas. As shown in table 10.2, Mexico has significant natural gas reserves: approximately 72 trillion cubic feet, compared with 97 trillion for Canada. Of these, about half are in southern Mexico and offshore in the Gulf of Campeche, largely in association with crude oil deposits. The remaining half are in northern Mexico and are mostly nonassociated gas. There is limited pipeline capacity between the two regions, so that northern Mexico is more closely tied to the southwest U.S. market.[26]

The reservations to NAFTA's investment provisions, combined with Pemex's capital constraints and its emphasis on developing oil resources, suggest that Mexico's sizable reserves of nonassociated gas are likely to remain largely untapped in the near future. Given expectation of rapid growth in demand, this implies that Mexico's gas imports from the United States are likely to rise dramatically (which in turn implies an increase in U.S. imports of Canadian gas). This will put further pressure on

Mexico to open its oil and gas sectors to foreign direct investment.

To meet the expected growth in demand for electricity, Mexico must either invest in additional generating facilities, or increase electricity imports, or both. The ability to expand imports is constrained by existing transmission capacity.[27] Except for a small section of northern Baja California, the Mexican transmission system is not operated synchronously with U.S. systems. This has limited trade to border regions in which exchanges can be made over alternating current systems rather than over more costly direct current lines. Demand growth must therefore be met by substantial construction of new generating plants, by long-distance direct current lines, or by modifying the existing system to achieve compatibility with U.S. grids.

The constraint on transmission capacity, together with the investment restrictions on hydrocarbons, will have implications for the location of independent generating facilities. As a result of relative fuel prices and environmental regulations favoring low-sulfur fuels, the most popular choice of generating technology by independent power producers in the United States has been combustion turbines fired by natural gas. If the desire to sell some electricity back to the United States is an important consideration for U.S. power producers locating plants in Mexico, then they will tend to locate in the border region to access existing interconnections to the U.S. grids. This will further increase demand for development of nonassociated gas deposits in northern Mexico, creating additional incentives for the government to liberalize the restrictions on foreign direct investment.

Summary and Conclusions

The potential gains from trade and investment in North American energy markets will not be realized unless NAFTA evolves beyond its current form. The extensive exemptions and special provisions granted to Mexico are likely to limit the opportunities for foreign investment and trade in a variety of energy-related goods. For example, in the case of petroleum and natural gas, the activities reserved for the Mexican state include foreign trade, exploration, refining, processing, transportation, storage, and distribution (including investment in and the provision of services for each of these activities). The production of artificial gas and some basic petrochemicals, as well as virtually all activities associated with nuclear energy, are also reserved for the Mexican state. While other provisions would seem to establish the right of end-users and suppliers to negotiate contracts (in such areas as cross-border trade in natural gas), any inconsistencies are resolved in favor of the exclusive rights granted to the Mexican state. The only significant exceptions are in the area of independent electrical generation (where significant investment opportunities are explicitly provided for by the Agreement), the opening up of Pemex and CFE procurement contracts to foreign bidders, the production of coal (of which Mexico has very little), and the production of some basic petrochemicals.

In their assessment of NAFTA, Hufbauer and Schott give a grade of ''C+'' to the energy provisions.[28] This represents either a very generous curve or substantial grade inflation. The exemptions and special provisions granted to Mexico, which in some cases go beyond what is required by the Mexican Constitution, are at odds with the stated objective of liberalization. It is possible that further liberalization will be forthcoming, in the form of either modifications to NAFTA or de facto liberalization resulting from Mexican acquiescence. In either case, however, the destiny of such liberalization lies in the hands of Mexico.

Perhaps the greatest hope for further liberalization resides with the implications of NAFTA for economic growth. NAFTA-induced growth in Mexican GDP will result in a disproportionate increase in energy demand, which, given supply constraints, will create an imperative for additional liberalization. This growth in demand and its consequences will be felt in all major areas within the energy sector. Perhaps the most important of these is oil. Mexico's National Energy Modernization Program calls for the preservation of existing levels of oil exports. However, Mexico faces severe constraints on its ability to expand capacity to meet growth in domestic demand. These constraints are exacerbated by restrictions in NAFTA relating to foreign direct investment and the provision of energy-related services. This suggests that Mexico will be forced either to retreat from its commitment to preserving current levels of petroleum exports, or to move down the path of further liberalization.

Notes

1. G. C. Watkins, "NAFTA and Energy: A Bridge Not Far Enough?" in Steven Globerman and Michael Walker, eds., *Assessing NAFTA: A Trinational Analysis* (Vancouver: The Fraser Institute, 1993), 193–225.

2. For a summary of energy-related constitutional provisions, see Gary Clyde Hufbauer and Jeffrey J. Schott, *North American Free Trade: Issues and Recommendations* (Washington, D.C.: Institute for International Economics, 1992) 75–76.

3. Federal Energy Regulatory Commission (FERC), "Small Power Production and Cogeneration Facilities; Regulations Implementing Section 210 of the Public Utility Regulatory Policies Act of 1978," *Federal Register* 45:38 (February 25, 1980): 12214–37.

4. See Daniel A. Hagen and James W. Vincent, "On the Pricing of Independently Generated Electricity," *Southern Economic Journal* 55, no. 4 (April 1989): 935–53.

5. Paul R. Portney, "Policy Watch: Economics and the Clean Air Act," *Journal of Economic Perspectives* 4, no. 4 (Fall 1990): 173–81.

6. Eric Bond and Stephen Guisinger, "Investment Incentives as Tariff Substitutes," *Review of Economics and Statistics* 67, no. 1 (February 1985): 91–7.

7. Gary Clyde Hufbauer and Jeffrey J. Schott, *NAFTA: An Assessment* (Washington, D.C.: Institute for International Economics, February 1993) 120.

8. Drusilla K. Brown, "The Impact of a North American Free Trade Area: Applied General Equilibrium Models," in Nora Lustig, Barry P. Bosworth, and Robert Z. Lawrence, eds., *North American Free Trade: Assessing the Impact* (Washington, D.C.: The Brookings Institution, 1992), 26–68; Drusilla K. Brown, Alan V. Deardorff, and Robert M. Stern, "North American Integration," *The Economic Journal* 102, no. 415 (November 1992): 1507–18; Steven Globerman, "The Economics of NAFTA," Manuscript. Presented at the Western Washington University Faculty Seminar, 8 March 1993; Hufbauer and Schott, *North American Free Trade;* Sidney Weintraub, "Modeling the Industrial Effects of NAFTA," in Nora Lustig, Barry P. Bosworth, and Robert Z. Lawrence, eds., *North American Free Trade: Assessing the Impact* (Washington, D.C.: The Brookings Institution, 1992), 109–43.

9. Brown, Deardorff, and Stern, "North American Integration," 1510.

10. Amulya K. N. Reddy and Jose Goldemberg, "Energy for the Developing World," Chapter 6 in *Energy for Planet Earth: Readings from Scientific American* (New York: W. H. Freeman and Company, 1991).

11. Drusilla K. Brown, Alan V. Deardorff, and Robert M. Stern, "A North American Free Trade Agreement: Analytical Issues and a Computational Assessment," *World Economy* 15, no. 1 (January 1992): 11–29.

12. Thomas Sterner, "Factor Demand and Substitution in a Developing Country: Energy Use in Mexican Manufacturing," *Scandinavian Journal of Economics* 91, no. 4 (1989): 723–39 and Thomas Sterner, "Energy Efficiency and Capital Embodied Technical Change: The Case of Mexican Cement Manufacturing," *The Energy Journal* 11, no. 2 (April 1990): 155–67.

13. Joy Dunkerley with Michele Gottlieb, "The Structure of Energy Demand and Energy Conservation," *The Energy Journal* 8, Special LDC Issue (1987): 49–52.

14. U.S. General Accounting Office (GAO), *Mexican Oil: Issues Affecting Potential U.S. Trade and Investment,* Report No. GAO/NSIAD-92-169, U.S. Government Printing Office (March 1992) 18.

15. Ramesh Bhatia, "Energy Demand Analysis in Developing Countries: A Review," *The Energy Journal* 8, Special LDC Issue (1987): 18–19.

16. Tim Josling, "NAFTA and Agriculture: A Review of the Economic Impacts," in Nora Lustig, Barry P. Bosworth, and Robert Z. Lawrence, eds., *North American Free Trade: Assessing the Impact* (Washington, D.C.: The Brookings Institution, 1992), 144–75.

17. Brown, Deardorff, and Stern, "North American Integration," 1514.

18. Donald W. Jones, "Urbanization and Energy Use in Economic Development," *The Energy Journal* 10, no. 4 (October 1989): 29–43.

19. Bhatia, 23.

20. Dunkerley with Gottlieb, 49.

21. Ibid., 37; Bhatia, 25.

22. E. R. Berndt and R. Samaniego, "Residential Electricity Demand in Mexico: A Model Distinguishing Access from Consumption." MIT Working Paper No. 1416–83, March 1983.

23. See Hufbauer and Schott, *North American Free Trade,* 187–93 and U.S. General Accounting Office (GAO).

24. U.S. General Accounting Office (GAO).

25. Ibid.

26. *Platt's Oilgram News,* "Investment Constraints on Pemex May Bode Well for U.S. Gas Sales to Mexico," 70:132 (9 July 1992): 2.

27. See Energy Information Administration (EIA), U.S. Department of Energy, *U.S. Electricity Trade with Canada and Mexico,* Publication No. DOE/EIA-0553, U.S. Government Printing Office (January 1992).

28. Hufbauer and Schott, *NAFTA: An Assessment,* 10.

PART 4

IMPACT ON OUTSIDERS

Chapter 11

NAFTA AND JAPANESE INVESTMENT

David W. Edgington and W. Mark Fruin

Japan and NAFTA

This chapter deals solely with Japanese investment as it is already of considerable importance to the economies of Canada, the United States, and Mexico.[1] Japan, as the most advanced of the Asian economies, is a harbinger of what other Asian economies are likely to do as they continue to grow and diversify their products and markets.

Over the last ten years foreign direct investment (FDI) from Japan has recorded substantial increases, and in each of NAFTA countries a significant number of people are employed in Japanese-owned businesses.[2] Japan ranks as both Canada's and Mexico's largest trading partner after the United States, and in terms of source of foreign investment Japan is fourth in Mexico[3] and third in Canada.[4] For the United States, Japan is its largest bilateral trade partner apart from Canada, and ranks fourth in cumulative FDI after several E.C. nations.[5] Future rounds of Japanese FDI will therefore have a direct impact on the overall health of each of the three North American economies.

But what does NAFTA mean for future patterns and levels of Japanese investment? It is probably too soon to assess changes in Japanese business strategies in North America following the Agreement. Yet what can be done is to appraise recent patterns of Japanese investment, and current Japanese reactions towards the broader challenges posed by globalization. While the continuing evolution of the details of NAFTA and its implementation makes definitive answers impossible, a number of trends are now visible. A broad conclusion which emerges from this material is that even without the formal NAFTA agreement many Japanese companies already think of North America in terms of one integrated production network. For example, Japanese auto firms drawn to manufacture in Canada have gone there knowing they had to rely on continental integration of production and an ability to export competitively to the United States.

The discussion below proceeds as follows: in the following section recent shifts in the overseas investment strategies of Japan's major multinational companies (MNCs), their changing organizational structures, and the implications of the tendency towards a tripolar global economy are discussed. Secondly, using unpublished Japanese FDI statistics, the importance of the NAFTA triad among Japan's worldwide investment is evaluated. An examination of where within the NAFTA region Japanese companies have located, and how and why they have distributed their investments follows. Thirdly, recent and proposed Japanese investments in the automobile sector as a case study of continental integration are scrutinized. Finally, the implications of these trends for future patterns of Japanese investment activity within NAFTA are postulated.

Globalization of Japanese Manufacturing Companies

As discussed in Edgington, Japanese FDI accelerated to substantial levels following the revaluation of the yen in 1985 (*endaka*).[6] Overseas production by major Japanese manufacturing companies and their suppliers grew rapidly in East and Southeast Asia, as well as North America and the European Community (E.C.). This was motivated in the former case mainly by cost pressures in Japan arising from the appreciation of the yen, and in the two latter cases by the need to avoid trade friction abroad. By the end of the decade Japanese FDI was growing more quickly than that of any other source nation, although its absolute global size was still substantially smaller than that from either the United States or the U.K.[7] In contrast, the early 1990s have seen a fall in Japan's FDI, due both to the impact of the "bursting of the bubble economy" and the global recession of 1991 to 1992.[8] It is likely, however, that overseas production by Japanese manufacturing companies will continue during the remainder of the decade.[9] Furthermore, along with higher levels of overseas production, Japanese manufacturers have now irrevocably modified their perceptions of how to conduct overseas business. From being disinclined to invest much outside neighboring Asian countries, up until the early 1980s, the largest Japanese companies have now followed western MNCs to operate fully on a global scale of production and markets.

To ascertain why Japanese investors have decided to establish firms in NAFTA (and will continue to do so), one must look first at the overseas strategies that Japanese MNCs have followed during recent years. Apart from the unique pressures associated with endaka and trade conflict, Japanese MNCs have been influenced by three general forces acting upon global capitalism. The first of these has been a general intensification of international competition among all triad-based MNCs and the consequent need to deepen their involvement in key overseas markets.[10]

A second factor has been the introduction of flexible manufacturing techniques, allowing efficient short-batch production to run parallel to changes in consumer and industrial demand, together with the shortening of product cycles and the greater use of just-in-time delivery systems.[11] This lean production system achieves its highest efficiency, quality, and flexibility when all activities from design to assembly occur in the same place.[12] These changes in production bring advantages to firms able to create a top-to-bottom manufacturing system in each of the world's major markets.

A third element fostering greater levels of overseas FDI has been the revolution in information technologies.[13] This facilitates the transfer abroad of top-level management and coordination functions—such as research and development, engineering, and finance—often leading to the establishment of global regional offices. While there are strong forces keeping these high-order management activities at home, the potential advantage of moving such operations overseas is that local subsidiary companies can have all of the necessary functions to become fully-fledged insiders in each of the Triad economies (North America, Europe, and the West Pacific).[14] This enables them to be more efficient competitors with local incumbents, and to respond more effectively to local consumer or industrial needs.

Japanese firms have responded to all of the above pressures and influences.[15] Over the 1980s they have outgrown their old image of reluctant multinationals, by locating production and even research and design functions in foreign markets.[16] To varying degrees they have also relaxed what was once a concentrated decision-making structure focused upon their domestic head office. As reported elsewhere, Japanese manufacturing companies have increasingly become insiders in each of the world's Triad economies.[17] This emerging trend towards use of a global regional structure has also been consistent with trade policy developments, both in Europe as it moved toward economic union, in North America as it moved to NAFTA, and also in Asia, where the economies of the newly industrialized countries began rapidly integrating with Japan's.

Besides more comprehensive localization, the globalization of Japanese firms has also implied more extensive intrafirm horizontal division of labor across countries and Triad regions for the supply of parts and products, as well as unhindered flows of technology, finance, and other materials between production units on a global scale.[18] For firms which have progressed fully to this position (Sony, Nissan, and Honda), the Japanese headquarters now considers each of the worldwide regional centers as sources of ideas, products, and other resources that can be harnessed for the benefit of the total organization. Significantly, this pattern contrasts sharply with the earlier dominant international production strategies of the 1970s and early 1980s when, for most MNCs, global strategies followed the New International Division of Labor (NIDL) thesis, concentrating on keeping costs low by exploiting fully both cheap labor locations and economies of scale.

Japanese Investment in NAFTA

Having explained why Japanese firms now feel the need to establish production and sales networks in each Triad, figure 11.1 displays the percentage of total annual Japanese direct investment in each Triad host region during the 1980s (NAFTA, the E.C., and the West Pacific) as well as to other countries.[19] Three patterns are evident. First, all Triad regions grew in importance relative to the rest of the world (for example, South America, the Middle East, and Africa). In part, this reflects the reduction of Japanese investment interest in energy and raw materials projects in countries such as Brazil and Saudi Arabia.

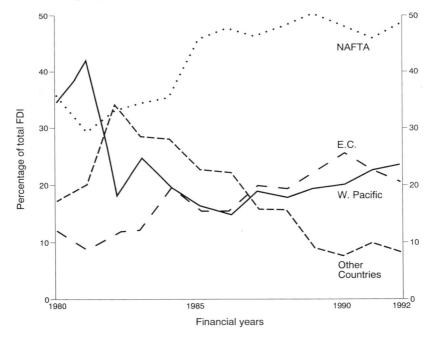

Figure 11.1   Percentage Share of Japanese Annual FDI Among Global Regions, 1980–1992

NOTE: 1992 figures based on half year data.

SOURCE: Japanese Ministry of Finance data, approval basis

Second, the E.C. (including all European countries and the former Soviet Union) and NAFTA grew in importance over the 1980s, although it has been NAFTA which shifted into first place since the mid-1980s. Third, the West Pacific (including Australia) lost share throughout most of the 1980s, first to NAFTA and then to the E.C., but regained some of its lost share towards the end of the period. This was mainly due to the 1991 to 1992 recession in Europe and North America, which left Asia-Pacific countries as the only global region showing any economic growth.

Table 11.1 shows that within NAFTA bloc, the United States remained consistently the number one host country to annual Japanese FDI over the last ten years; and was increasingly favored over Canada and Mexico. Up to fiscal year (FY) 1992 (first half), the cumulative share of Japanese investment in NAFTA was 94.6 percent for the United States, 4.1 percent for Canada, and only 1.2 percent for Mexico. Table 11.1 demonstrates that there is a great discrepancy in these percentages based upon the relative market size (measured by GDP), as well as population size of Canada, Mexico, and the United States. For example, Mexico has about 25 percent of the population and about 3 percent of the combined GDP, but has attracted less than one percent of annual Japanese FDI since 1987. Table 11.1 displays equally wide differences between the United States and Canada in terms of investment patterns. In the manufacturing sector (not shown in table 11.1), cumulative Japanese annual direct investment in the United States amounted to $43.3 billion by the end of FY 1991 (or 88.7 percent of all Japanese manufacturing in NAFTA) compared with $2.9 billion in Canada (5.9 percent), and just $1.3 billion (2.7 percent) in Mexico.[20]

It is instructive to compare further the patterns of Japanese investment among the three countries. A complete comparison of Japanese cumulative investment profile in the United States, Canada, and Mexico up to FY 1991 is shown in figure 11.2, based on the percentage distribution among different sectors for each country. Due to the problems inherent in the data, this analysis of the relative importance of Japanese FDI by broad-scale sector is only a first step towards identifying the activities

TABLE 11.1

Japanese FDI in NAFTA: GDP, Population,
and Land Area, 1989
(U.S. million dollars)

	Canada (%)		United States (%)		Mexico (%)	
1980	112	(6.7)	1,484	(88.3)	85	(5.1)
1981	167	(6.4)	2,354	(90.4)	82	(3.2)
1982	167	(5.5)	2,738	(89.8)	143	(4.7)
1983	136	(4.8)	2,565	(90.9)	121	(4.3)
1984	184	(5.1)	3,359	(93.3)	56	(1.6)
1985	100	(1.8)	5,395	(96.4)	101	(1.8)
1986	276	(2.6)	10,165	(95.6)	226	(2.1)
1987	653	(4.2)	14,704	(95.6)	28	(0.2)
1988	626	(2.8)	21,704	(96.8)	87	(0.4)
1989	1,362	(4.0)	32,540	(94.7)	36	(0.1)
1990	1,064	(3.9)	26,128	(95.5)	168	(1.0)
1991	797	(4.2)	18,026	(94.8)	193	(1.0)
1992*	316	(3.8)	8,038	(95.8)	40	(0.5)
GDP (U.S. billion dollars)	531.6	(9.0)	5,200.8	(87.6)	201.4	(3.4)
Population (million)	26.3	(7.3)	248.8	(69.0)	85.0	(23.6)
Land Area (million kms²)	9,976	(46.8)	9,373	(44.0)	1,958	(9.2)

*half-year figures

SOURCES: Japanese Ministry of Finance data, approval basis; *Business Week,* 1992.

and areas of Japanese companies' operations in NAFTA.[21] Nonetheless, it reveals a number of interesting contrasts between the three countries—in part reflecting differences in Japanese investment motivations. Thus, investment in Canada has been to assure exports of food, minerals, metals, and resources for the Japanese market, or to provide local commercial conduits for Japanese exports. It is therefore not surprising that

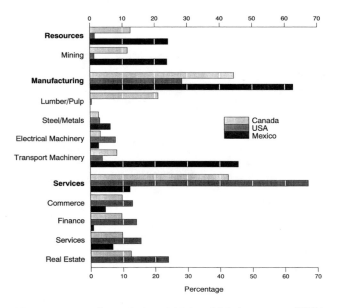

Figure 11.2　Cumulative 1954–1992 Japanese FDI by Sector, Canada, United States, and Mexico (Relative Percentage)

NOTE: 1992 figures based on half year data.

SOURCE: Derived from Japanese Ministry of Finance unpublished data, approval basis

figure 11.2 shows Canada's profile of Japanese investment, when compared to the United States and Mexico, to have been more dominant in sectors such as mining, lumber, and pulp. In the United States, by contrast, it is the service sectors which are relatively more important. Here Japanese investment has traditionally taken place largely in commerce, banking and finance, and insurance; and it has only been in the 1980s that the United States saw an upsurge of Japanese investment in manufacturing (especially in electrical/electronic equipment and transport equipment), together with a rise in additional services-based investments (particularly finance and real estate development). Mexico exhibits a relative focus on Japanese investment in mining (oil and industrial salt) as well as metals (steel products) and transport equipment.

This analysis suggests that the major motivations underlying the patterns of Japanese investment in Canada and Mexico have been quite different from those in the United States. Thus the focus of postwar Japanese investment in Canada has been in resources; Japanese companies use Canada more heavily as a resources location than either the United States or Mexico (other than mining). By comparison, virtually all investment in the United States was oriented to the local market. For instance, much Japanese FDI in manufacturing was prompted by Japanese government pressure to decrease trade friction through local production. By way of illustration, this was the main reason for major automobile and electric/electronics firms deciding to build large-scale manufacturing plants in the United States during the 1980s.[22] Canada unquestionably has been able to attract substantial Japanese investment in manufacturing. Yet while Japanese investment in U.S. manufacturing is oriented to medium- to high-technology operations, corresponding Canadian investment has been directed to lower value-added wood pulp and medium technology car assembly.[23] Also for the United States, services and real estate was more important, again reflecting the importance of the U.S. market.

For Mexico, mining and transport equipment were the two dominant sectors. Japanese MNCs use Mexico more heavily as a manufacturing location than they use their Canadian affiliates (although the total dollar values of sale and assets are much larger in Canada). Also of significance is that in the 1980s the United States replaced the Mexican market as the chief target for Japanese producers expanding their operations in Mexico. Intense global competition in autos and consumer electronics promoted the location of Japanese plants in Mexico to take advantage both of lower labor costs as well as proximity to the United States. These plants, in both the maquiladoras as well as other locations, supply components to Japanese industries located elsewhere in Mexico and in the United States and Canada, as well as finished goods. The ten largest Japanese manufacturing operations in Mexico are shown in table 11.2. The large numbers of workers involved in each company attest to the labor-intensive nature of these subsidiaries.[24]

Significantly, recent exports to the United States from Japa-

TABLE 11.2.

Top Ten Japanese Manufacturing Companies in Mexico: By Employment Size, 1991

Name	Year of Establishment	Major Products	Markets	Employment
1. Nissan	1966	Cars/Trucks/Parts	Local/Export	7,786
2. Yazaki	1983–1987	Auto Wiring	Export	7,100
3. Matsushita	1974–1978	CTVs	Export/Local	2,375
4. Kyocera	1983–1990	Industrial Ceramic Components	Export	1,450
5. Clarion	1984–1986	Car Radio	Local/Export	1,194
6. Mitsubishi	1973	Industrial Salt	Export	1,100
7. Toshiba	1986	CTV Chassis	Export	749
8. Nihonbanshoji	1976	Glass (Auto)	Local	600
9. Mitsubishi Electronic	1976	Auto Electronic Parts	Local/Export	690
10. SMK	1990	Electroic Parts	Export	509

NOTE: The Mexican subsidiaries of Japanse corporations have been combined in certain cases.

SOURCE: Derived from Nihon Keizai Shimpo, 1992.

nese-owned plants in Mexico are no longer limited to labor-intensive, subassembled products. There is a gradual shift to production of goods that require more sophisticated technology, evident in Japanese-controlled production of color televisions and certain automobile components.[25] The impact of a NAFTA on the maquiladoras and Japanese investment in these in-bond factories have been contentious issues in the negotiations.[26] It appears, however, that, subject to minimum production and export levels, maquiladoras have largely retained their duty-free status for imported parts and components.[27]

Levels of overall investment flows between NAFTA and Japan provide only a framework and a point of departure for analyzing the depth and breadth of the relationship between the two economies. The next section shifts focus by examining patterns of Japanese investment in North American automobile production, as this is a sector which features strongly in all three countries concerned.

Japanese Investment in North American Auto Production

As pointed out by Eden and Molot the auto industry is clearly the most integrated North American industry, and so it may serve to indicate how other industries respond to NAFTA in the 1990s.[28] Certainly, Japanese investment in the industry has been of increasing importance for all three countries. Thus for Mexico, transport equipment accounts for about 70 percent of all Japanese investment in the manufacturing sector; for Canada, it is now the second most significant Japanese investment sector in manufacturing behind timber products, pulp, and paper; and in the United States it lies third behind electrical machinery and chemicals.[29]

The Canadian government, in order to stimulate Japanese investment, gave preferential treatment to those Japanese automakers with plants in Canada when determining the allocation of voluntary export restrictions (VERs) in the early 1980s. Consequently, special import duty reductions for imported parts and components were negotiated for guaranteed levels of output and exports, and this allowed Canada to attract the production bases of three Japanese automakers aimed at the U.S. market (Honda, Toyota, and Suzuki/GM). By the end of the 1980s these companies had set up assembly plants in southern Ontario. In total, they accounted for about 25 percent of Japanese auto assembly investment and about 20 percent of Japanese auto production in the new North American transplants, even though Canada consisted of only 10 percent of the joint U.S./Canadian market. The U.S.-Canadian Free Trade Agreement (FTA) (which commenced operation in 1989) disrupted this arrangement as it phased out the special duty reductions for Japanese transplants in Canada by the middle of the 1990s.[30] Toyota and Honda have especially felt discriminated against by this action, since they entered Canada as assemblers with the initial knowledge and expectation that they could bring in parts duty free. At the coercion of the United States this privilege was taken away unilaterally by FTA through a 50 percent local content rule, which under NAFTA is to be raised eventually to 62.5 percent.[31]

In the United States eight major Japanese car makers opened transplant manufacturing facilities, together with nearly three hundred Japanese parts suppliers. All told, they have created an entire second system of automobile production in the lower Midwest. By the early 1990s these plants were set to produce roughly 20 percent of all cars manufactured in the United States.[32]

In Mexico, Nissan is at present the lone Japanese automaker which supplies Sentras and minivans to the Mexican market from its plant near Cuernavaca, about forty miles south of Mexico City (originally set up in 1966). The 1980s recession in Mexico, and later deregulation of import tariffs and other controls, prompted Nissan to rethink its strategy and redirect production in both new and established plants to export markets, primarily but not limited to the United States. In 1992 it spent $1 billion on expansions and a new assembly plant in Aguascalientes to make Sentras for export, leading to an expectation that Japanese suppliers would also subsequently set up nearby to assist in production. Reflecting the lower costs of assembly labor (approximately 10 percent of similar wages in Canada and the United States), Nissan's new plant at Aguascalientes will have only half the automation of its transplant in Smyrna, Tennessee.[33] Notably, while moving from its domestic orientation to a more international one, Nissan did not abandon the domestic market. Despite its diversification into exports, Nissan continued to strengthen its position within the domestic market and has been the top seller of automobiles in Mexico since the late 1980s.[34]

Moreover, unlike America's Big Three automakers (and some Japanese suppliers to transplants in the United States and Canada), Nissan has no maquiladoras plants. It has been able to export from its Cuernavaca plant and from its new plant in the state of Aguascalientes due to high productivity and quality levels. While the Nissan plant in Cuernavaca primarily produces more economical vehicles for Canada and Latin America, the newer Aguascalientes plant manufactures higher-priced and more sophisticated versions for the United States and Japanese markets.[35] In summary, Mexico is set to be further integrated into the North American auto production system.

Future Prospects

Japanese overseas investment paused in 1991 and 1992 as recession hit their markets in North America, and as the speculative boom in Japanese stocks and property turned into a spectacular bust.[36] But while the expansionist strength of Japanese investments may have peaked, they will not go away. Japanese firms have built such a momentum that they will now consolidate their position, and in many cases will resume their growth in the 1990s using local resources rather than Japanese ones.[37]

Most of Japan's major twenty international manufacturing firms are now set up in NAFTA (see table 11.3). Accordingly, a recent Ex-Im Bank Survey of Japanese manufacturing companies reported that in the near future, the main stream of investment in NAFTA would shift from major new projects to the completion of ongoing plans and the expansion or renewal of

TABLE 11.3

Manufacturing Investments in NAFTA by Twenty Major Japanese Multinational Corporations

	Canada	United States	Mexico
A. Auto sector			
Honda	X	X	
Mazda		X	
Mitsubishi Motors		X	
Nippondenso		X	
Nissan		X	X
Suzuki	X		
Toyota	X	X	
B. Electronics			
Canon		X	
Fujitsu		X	
Hitachi	X	X	X
Matsushita	X	X	X
Mitsubishi Electric	X	X	X
Nec		X	X
Sanyo	X	X	X
Sharp		X	X
Toshiba		X	X
C. Other			
Asahi Optic		—	
Brother		X	
Canon		X	
YKK	X	X	

SOURCE: Company reports and interviews, 1990, 1991.

existing production facilities and research and development investment.[38] What matters therefore from a Canadian, U.S., or Mexican perspective is which part of NAFTA factory obtains investment capital when it comes time to expand.

In this regard, Toyota is reported to be wanting to catch up with Nissan overseas and expand its production in North America by one hundred to two hundred thousand vehicles a year despite the over capacity problems that exist in this market.[39] An additional factor behind Toyota's review of its production network in NAFTA is that its agreement with General Motors at the joint venture NUMMI assembly plant in California expires in 1996 due to limits set by the U.S. Federal Trade Commission. The company is reported to be attracted by the lower wage costs which can be enjoyed through an assembly operation in Mexico. At the same time however, it has to take into account a lack of sophisticated supply infrastructure which would mean shipping in parts from Toyota suppliers located in the U.S. Midwest, thereby increasing transportation costs. In addition, NAFTA's local content rules are pertinent. To discourage Japanese investment using either Mexico or Canada as an export base to the United States, Detroit's lobbyists pushed hard for high North American-content requirements. This could mean that Toyota would have to commence engine production in North America to move autos across the Mexican and Canadian borders into the United States. In this case, Toyota's Cambridge, Ontario, plant is disadvantaged as a suitable location for such an extension because of its capacity—only eighty thousand units per year compared with a planned four hundred thousand units per year of Camrys at Georgetown, Kentucky.

Honda is also considering expansion within NAFTA. For Honda, the huge U.S. market—in which Honda's share of car sales has more than doubled to almost 10 percent over the past decade—remains a significant inducement for its additional investment in NAFTA. By contrast, Canada has been put at a perceived disadvantage because of the U.S. Customs Service action against Honda, mentioned earlier. Once NAFTA is ratified, Honda should escape the $20 million customs penalty imposed in 1992. This is because while Honda is not excluded by any specific mention in NAFTA, the company's appraisal of NAFTA's more explicit rules of origin is that Canadian-made Civics have almost 60 percent North American content.[40] However, there remains the apprehension of possible further discrimination by the United States. While NAFTA regulations at least formally give Honda secure access to the U.S. market from their

Canadian investments, this access is still not quite as guaranteed as the access they might expect to achieve by building or expanding plants directly in the United States instead.

Besides these case studies of planned plant expansions there is also the possibility of further research and development and other higher-order management facilities in NAFTA. For instance, many Japanese firms wish to strengthen their research and development and design bases, both to develop products for the local consumer and industrial markets and to inspect the quality of parts that use locally available materials.[41] Table 11.4 identifies the existing locations of higher-order management functions in North America at the beginning of the 1990s for twenty major Japanese companies such as Toyota, Honda, Nippon Denso, Sony, Sharp, and others. This analysis indicates that none had located in either Mexico or Canada—all were based in the United States. It is likely that such a pattern will continue in the future.

TABLE 11.4

Location of Japanese Offshore Research and Development Centers, Regional Management Centers, and International Purchasing Offices (IPOs) in NAFTA for Twenty Major Industrial Companies

Research and Development Centers		Regional Management Centers		IPOs	
United States	23	United States	6	United States	2
Los Angeles	6	New York	3	New York	1
Ann Arbour/Detroit	6	Los Angeles/		Boston	1
Princeton, N.J.	3	Torrence	1		
San Diego	2	San Francisco	1		
Chicago	1	Detroit	1		
San Jose	2				
Colorado	2				
Santa Clara	1				

SOURCE: Company interviews, 1990, 1991.

Conclusion

This chapter has used current trends to point to a number of characteristics of Japanese investment (and the likely characteristics of other Asian investment) in North America in the post-NAFTA environment. First, despite initial suspicion concerning NAFTA, it is likely that Japanese production will continue to move off-shore, and that Japanese companies will be increasingly drawn into insider positions in each of the Triad regions. Incremental expansion within the NAFTA region will take place through the 1990s because of its overall market size and growth of incomes. This will be the case even though higher shares of Japanese investment in the short term may favor faster growing Asia-Pacific markets. Moreover, further Japanese investment in NAFTA is likely to contain more sophisticated research, design, and management functions, reflecting the movement of Japanese firms into a new stage of globalization and localization.

The auto industry was used to point to trends which apply to other sectors. Here, existing auto trade and investment linkages within North America have been characterized as a "hub and spoke" relationship, with the U.S. markets as the central hub, linked bilaterally to the northern and southern spokes. It remains to be seen how NAFTA will alter this relationship. However, based on current trends it is likely that the United States will continue to attract the lion's share of manufacturing investments due to its larger market size. In addition, investments in Mexico will increase substantially in light of its growing importance as a market for motor vehicles.

Normally, assuming that Mexico could only provide cheap labor, Mexico and Canada would be expected to be complementary to each other and attract incremental Japanese investment more or less equally. This is because Canada would be expected to have higher wages but more efficient production. However, in a situation where Mexican labor, with suitable training, is known to be capable of carrying out sophisticated assembly work, the Canadian advantage could disappear over time, unless its productivity continues to increase.[42] In the important auto sector, as argued elsewhere, unless Canada lowers its Most Favored

Nation tariff on imported Japanese parts from 9.2 percent to the U.S. rate of 2.9 percent or less, the Japanese manufacturers will find it less costly to assemble motor vehicles in the United States to serve both the U.S. and Canadian markets.[43] With new competition arising from Mexican access to the United States, as provided under NAFTA, the continuing high share that Canada enjoys of total Japanese North American auto production would be questioned. If Mexican plants can be upgraded on a level comparable to assembly plants in Canada, then the latter will face severe competition.[44]

Conversely, with no particular incentive to assemble in Canada (through duty drawbacks and duty remissions) the Japanese auto producers could theoretically shift more of their assembly to the United States or Mexico, purchase no parts in Canada, and as long as the vehicles met the requisite North American content, still sell them in Canada duty free. However, changes in tariffs triggered by the free trade agreement, per se, are not likely to cause repatriation of Japanese plants across the U.S. border. This is true even with regard to Mexico, especially as most Japanese producers have already established production facilities in the maquiladoras prior to NAFTA arrangements (see table 11.2). Long-term adjustments after NAFTA may occur, but these are expected to depend on other factors, such as changes in currency exchange rates and the relative growth rates of specific markets.[45] The broader question for Canada remains how to attract Japanese investment through its own advantages, based on raw materials, cheaper energy, services, and technology-intensive sectors.

Notes

1. For some commentators, Japan was the fourth party at the table in NAFTA negotiations, see Eric Hartman, *The North American Free Trade Agreement's Auto Text in Strategic Context* (Washington, DC.: Northeast-Midwest Institute, Centre for Regional Policy, 1992).

2. Neil Reid, "Japanese Direct Investment in the United States Manufacturing Sector," in J. Morris, ed., *Japan and the Global Economy: Issues and Trends in the 1990s* (London: Routledge, 1991), 61–90; Gabriel Szekely, ed.,

Manufacturing Across Borders and Oceans: Japan, the United States and Mexico, Monograph Series, 36 (La Jolla, Calif.: Center for U.S.-Mexican Studies, University of California, San Diego, 1991); David W. Edgington, *Japanese Direct Investment in Canada: Recent Trends and Prospects,* B.C. Geographical Series, No 49 (Vancouver, Department of Geography, University of British Columbia, 1992).

3. Szekely.

4. Edgington, *Japanese Direct Investment in Canada.*

5. Reid.

6. David W. Edgington, "The Globalization of Japanese Manufacturing Corporations," *Growth and Change* 24 (1993): 87–106.

7. *Focus Japan,* Japan Scene: JETRO Report on Overseas Direct Investment, supplement, 18:1 (January 1991).

8. Chris Wood, *The Bubble Economy: The Japanese Economy Collapse* (London: Sidgwick and Jackson, 1992).

9. Bill Emmot, *Japan's Global Reach: The Influences, Strategies and Weaknesses of Japanese Multinational Companies* (London: Century, 1992).

10. Erica Schoenberger, "U.S. Manufacturing Investments in Western Europe: Markets, Corporate Strategy, and the Competitive Environment," *Annals of the Association of American Geographers* 80 (1990): 379–93.

11. Kim B. Clark and T. Fujimoto, *Product Development Performance: Strategy, Organization and Management in the World Auto Industry* (Boston: Harvard Business School Press, 1991); W. Mark Fruin, *The Japanese Enterprise System: Competitive Strategies and Cooperative Structures* (Oxford: Clarendon Press, 1992); W. Mark Fruin and T. Nishiguchi, "Supplying the Toyota Production System: Interorganizational Corporate Evolution and Supplier Subsystems," in B. Kogut, ed., *Work and Country Competitiveness* (New York: Oxford University Press, 1993), 225–46.

12. James P. Womack et al., *The Machine That Changed the World* (New York: Rawson Associates, 1990).

13. John V. Langdale, "The Geography of International Business Telecommunications: the Role of Leased Networks," *Annals of the Association of American Geographers* 79 (1989): 501–22.

14. Kenichi Ohmae, *The Borderless World* (New York: Harper Business, 1990).

15. Honda seems to have been the first to see the advantages of setting up a full manufacturing facility in each Triad economy to serve regional markets (Womack et al., *The Machine That Changed the World* [New York: Rawson Associates, 1990:205).

16. Malcolm Trevor, *Japan's Reluctant Multinationals: Japanese Management at Home and Abroad* (London: Frances Pinter, 1983).

17. David W. Edgington, "The Globalisation of Japanese Manufacturing."

18. Ibid.

19. Difficulty arises in deriving reliable levels of actual Japanese investment

in the NAFTA in any time period from the available statistics. For instance, Ministry of Finance data are based upon notifications by prospective Japanese investors to the Bank of Japan under the Japanese overseas investment legislation. While this probably represents a close fit with actual flows of investment out of Japan (with some delay of course) it does not match investment data for a similar period from either the U.S. Department of Commerce or Investment Canada. Notably, the Japanese data do not take into account investments from Japanese subsidiaries in the NAFTA which use either reinvested earnings or funds raised locally. Another but related complication concerns assessing the activities of Japanese multinationals in North America from broad-scale investment statistics. In particular, Japanese manufacturing subsidiaries have a high propensity to rely on importing finished products into the market rather than manufacturing. See K. Noguchi and Andrew Anderson, *An Analysis of the Activities of Japanese Multinational Enterprises in the United States: 1977–1989*, mimeo, Faculty of Management, University of Toronto (1991) and Alan M. Rugman, *Japanese Direct Investment in Canada* (Ottawa: Canada-Japan Trade Council, 1990).

20. Unpublished data, Japanese Ministry of Finance.

21. See note 23.

22. See Reid; Richard Florida and Martin Kenney, "Japanese Foreign Direct Investment in the United States," in Jonathan Morris, ed., *Japan and the Global Economy: Issues and Trends in the 1990s* (London: Routledge, 1991), 91–114.

23. It is true, however, that at a finer scale of analysis (revealed mainly through company interviews) recent patterns of Japanese direct investment in Canada suggest a moderate degree of diversification during the 1980s. For instance, there are now more varied fields of investment than ever before, ranging from high voltage electronics, satellite communications, information software, laser equipment, and other technology activities, together with banking, finance, and other services. The diversity of this new wave of investment has improved both the technological and employment impact of Japanese business in Canada compared with a decade ago, when Japanese investment was directed overwhelmingly into the resources sector. See David W. Edgington, "Japanese Perceptions of the Canada-U.S. Free Trade Agreement," *Canadian Journal of Regional Science* 13 (1990): 349–66.

24. Japanese companies found that Mexico's maquiladora program offered attractive fiscal incentives and a convenient base to support the operations of their large manufacturing firms in the United States. While U.S. tariffs are payable on imported parts and the value-added in Mexico, maquiladora production can circumvent U.S. voluntary export restraints on exports from Japan. In the 1980s sixty Japanese plants and their suppliers located in maquiladoras. While this participation in the maquiladora program is rather modest (only seventy out of a total 1,924 maquiladora were Japanese owned by mid-1990), their facilities were highly visible because of a heavy concentra-

tion of investment in the electronics (56 percent) and automobile (24 percent) industries. Within each of these sectors, Japanese investment was further concentrated in specific subsectors, namely color television production in the electronics sector and wireharness production for passenger cars in the auto parts sector. See Akihiro Koido, "The Color Television Industry: Japanese-U.S. Competition and Mexico's Maquiladoras," in Gabriel Szekely, ed., *Manufacturing Across Borders and Oceans: Japan, the United States and Mexico,* Monograph Series, 36 (San Diego, Center for U.S.-Mexican Studies, University of California, San Diego, 1991), 51–75.

25. Ibid.

26. In 1992 the Matsunaga/Moctezuma report on Mexican-Japanese relations noted that Japanese companies in Mexico had expressed their concerns regarding the rules of origin and the maquiladora regime under the NAFTA. Anxieties had been manifested over the possibility of losing the status they had earned after many years of hard work in Mexico. See Nobuo Matsunaga and Julio Rodolfo Moctezuma et al., *Final Report, Japan-Mexico Commission for the 21st Century,* mimeo, Tokyo (1992) 19.

27. Personal communications with C. Thomas, Council for the Secretariat of Commerce and Industry of Mexico, March, 1993.

28. Lorraine Eden and Maureen A. Molot, *Continentalizing the North American Auto Industry* (Ottawa, Centre for Trade Policy and Law, Carleton University, Occasional Paper No. 26, 1992).

29. Reid conducted a more sophisticated sectoral distribution of Japanese manufacturing investment using Japan Economic Institute data. He found that at the end of 1987 motor vehicle assembly and parts plants were the leading sector, accounting for over 20,000 jobs or 11.1 percent of total jobs in U.S.-Japanese manufacturing subsidiaries.

30. Edgington, *Japanese Direct Investment in Canada.*

31. Under the new NAFTA pact, 50 percent North American content in auto production will be sufficient for the first four years, after which it rises to 56 percent. After eight years, regional content must be at least 62.5 percent to qualify for tax-free shipment across the Canadian-U.S. border. Prior to the NAFTA, all three Japanese transplants in Canada felt confident that they could meet the 50 percent North American local content ruling of the U.S.-Canada FTA; Honda in particular, based on the knowledge that it was importing all power train units for its Canadian plant from its engine factory in Ohio. However, according to the U.S. Customs Service, all Canadian-built Honda Civics shipped to the United States in the first fifteen months after the FTA took effect in 1989 failed the North American content test. The major problem appeared to be that Honda's U.S.-made engines were found by the Customs Service to be less than half North American. Under special FTA rules, this meant that it was counted wholly as a foreign part and Honda received no credit for its North American content, even though both the engine block and

head assembly were produced in Ohio by Americans (*Business Week,* 18 November 1991). Negotiations under the NAFTA expressly readjusted the technical interpretation of local content regulations to avoid these problems in the future (*Globe and Mail* Toronto, 14 March 1992).

32. Florida and Kenney.

33. *Business Week,* "Detroit South. Mexico's Auto Boom: Who Wins, Who Loses," (16 March 1992): 98–103.

34. One estimate has the Mexican auto market increasing by 436 percent from 1985 to the end of the century, compared with stability or even decline in the United States and Canada (Ibid.).

35. Ibid.

36. Wood.

37. Emmot.

38. Shigeki Tejima, "Japanese Foreign Direct Investment in the 1980s and Its Prospect for the 1990s," *Exim Review* 11, no. 2 (1992): 25–51.

39. Globe and Mail [Toronto], 14 November 1992

40. Ibid., 2 November 1992

41. David W. Edgington, "The Globalization of Japanese Manufacturing."

42. Szekely.

43. Edgington, *Japanese Direct Investment in Canada.*

44. Womack argues that because of their location proximate to the U.S. border, Mexican factories are likely to attract Japanese FDI away from East Asia. Moreover, if Mexican plants can be technologically upgraded—and there is some evidence that at least the Ford plant at Hermosillo functions on a level comparable to assembly plants in Canada and the United States (Womack, 265)—and integrated into U.S. just-in-time delivery systems, U.S. and Canadian plants are likely to face sharp competition. Shaiken and Herzenberg have already shown that productivity in automobile engine production is as high in Mexico as in the United States and Canada, in spite of lower wages and lower levels of formal education (Harley Shaiken and Stephen Herzenberg, *Automation and Global Production: Automobile Engine Production in Mexico, the United States and Canada,* Monograph Series No. 26 (La Jolla, Calif.: Center for U.S.-Mexican Studies, University of California, San Diego, 1987). Mexico is also considered by Womack to be the preferred production location for low-cost entry level cars and trucks for the continental market (currently being imported into the United States and Canada from Korea and Japan), while the U.S. Midwest and Ontario is likely to supply larger trucks and cars for all of North America.

45. Japanese companies in Canada appear to have a cautious reaction to the NAFTA. Regarding whether the NAFTA would or would not have an impact on business plans, responses to a 1992 survey were divided almost evenly into yes (43.7 percent) and no (56.3 percent). Asked if they would newly construct plants in Mexico or relocate existing plants to Mexico to seek cheaper labor if the NAFTA were executed, of forty-two respondents in the manufacturing

sector, none said yes, thirty-five replied no, six answered maybe, and one firm responded that it was still looking at the situation. See JETRO. *The Fourth Jetro Survey of Japanese-Affiliated Firms in Canada,* mimeo, Toronto (1992).

Additional References

Eden, Lorraine and Maureen A. Molot. *From Silent Integration to Strategic Alliance: the Political Economy of North American Free Trade* (Ottawa, Centre for Trade Policy and Law, Carleton University, Occasional Paper No. 17, 1991).

Shimpo, Nihon Keizai. *Japanese Overseas Investment* (Japan: Nihon Keizai Shimpo, in Japanese, 1992).

Chapter 12

EXTENSION OF NAFTA TO LATIN AMERICA

Michael Gestrin and Leonard Waverman

Introduction

To the extent that the 1980s came to be viewed as a lost decade for Latin America, the 1990s are likely to be remembered as the decade of Western Hemispheric economic integration.[1] Since the mid-1980s most Latin American governments have been implementing market reforms aimed at achieving much higher levels of international economic integration. Concurrently, the region's historical diversity in terms of its international trade and investment relationships has been threatened by several developments, including the difficult negotiations among the leaders of the Triad powers (Japan, the United States, and the E.C.) during the Uruguay Round and the potential for trade and investment diversion created by the opening up of Eastern Europe.

To date the process of economic regionalism has been characterized by the negotiation, and in some cases, the revival, of numerous trade and investment agreements among various countries. The United States has negotiated at least fifteen trade and investment framework agreements with thirty-one Latin American and Caribbean countries since mid-1990.[2] While the North American Free Trade Agreement (NAFTA) is by far the largest and most comprehensive regional trade agreement, it is not the only meaningful one. Other active trade groups in the region include the Andean Group (Ecuador, Bolivia, Colombia, Venezuela and Peru), the Central American Common Market

(CACM), the Caribbean Common Market (CARICOM), the Group of Three (Mexico, Colombia, and Venezuela), and Mercosur (Brazil, Argentina, Paraguay, and Uruguay; Bolivia is an associate member).

A number of questions arise, however, with respect to the future of economic integration in the Western Hemisphere. For example, what administrative form will closer hemispheric relations take? What are the main factors which will shape the divergent policy options open to the region's leaders in this regard? At what rate will hemispheric integration progress? And to what extent is the region subject to the bicycle principle of trade liberalization—that if it stops moving, it falls over? These are the main questions which this chapter will address.

Two main themes are emphasized in this study. First, that the political costs associated with the ratification of NAFTA in the United States will mitigate against the Agreement's chances for playing a significant role as an administrative vehicle to further regional economic integration during the 1990s. Second, economic integration in the Western Hemisphere will proceed rapidly during the 1990s as regional trade groupings are widened and deepened and as foreign investment and trading relationships expand in response to the region's numerous unilateral reform programs.

This chapter is structured as follows: section two looks at the Western Hemisphere in terms of its place in the global trade and investment regime; section three identifies the main reasons for Mexico's interest in negotiating a NAFTA and compares Mexico's situation in this regard with other Latin American economies; section four outlines the forces which mitigate strongly against an extension of NAFTA in Latin America during the 1990s; section five explains why Western Hemispheric economic integration will likely proceed with or without an expanded NAFTA; and the last section summarizes the key findings.

Foreign Direct Investment and the Western Hemisphere

One of the most distressing trends of the 1990s for policymakers in developing countries was the relative concentration of foreign direct investment (FDI) stocks and flows among the developed countries of the Triad. Table 12.1 summarizes these developments. Between 1985 and 1990 FDI stocks in the less developed countries (LDCs) increased in book value from $182.6 to $310.0 billion, or by 70 percent. Global FDI stocks, however, increased in value from $727.1 to $1,638.9 billion during the same period—an increase of 125 percent. Global exports only increased by 84 percent during the same period. Therefore, between 1985 and 1990 the developing countries witnessed their share of global FDI stocks decrease from 25.1 percent to 18.9 percent.

Among the developing regions two distinct patterns emerge. Developing countries in the Western Hemisphere accounted for 12 percent of total inward FDI stocks in 1985, but their share was almost halved by 1990, falling to 7.3 percent. This downward spiral owed much to the effects of the debt crisis and the underlying factors which led to it, and is therefore likely to experience a strong reversal during the 1990s if economic reform in the region continues.

The Asian countries, on the other hand, almost maintained their share of global FDI stocks. Their share experienced a small drop from 10.1 to 9.5 percent of the total over the same five year period. Several Latin American governments have identified successful competition with the East Asian Newly Industrialized Economies (NIEs) for international capital as a prerequisite for economic success in the 1990s. As Alieto Gaudagni, Argentina's secretary for international economic relations, put it, in reference to North American FDI, "at the minimum, we would like priority to be given to us in Latin America, not to Pacific nations."[3]

Two main challenges confront Latin American policymakers in their attempts to restore their share of global FDI stocks to predebt crisis levels. The first is the possibility that the opening of Eastern Europe will divert European Community (E.C.) investment. The second challenge is to attract U.S. and Asian FDI.

FDI from the E.C. has been significant in several Latin American economies, most notably Brazil. While it is too early yet to

TABLE 12.1

Global Inward FDI Stocks by Region: 1990 & 1985 (U.S. billion dollars)

	1990 Inward $	%	1990 Outward $	%	1985 Inward $	%	1985 Outward $	%
Developing Countries	310.0	18.9	51.2	3.1	182.6	25.1	21.9	3.2
Western Hemisphere	119.6	7.3			87.0	12.0		
Asia	155.1	9.5			73.3	10.1		
Middle East	12.0	0.7			6.5	0.9		
Rest of Asia	143.0	8.7			66.8	9.2		
Africa	35.3	2.2			22.3	3.1		
Developed Countries	1328.9	81.1	1593.0	96.9	544.5	74.9	656.9	96.8
North America	504.7	30.8	501.2	30.5	247.0	34.0	289.7	42.7
E.C.	646.6	39.5	714.8	43.5	224.6	30.9	268.1	39.5
Japan	9.9	0.6	201.4	12.2	4.7	0.6	44.0	6.5
World Total	1638.9	100.0	1644.2	100.0	727.1	100.0	678.2	100.0

SOURCE: J. Rutter, "Recent Trends in International Direct Investment," U.S. Department of Commerce (Washington, D.C., 1992), appendices 3, 8.

know whether or not significant diversion will result from developments in Europe, the planned adoption on 1 July 1993, of trade measures favoring European banana growers over Latin American producers does suggest that non-Lome Convention Latin America looms small in the E.C.'s collective international economic outlook. The plan's tariffs and quotas will cut European banana imports from Latin America by more than half. It is estimated that these restrictions will cost Latin America $1 billion in export revenues and 170,000 jobs by 1995. Another E.C. measure recently approved will see apple imports from Chile reduced by 19 percent.[4] Continued problems in agriculture are particularly troublesome to Latin American policymakers since this sector is expected to play a significant role in the region's economic restructuring during the 1990s.[5] More generally, this case is illustrative of the sort of factors which have given rise to the feeling that secure access to the North American market is increasingly vital to the region's future economic prosperity.

The second challenge to Latin America will be to increase its share of Triad-based FDI if the trend towards greater concentration of FDI within the Triad at the expense of LDCs witnessed during the 1980s continues. Competition with the Asian Newly Industrialized Countries (NICs) for FDI will likely be a more prominent theme in Latin American policy formulation during the 1990s, and in this regard, the primary goal will be the attraction of American investment away from potential East Asian candidates.

Mexico's Pursuit of NAFTA

Three factors motivated Mexico to shift the primary focus of its international economic policy from multilateralism to regionalism in 1989. These were: (1) the ratification of the U.S.-Canadian Free Trade Agreement (FTA), which Mexico perceived as a threat to some of its key exports to the U.S. market; (2) Europe 1992 and the opening up of Eastern Europe, which Mexico felt might jeopardize its export markets and divert investment; and (3) the realization that Mexico was not a serious target for Japanese FDI aimed at serving the American market.[6]

Indeed, to a greater degree than any other economy in Latin America, the Mexican economy is tied to the U.S. market, a dependence which had been increasing even before President Carlos Salinas approached the Bush administration around mid-1989. Table 12.2 summarizes the evolution of Mexico's trade with the Triad during the 1980s.

What table 12.2 indicates is the increasing share in total Mexican trade accounted for by the American market. This trend is not surprising given the relatively open trading relationship which has evolved between the two countries during the 1980s. By 1992 76.5 percent of Mexico's exports were going to the U.S. market, up from 65.8 percent in 1985. Mexican imports experienced a similar concentration, rising from 66.6 to 71.3 percent over the same period.

United States exports enter the Mexican market with a 13 percent average tariff while Mexican exports to the United States only face a 5 percent average tariff.[7] What this indicates is the extent to which the desirability of a NAFTA from the Mexican perspective lies not so much in the Agreement's impact upon Mexico's access to the U.S. market but in the anticipated "seal-of-approval" effect which such an agreement would have in the international investment community. As mentioned above, the fears which motivated Mexico to pursue NAFTA were largely related to concerns about the economy's ability to attract foreign investment in the face of rising global and regional competition for international capital.

Mexico hopes to gain in three main ways from joining NAFTA: first, joining the Agreement will serve to send a clear message to the international business community that Mexico's market reforms are irreversible; second, that investors in Mexico and thus exports will enjoy more secure access to the American market than exports from other parts of the world; and third, in an historically ironic twist, it is hoped that by integrating more closely the Mexican and American economies, the Agreement will lessen the Mexican economy's dependence upon American capital by attracting capital from other Triad members interested

TABLE 12.2

Mexico's Trade with the Triad, 1985–July 1992 (U.S. million dollars)

	1985		1986		1987		1988		1989		1990		1991		1992*	
	$	%	$	%	$	%	$	%	$	%	$	%	$	%	$	%
Exports to																
United States	13,341	65.8	10,424	70.1	13,265	64.6	13,454	65.9	16,163	70.1	18,837	70.3	28,969	74.5	18,515	76.5
E.C.	4,030	19.9	2,260	15.2	2,997	14.6	2,682	13.1	2,649	11.5	3,366	12.6	3,332	8.6	2,042	8.4
Japan	1,709	8.4	1,115	7.5	1,347	6.6	1,228	6.0	1,311	5.7	1,502	5.6	1,583	4.1	682	2.8
Western Hemisphere	1,199	5.9	1,073	7.2	1,599	7.8	1,531	7.5	1,645	7.1	1,785	6.7	1,601	4.1	922	3.8
World	22,105		16,120		20,409		23,046		26,812		38,868		24,193			
Imports from																
United States	8,954	66.6	7,574	65.8	8,252	64.7	13,043	66.7	15,554	68.2	18,160	64.7	33,276	70.8	23,671	71.3
E.C.	1,744	13.0	1,695	14.7	2,050	16.1	2,880	14.7	2,737	12.0	4,286	15.3	5,935	12.6	3,955	11.9
Japan	723	5.4	698	6.1	837	6.6	1,171	6.0	818	3.6	1,065	3.8	2,822	6.0	2,265	6.8
Western Hemisphere	630	4.7	400	3.5	387	3.0	756	3.9	968	4.2	1,451	5.2	1,428	3.0	824	2.5
World	13,441		11,507		12,758		19,558		22,792		28,066		47,033		33,212	

*January–July 1992, inclusive

SOURCE: International Monetary Fund, *Direction of Trade Statistics*, December 1992 and Yearbook 1992.

in serving the American market from a relatively low cost production platform.

Table 12.3, which shows Mexican imports of machinery for 1983, 1986, and 1991, suggests that Mexico's dependence upon the United States has remained more or less constant into the 1990s, relative to the other Triad members, at around 72 to 76 percent. The Japanese share has steadily increased from 8.9 to 11.4 percent while the E.C. share has decreased from 19 to 15 percent between 1983 and 1991.

Latin America and NAFTA

The urgency of NAFTA for Mexico stemmed in large measure from the latter's heavy reliance upon the U.S. market in terms of both trade and foreign investment. For other Latin American economies the U.S. market is less important. Table 12.4 shows the relative shares of the Triad members in the exports of four Latin American economies from 1985 through 1991—Argentina, Chile, Brazil, and Venezuela.

TABLE 12.3

Mexican Imports of Capital Goods* from the Triad (U.S. thousand dollars)

	1983		1986		1991	
	$	%	$	%	$	%
United States	2,710,739	72.1	4,837,891	76.1	10,798,377	73.6
E.C.**	713,530	19.0	874,595	13.8	2,192,623	15.0
Japan	333,690	8.9	642,903	10.1	1,672,709	11.4
Total	3,757,959		6,355,389		14,663,709	

*SITC, Revision 3, 71–77

**France, Germany, Italy, Sweden, United Kingdom

SOURCE: Organization for Economic Cooperation and Development, *Foreign Trade by Commodities*, Series C (1991).

TABLE 12.4
Exports From Four Latin American Countries by Region

Exports	To	1985	1986	1987	1988	1989	1990	1991
Argentina	United States	29.8	22.7	31.3	28.5	29.8	29.0	21.1
	E.C.	59.7	64.8	61.1	63.7	63.4	64.3	69.8
	Japan	10.5	12.6	7.5	7.8	6.8	6.7	9.1
Chile	United States	34.2	33.0	33.8	28.6	26.3	24.5	26.1
	E.C.	50.8	51.9	49.5	53.3	53.5	52.7	47.1
	Japan	15.0	15.1	16.7	18.1	20.2	22.8	26.8
Brazil	United States	45.6	46.1	46.0	42.9	39.6	37.3	33.0
	E.C.	45.2	42.9	43.5	46.0	49.0	49.5	52.5
	Japan	9.2	11.0	10.5	11.2	11.4	13.2	14.5
Venezuela	United States	42.8	27.5	32.5	23.6	31.6	46.2	40.0
	E.C.	18.8	9.6	7.2	6.0	7.6	11.4	8.1
	Japan	2.7	2.0	0.3	2.2	2.4	2.5	2.1

SOURCE: International Monetary Fund, *Direction of Trade Statistics Yearbook*, 1992.

Two aspects of table 12.4 stand out. The first is the low share of exports from these economies going to the U.S. market. Indeed, for Argentina, Chile, and Brazil, the E.C. accounted for the largest share of exports. In 1991 the E.C. accounts for approximately 70, 47, and 53 percent of the exports for these three economies, respectively. The United States is only the most important market for Venezuela, accounting for 40 percent of this country's exports. Recall from table 12.2 that in 1991 75 percent of Mexico's exports were destined for the U.S. market.

The other striking feature of table 12.4 is the clear evolution of Triad linkages among three of the four countries. Chile, in particular, has strengthened its position in the Japanese market, probably through its dominant global position as an exporter of fish products. In 1985 15 percent of Chilean exports went to Japan. By 1991 this proportion had increased to 27 percent. Chile currently ranks as the world's second largest supplier of salmon behind Norway and has reduced its dependence upon copper exports from a high of approximately 70 percent of total export value during the 1970s to approximately 30 percent in the early 1990s.[8] Brazil and Argentina have become increasingly oriented towards the E.C. market between 1985 and 1991. In both countries the increased E.C. share has come at the expense of the U.S. market share.

The main point which table 12.4 conveys is the degree to which Latin America is heterogeneous in terms of its international economic interests (at least from an export perspective). Unlike Mexico, there is no unambiguous dependence upon the U.S. market, not is there any clear trend working in this direction. This is not to suggest that access to the U.S. market might not be a desirable goal for many Latin American economies— but it does show that the forces of market dependence felt by Mexico are clearly neither uniform nor acting as strongly in the rest of Latin America as they were in the Mexican case.

Table 12.3 considers Mexico's imports of capital goods from the members of the Triad and finds the United States to be Mexico's main source of imported machinery, with a share just above 70 percent; the E.C.'s share has declined while the Japanese share has increased (from 19 percent to 15 percent and from 8.9 percent to 11.4 percent, respectively). Table 12.5 considers imports of machinery from the members of the Triad by Argentina, Brazil, Chile, Colombia, Venezuela, Ecuador, and Peru. The trends in capital imports for these countries lie in sharp contrast to those found in the Mexican data.

Three features distinguish the seven countries in table 12.5 from Mexico in terms of capital imports from the Triad. First, in all seven countries the share of the United States as a supplier of machinery increases between 1986 and 1991, while for four of the seven, the U.S. share increases by at least 9 percent. Second, the share of the E.C. as a supplier of machinery to the region remains more or less constant in the seven countries. Only in Argentina and Peru are there significant changes in the European share. Third, in all seven countries the Japanese share in machinery imports drops, in some instances drastically. For example, in Argentina, Chile, Venezuela, and Peru, Japan's share of imports is almost halved, while in Ecuador, Japan's share falls to less than a third of its 1986 level by 1991.

These figures hint at two possible developments in the region. The first is that there is a process of regionalization underway, and that this process is reflected in the increased reliance upon the United States for intermediate goods. The second less desirable trend suggested by the data is the diversion of Japanese investment away from Latin America and towards Mexico (recall that table 12.3 showed Japan's share of Mexico's machinery imports steadily increasing).

Mexico has stronger linkages with the U.S. economy than any other Latin American country, and therefore has more to lose from American protectionism. However, Latin American countries are still motivated to secure better access to the U.S. market in order to offset potential protectionism in the E.C. market, as well as to be able to attract foreign investment (or, at a minimum, to avoid investment diversion to Mexico).

Prospects for Widening NAFTA

One of the main impediments to any extension of NAFTA to include other Latin American economies derives from a combi-

TABLE 12.5

Triad Shares of Capital Imports in Latin America (percentage shares)

From/To	Argentina		Brazil		Chile		Colombia		Venezuela		Ecuador		Peru	
	1986	1991	1986	1991	1986	1991	1986	1991	1986	1991	1986	1991	1986	1991
United States	29.2	45.7	39.3	42.6	39.0	49.5	50.2	52.2	58.7	67.7	44.7	63.2	43.0	44.4
Europe*	48.1	41.8	39.4	40.0	35.4	36.8	35.2	33.3	30.5	26.1	29.2	28.1	39.5	45.5
Japan	22.7	12.5	21.3	17.4	25.7	13.6	14.6	14.5	10.7	6.2	26.2	8.7	17.6	10.0

*France, Germany, Italy, Sweden, and the United Kingdom.

SOURCE: OECD, Foreign Trade by Commodities, vols. 1–4, series C (1991).

nation of two factors. The first is the importance of other issues to President Clinton. The domestic economy, the Uruguay Round, U.S.-Japanese economic relations, and the evolving situation in Russia are only some of President Clinton's more pressing concerns. The second consists in the high political cost of NAFTA. The Clinton administration will have to expend enormous amounts of political capital to have NAFTA approved by Congress in the fall of 1993. Now that the current administration has committed itself to looking very closely at the environmental and labor standards of its free-trade partners, as well as the danger of import surges, the political costs of expanding the Agreement into Latin America could be quite high. In addition, these side agreements may make NAFTA unpalatable (and uneconomic) to Latin American countries given their lower dependance on the U.S. market.

The region is unilaterally reforming itself in such a way that American businesses are likely to benefit from increased investment and trade opportunities without the need for the current administration to step in and associate itself with plant relocations, poor environmental conditions, and low labor standards by proposing to add more Latin American countries to NAFTA roster.

The benefits in terms of expanding export markets for U.S. producers also may be limited if current data are relied on. However, given the significant number of NTBs and the recent history of the debt crisis, current trade figures may not be good indicators of the region's potential as an export market. Table 12.6 summarizes the share of the main Latin American trade groupings in U.S. exports between 1986 and 1991. Mexico's share of total U.S. exports has increased steadily over this period from 5.7 to 7.9 percent. In contrast, the combined market of Chile, Mercosur, and the Andean group only accounted for 4.5 percent of U.S. exports in 1991, while the entire Latin American market accounted for 7.2 percent of U.S. exports. Furthermore, while the significance of the Mexican market to U.S. exporters has been steadily increasing, the rest of the Latin American market has experienced a decrease in its share of U.S. exports. Although this situation is likely to reverse itself during the 1990s, it remains that the small size of the Latin American market, combined with the high costs which would be associated with the negotiation of these countries into NAFTA, mitigates against the extension of NAFTA into the region.

The Evolution of Latin America's Regional Trade Agreements

In 1950 Raúl Prebisch, secretary general of the U.N. Economic Commission for Latin America, wrote that the Latin American economies could not depend on exports of primary products, but instead had to turn to import substitution policies to manufacture goods that were being imported from the developed economies. The main policy instrument of the structuralist school, as it came to be known, consisted in prohibitive import barriers against manufactured goods; these barriers, however, were intraregional as well as interregional in their scope. By the late 1950s it became clear that each Latin American country was attempting to develop indigenous industrial capacity which could not be supported efficiently by the size of the available markets. This realization gave rise to a new policy focus based upon the pursuit of intraregional trade liberalization behind import barriers against the United States and Europe. The Treaty of Montevideo of 1960 established the Latin America Free Trade Association (LAFTA) involving all countries in Latin and South America (except Guyana, Surinam, and French Guyana).

The LAFTA represented a structuralist approach utilizing a product-by-product annual negotiations strategy. The Association was flawed in three ways. First, it was too large and ambitious. Second, it had a rigid agenda not well-suited to the negotiation of preferences. Third, it allowed "free riding" since any country could use a Most Favored Nation (MFN) clause to benefit from the tariffs lowered by other countries without lowering its tariffs in return.

In 1960 a second area-wide group was formed. The Central American Common Market (CACM) joined Costa Rica, Guate-

TABLE 12.6

Relative Shares of Triad Export Markets (U.S. million dollars)

U.S. Exports to:	1986 $	1986 %	1987 $	1987 %	1988 $	1988 %	1989 $	1989 %	1990 $	1990 %	1991 $	1991 %
Mexico	12,392	5.7	14,582	5.8	20,473	6.4	24,969	6.9	28,375	7.2	33,276	7.9
Chile	824	0.4	796	0.3	1,063	0.3	1,411	0.4	1,672	0.4	1,840	0.4
Mercosur*	5,099	2.3	5,405	2.1	5,619	1.8	6,136	1.7	6,693	1.7	8,795	2.1
Andean Group**	5,866	2.7	6,573	2.6	7,976	2.5	6,427	1.8	6,741	1.7	8,593	2.0
Latin America (less Mexico)***	18,679	8.6	20,413	8.1	23,105	7.2	24,086	6.6	25,585	6.5	30,195	7.2
NICs****	18,289	8.4	23,548	9.3	34,662	10.9	38,458	10.6	40,819	10.4	45,666	10.8
World	217,292		252,884		319,413		363,807		393,106		421,755	

*Mercosur: Brazil, Argentina, Paraguay, Uruguay

**Andean Group: Ecuador, Bolivia, Venezuela, Colombia, Peru

***Latin America (less Mexico): includes the Caribbean

****NICs: Hong Kong, Singapore, Taiwan, Korea

SOURCE: International Monetary Fund, *Direction of Trade Statistics Yearbook*, 1992.

mala, El Salvador, Honduras, and Nicaragua in an ambitious scheme to create a customs union over a ten year period. Intra-CACM trade did grow rapidly in the 1960s (from 7 percent to 20 percent of all CACM trade) but the ambitious goals were never reached. The 1969 war between El Salvador and Honduras and the continuing political turmoil of the 1970s and 1980s impeded the expansion of intraregional trade.

The Andean Group was formed in 1969 by Chile, Bolivia, Colombia, Ecuador, and Peru as a response to the perceived failures of the LAFTA. This was another enormous and ambitious scheme, patterned after the E.C. Its goals at the outset were for a customs union, common treatment of foreign investment, and macroeconomic policy harmonization. Chile left in 1973 after Pinochet's coup and Venezuela joined in 1976. The Andean Group did encourage intraregional trade, which grew from .1 percent of total trade in 1960 to 5.4 percent in 1980.

By the 1970s LAFTA was viewed within Latin America as a failure. It was therefore replaced in 1980 by the Latin American Integration Association (ALADI). This continent-wide scheme had as its long-term goal the creation of a Latin American common market. No fixed timetable was established. The basic mechanism of liberalization in ALADI was regional tariff preferences (RTPs) where percentage reductions on external tariffs were established for insiders. ALADI, like its predecessors, is discriminatory since it promotes intraregional trade at the expense of more efficient trade with countries outside Latin America. Trade diversion has not been a substantial feature of the E.C. or NAFTA since external tariffs are low. Latin American countries, on the other hand, had high external barriers in 1980. Trade diversion as a result of ALADI was likely.

The debt crisis which began 1982 undermined the potential benefits of ALADI. It was not until 1990/1991 that intraregional trade reached the levels set in 1981. The debt crisis and the concomitant drought of international credit meant that Latin American countries were motivated to run large current account surpluses—not a goal which helped intraregional trade. Latin American countries had an aggregate current account deficit of $7 billion in 1981 and a $40 billion surplus just three years later.[9]

The 1980s have seen a proliferation of regional economic integration schemes and, more significantly, a wave of unilateral liberalizations. The trade and investment regimes of Chile, Mexico, Peru, Argentina, Venezuela, and Colombia have provided regional integration schemes with a sound basis for continued viability. In fact, many Latin American integration schemes are more ambitious than NAFTA. For example, in March 1991 the Ascunción Treaty established Mercosur, culminating an integration process began by Argentina and Brazil in 1985. Between 1986 and 1990 twenty-four protocols were signed by Brazil and Argentina covering sectoral trade liberalization and cooperation in commercial, scientific, and technological areas. A 1988 treaty added coordination of monetary, capital markets, and fiscal and exchange rate issues. In 1990 Argentina and Brazil implemented a four year program for the elimination of all tariff and nontariff barriers to trade.

The recent developments outlined above indicate that Latin America is moving rapidly away from the inward-looking policy tradition of the 1950s towards a more open, heterodox policy stance. This movement seems at once motivated by a growing awareness of the costs of autarky as well as of the potential benefits of regional integration.

Continued Economic Integration in Latin America

Even in the absence of an expanded NAFTA, increased economic integration in the Western Hemisphere is likely. Linkages continue to grow based upon the unrealized potential in the region for more intraregional trade and investment, as well as upon the attractiveness of the region for foreign investors if the reforms are sustained.

Table 12.7 compares intra- and extraregional trade patterns for Latin America, the E.C., and Asia. What the data reveal is the extent to which Latin America has lagged behind other trade groupings in terms of both intra- and extraregional trade activity. During the period 1985 to 1988 in particular, Latin American trade lagged behind trade levels in the E.C., Asia, and the growth rate in world trade. During the 1988 to 1991 period, however, after the initiation of many of the market reforms in the region, trade activity increased dramatically. During this period, world exports grew at an average of 8.8 percent per annum. In Latin America intraregional trade grew at an average rate of 11.5 percent per annum while the region's trade with the rest of the world grew at a rate of 9.8 percent per annum. These figures pale in comparison, however, to the level of trade activity in Asia.

Another indication that regional economic integration is likely to proceed in the absence of formal trade agreements linking Latin America to the North American market is found in the FDI activity of U.S. firms in Latin America. Table 12.8 gives U.S. FDI stocks in Latin America for the years 1986 through 1991 and the shares of individual Latin American countries in total U.S. FDI stocks.

TABLE 12.7

Growth in Intra- and Extraregional Trade (Average Annual Growth Rates)

	1985–1988	1988–1991
Western Hemisphere		
Intraregional Exports	7.1	11.5
Exports to World	3.4	9.8
European Community		
Intraregional Exports	21.6	10.4
Exports to World	18.0	9.0
Asia		
Intraregional Exports	24.7	19.7
Exports to World	20.8	12.5
World Exports	14.1	8.8

SOURCE: International Monetary Fund, *Direction of Trade Statistics Yearbook,* 1992; Authors' calculations.

TABLE 12.8

U.S. FDI Stocks
(U.S. million dollars)

	1986		1987		1988		1989		1990		1991	
	$	%	$	%	$	%	$	%	$	%	$	%
Developing Economies	61,072	23.5	70,676	22.9	80,060	26.2	90,374	24.3	102,360	24.1	111,608	24.8
Mexico	4,623	1.8	4,898	1.6	5,712	1.9	7,341	2.0	9,398	2.2	11,570	2.6
Latin America	36,851	14.2	44,905	14.6	53,506	17.5	62,485	16.8	71,593	16.9	77,342	17.2
South America	19,813	7.6	20,690	6.7	21,815	7.1	23,045	6.2	23,760	5.6	25,998	5.8
Argentina	2,913	1.1	2,673	0.9	2,597	0.8	2,604	0.7	2,956	0.7	3,412	0.8
Brazil	9,268	3.6	10,288	3.3	12,609	4.1	14,733	4.0	14,918	3.5	15,222	3.4
Chile	265	0.1	343	0.1	672	0.2	1,075	0.3	1,368	0.3	1,555	0.3
Colombia	3,291	1.3	3,241	1.1	2,248	0.7	1,659	0.4	1,728	0.4	1,744	0.4
Ecuador	413	0.2	466	0.2	431	0.1	382	0.1	387	0.1	337	0.1
Peru	1,103	0.4	1,084	0.4	976	0.3	766	0.2	410	0.1	352	0.1
Venezuela	1,987	0.8	2,036	0.7	1,903	0.6	1,362	0.4	1,490	0.4	2,785	0.6
Other	572	0.2	560	0.2	379	0.1	463	0.1	503	0.1	590	0.1
World	259,800	100.0	307,983	100.0	305,893	100.0	372,419	100.0	424,086	100.0	450,196	100

SOURCE: United States Department of Commerce, Survey of Current Business, various August issues. 1987–1992.

The two countries in Latin America which have undergone the most drastic market reforms, and in which the reforms have been most successful, are also the only two economies in the region which have increased their share of total U.S. FDI stocks. Mexico has increased its share of U.S. FDI stocks from 1.8 percent in 1986 to 2.6 percent in 1991. Chile has experienced even more impressive gains, tripling its share from 0.1 to 0.3 percent. While in value terms Chile's share seems low, it is testament to the confidence which the reforms have engendered that Chile is the only country in South America which increased its share of U.S. FDI. What should also be noted is that the increases in Mexico's share of U.S. FDI began before NAFTA negotiations got underway, and, although they seem to have accelerated as the prospects for a NAFTA became more certain in 1991, the experiences of Mexico and Chile both suggest that reform alone will attract foreign investment.

Conclusion

The latent potential for closer economic integration of the economies of the Western Hemisphere created by decades of protectionist, autarkic economic policies throughout Latin America is beginning to realize itself into the 1990s. Within this context, NAFTA should be viewed as the framework which has established the critical early norms and standards against which future attempts at integrating North American and Latin American economies will be judged.

The history of NAFTA negotiations has seen these standards raised by U.S. domestic political levers to a height at which even Chilean reformers might balk. Chile, often held up as the perfect candidate for quick accession, is characterized by environmental and labor problems which, given the precedent set in NAFTA side agreements, will carry a political price in Congress. Should Chile suddenly become a serious candidate for accession, the negotiations will undoubtedly bring to the fore issues such as the rapid depletion of Chile's coastal fish stocks, lax enforcement of environmental regulations, and the 42 percent of the population which lives below the poverty line.[10] The point is not whether these are legitimate reasons for not including Chile (or any other Latin American country) in NAFTA—the point is that President Clinton's introduction of the side agreements has afforded protectionist interests powerful weapons with which to fight any widening of the Agreement.

Despite these problems, the prospects for continued integration of the economies of the Western Hemisphere remain strong for the simple reason that NAFTA is not the only game in town. The numerous trade and investment agreements which have either been brought back to life after years of near-redundancy (CACM) or have been newly created (Mercosur, the Group of Three) have given rise to a substantial increase in intra- as well as extraregional trade and investment in the early 1990s.[11] In addition, a wave of unilateral market-oriented reforms has characterized most recent policymaking in Latin America. These reforms have gone a long way to restore confidence and attract investment to the region—and the scope for further unilateral action on the part of the region's governments is substantial.

Therefore, when NAFTA is extended into Latin America, it probably will not be because the present signatories felt driven to radically change the face of hemispheric economic relations. Rather, it will be because high levels of economic integration will have become an unmistakable feature of the Western Hemisphere, much as NAFTA, and FTA before it, reflected what had already taken place.

Notes

1. The authors recognize several historical and cultural inaccuracies inherent in referring to South America, Central America, and the Caribbean nations as Latin America. However, for lack of a suitably short and more accurate label, this is the term we will use in making general reference to the entire region described above.

2. United Nations Centre on Transnational Corporations, "FDI and Industrial Restructuring in Mexico; Government Policy, Corporate Strategies and Regional Integration," Series A, No. 18, *Current Series* (1992) 78.

3. Peter Cook, "Latins Dance to New Free-Trade Tunes," *Globe and Mail,* 8 January 1993, B1.

4. James Brooke, "EC tariffs trigger banana revolt," New York Times Service, *Globe and Mail* (Toronto, 7 April 1993): B1

5. See, for example, Ian Goldin and Dominique van der Mensbrugghe, "The forgotten story: agriculture and Latin American trade and growth," in Colin I. Bradford Jr., ed., *Strategic Options for Latin America in the 1990s,* (Paris: OECD, 1992).

6. United Nations Centre on Transnational Corporations, 19

7. Ibid., 77.

8. Cook.

9. Sebastian Edwards and Miguel Savastano, "Latin America's Intraregional Trade: Evaluation and Future Prospects," in David Greenaway et al., eds., *Economic Aspects of Regional Trading Arrangements* (New York: Harvestor Wheatsheaf, 1989).

10. For more examples, see Catharine Orenstein, "Latin America's Dark Side," *New York Times,* 16 May 1993, 38.

11. James Brooke, "Latin America's Regional Trade Boon," *New York Times,* 15 February 1993, C1.

PART 5

CONCLUSION

Chapter 13

RAPPORTEUR'S COMMENTS: MAKING SENSE OF NAFTA

Robert S. Spich

Introduction

As a formal observer, notetaker, and questioner at this book's founding conference, the task of drawing common conclusions about the complex North American Free Trade Agreement (NAFTA) discussions is daunting. Watching others struggle with this same task at recent panel discussions of the economic transition of Eastern Europe, the wisdom of fools treading where the wise do not, seems well corroborated. One member of this conference offered an elegantly simple solution: "why don't you simply declare NAFTA a 'win-win-win' situation and then let us all go home!" In reality, this conference has implemented this very solution. With few reservations, there was a consensus that investment activity is essentially a winning proposition for all parties.

This commentary does not summarize the collective ideas of the authors. They do that better themselves in their own chapters. Nor does it draw a common conclusion about foreign direct investment (FDI) in NAFTA. Such a conclusion over this varied field of topics would be too general and simplistic. Given the dynamic nature of the Agreement and the many unresolved issues, some of the writing contains observations and commentary that must, by nature, be both smart speculation and intelligent conjecturing.

However, the speculation and conjecture by the authors is

focused. Their thinking about investment in integrating markets reflects a systematic identification, analysis, and prognosis about a number of important aspects of investment activities. These include: the trends in FDI, the nature of the facilitating conditions necessary to make capital flow more easily, the identification of barriers that need to be lowered and the incentives that need to be offered, the strategic locations of this investment, the direct and indirect impacts of investment, and contingency issues that derive from its successes and failures. Insightful commentary on these issues runs throughout this book.

In contrast, this chapter looks at some broad issues of how one thinks about and analyzes issues in NAFTA debate. It rests on the assumption that how one feels and acts about an issue depends in large part on how one thinks and talks about it. Thus there is a legitimate need to look at how the sense-making analysis frames, develops, evaluates, and communicates issues of this very complex, evolving institution. Two aspects of this debate will be reviewed here: the criteria and trade-off analysis of assessment studies, and archetype themes and imminent issues.

The Challenge of Good Assessments: Tradeoffs and Criteria

Most NAFTA observers soon realize that there can be no simple, clear, objective, and complete theory about *this* particular agreement to either assess it or guide decisions. The various public and private parties are struggling along attempting to make sense of this "thing" as it develops. They need to imagine and speculate about the direction and outcomes of NAFTA, often without the help of solid assessment and analysis.

Just what does a good assessment do? What questions does it try to answer? What criterion does it offer to judge this or that proposal? What tradeoffs does the research make and how are they justified? What if the object of analysis is a moving target like NAFTA? No assessment can pretend to please all parties. In a sense, there are never any answers to what is the right and wrong thing about NAFTA. There are only arguments and some arguments are better than others. The quality of those arguments depends on how well the assessment criteria are met and the tradeoffs are calculated. Five criteria are discussed below.

The tradeoff analysis begins with the goals of any assessment effort. All assessments goals have three basic characteristics. First is the clarity of statement and focus of effort. A good NAFTA assessment should be able to state its purpose in a single paragraph statement. That statement identifies what the specific issue of interest is, why it is important (theoretical and practical interests), how it will be studied, and the expected value of the results. Secondly, the assessment must judge what the added-value of the study might be. This depends on how well the paradigm for an issue area is developed. A new paradigm is characterized by general and broad "ground-breaking/definitional" work as seen in the early descriptive analyses of NAFTA. It is followed by more rigorous studies that "fill in" the details with empirical work and further refinement of theory. Much of the work in this book is of this latter type. Given a paradigm's development, research work should assess where the most added value can be provided to further that paradigm's development. Lastly, realism and do-ability must guide the goal selection. This means a good match of research effort to resources available.

The inclusion/exclusion choice is a second assessment decision. No matter what topic is chosen for study, something else inevitably is left out. Whatever is chosen therefore needs a rationale and argument to provide it with initial legitimacy, do-able discovery, and a modicum of acceptance. What is not chosen likewise needs its justification. An assessment thus creates credibility and market for its domain by virtue of its choice of topics for study and the convincing rationales that support them.

The level-unit of analysis presents a third assessment criteria. An agreement like NAFTA has an impact on the widest possible spectrum of interests. Local and regional border economies have the most salient interests because of proximity effects. National interests are obvious in the institutional impacts and uneven adjustment outcomes that will have to be dealt with within a national system. Nonagreement parties, like Japan and the European Community (E.C.), have their own perspectives on the issues in terms of barriers and opportunities afforded by the Agreement. The relationship to supranational organizations, like the General Agreement on Trade and Tariffs (GATT), also needs to be explained.

Yet given the extent of this domain, there are inevitable hierarchies and interdependencies of issues between and among the various levels of analysis. National immigration policy for NAFTA, for example, could not be made without a specific analysis of the Southwest, the U.S. region that is affected the most by the Agreement. In similar fashion, how will U.S. investment tax credit policy in NAFTA affect the California structural adjustment program in the Los Angeles basin? There are at least three levels of impact in one policy decision. How do state and regional investment incentive policies interact for business? Do they complement or contradict each other? Such multilevel policy linkages and their implications should be an explicit part of any assessment analysis.

Data remain a constant problem for assessment. Whether the study is descriptive or predictive, the quality of the data often determine the final value of the study effort. In new ventures like NAFTA there are the standard problems of data availability, compatibility, reliability, and the like. Since much of the data are provided by official organizations, there is little direct control over data problems. Perhaps a real contribution in future NAFTA assessment will be a specification of the data needs and collective efforts to agree on standards, access, and cost sharing. With good databases in place, quality second-order studies will be facilitated.

Finally, the role of theory is critical to guide assessment. The value of theory lies in its use to specify an issue's parameters, identify key variables, hypothesize relationships, suggest meaningful criterion, and test for a study effort. Theory is never absent from an investigative effort. It may however be implicit, unspecified, assumed, or ignored. Practice shows that good theory which is explicit and clear tends to characterize quality studies. The value in specifying the theoretical base of a study, even if only in an introductory note, lies in the assistance it provides the readers and users of the study to understand the assumptions and beliefs that motivate and structure the argument. Too often readers have to struggle guessing what the authors are saying because they are not given the intellectual framework that the researchers assume is clear. With institutions such as NAFTA where a complex set of interacting theories will be needed to provide insight into any issue, the specification of the theory base for an assessment study would add considerable value and longevity to a study.

The present volume demonstrates how to deal with the difficulties of assessment analysis. It represents an assessment "guide book" for the more seasoned traveler who wants and needs to understand the details of NAFTA. The writers, some with direct experience in NAFTA agreement negotiations, bring both tools of analysis and experience of broadened views to their work. Even though NAFTA agreement provides too short an experience base and too little data, these researchers have made important contributions based on projections and interpolation of existing data. The product of their effort is both substantive analysis as well as models for future analysts.

They do a particularly good job at the task of analyzing the specifics of country, industry, and economic sector effects of economic integration. In this case the chosen terrain of analysis is FDI effects of NAFTA on the three country members. The goal is to provide insights into how the investment dimension of NAFTA agreement create both opportunities and barriers to investment decisions. For example, Rugman and Verbeke provide an important theoretical and conceptual framework to understand how investment decisions can be analyzed for NAFTA agreement. Globerman takes on the difficult task of identifying two important aspects of the economic theory behind NAFTA. He first summarizes and assesses the existent literature dealing with the economic affects of NAFTA. More importantly, he identifies and analyzes the major assumptions that underlie many of these studies. In knowing the assumptions, one can better assess the value and relevance of a study for policy decisions.

The level of analysis of this book is clearly national, with supporting studies at the industry and international level. Country perspectives are presented by well-known and experienced observers in Nymark and Verdun, Graham, and Edgington and Fruin. Specific industry studies of energy and forestry provide valuable insights into the dynamics and issue linkages that NAFTA provides for these industries. The Hagen, Henson, and Merrifield study merits specific attention as an excellent industry study. The Roberts and Vertinsky analysis is also specific, clear, and practical in value. Future industry studies could use these chapters as models. An international perspective provides insight into what external (exogenous) investment effects of fourth party interests in NAFTA might be (Edgington and Fruin), and NAFTA impacts on the potential for Latin American integration (Gestrin and Waverman, Ortiz).

As a group, these writings and investigations provide a solid example of the kinds of analysis that will be needed in future years to provide both public and private policy guidance for the evolving agreement.

Archetypal Themes and Imminent Issues

The second focus of this chapter looks at some archetypal themes and imminent issues that subtlety color and influence the thinking in NAFTA debate. These often appear as implicit assumptions, untested beliefs or mistaken notions about NAFTA. Such ideas often underlie the thinking about an issue. Dealing with them openly might serve future analyses and debates.

Anchoring Perspectives Correctly

Labeling, that is using intentional metaphors and descriptions for an issue, can be a problem because it tends to anchor perspectives and frame an issue in a particular way. Wrongly labeling a phenomenon may set a reader's initial expectations off in a direction that was not intended by the authors. This is especially important in sensitive issues of national interest like culture, employment, health care, and the rights of ethnic/ indigenous peoples—salient issues for all three NAFTA countries. Once people are "locked in" to a suggested perspective, they tend to interpret subsequent arguments and information in a particular way consistent with that original view of events. This may interfere with clear understanding and accurate interpretation of the intentions and ideas presented. This is especially true for prescriptive studies where interpretation of events and strategic decisions need to be made.

In this case, NAFTA can be labeled with multiple metaphors and historical events. Is NAFTA simply a convenient strategic alliance or a de facto formalization of an inexorable historical process of integration, the result of the trends of internalization, interdependence, and bloc politics that appear to be happening elsewhere in the world? Is it the beginning dream of the internationalist's "one-world" vision or a bad dream for national interests and tendencies? Is NAFTA a North American "catch-up" with the E.C. or the "last hurrah" of a desperate world power in transition? Or does NAFTA represent a more sinister process by which a very large and powerful nation state absorbs its willing neighbors? Whatever their form, labels must not be mistaken as simply neutral descriptions. Being careful about the words one uses to describe and define NAFTA has important bearing on how issues are seen and discussed.

NAFTA as Schumpeterianism Disguised

Schumpeter talks of the creative destruction of capitalism and its marvelous outcomes.[1] While not avoiding the issue of costs and their method of sharing, he does not dwell on the pain of adjustment, but rather celebrates the joys of wealth creation.

NAFTA is not too unlike that kind of thinking. It talks optimistically of the good things to come and offers light commentary on the pain. Would it not be better to clarify our understanding of NAFTA process of wealth creation with a better theory of integration and its making/breaking subprocesses? Even U.S. Congressman Richard Gephardt (D-Mo.) has stated that NAFTA will be "in our deep best interests," if it is concluded with a clear understanding of what is in store for the American people.[2]

One idea that may help explain the integration process has to do with the rates of absorption of change and the kinds of political economies that seem to do it best. Recent literature on planned change and structural adjustments of U.S. industries offers some useful insights here.[3]

The Eastern European nations are presently going through a transition process that merits attention to the differential rates of adjustment between technological/production/economic systems and the apparently slower moving political/social/cultural systems—the "people part."[4] Their transition was predicated, in Western eyes at least, on a dual development model: political development would parallel economic development. Implicit theory suggested that market economies thrive better in open, representative, and democratic systems. Thus economic reform and political reform were to go hand-in-hand.

It seems that reform is easier to imagine than to make happen. With political and sociocultural institutions, there seems to be a large and direct lag affect as the "people part" of the change struggles to catch up with the technical/physical change.[5] Social system changes are both complex and less satisfying because people do not behave like passive technology. Results are hard to plan for, achieve, measure, and report. And conditions and situations can change rapidly. Thus there is a tension between the rates of development between the solid physical/technological development and the more amorphous "people" systems. This lagged tension must be planned for in order to aid transformation and reduce conflict and resistance to change.

In Eastern Europe there is some question as to whether its development will both lag and founder because the "people" systems are taking more time to develop and adjust. Since transitions to market economies involve the cost and pain of structural dislocation there is some question about whether open democratic systems serve well here. An open, democratic system may not serve well. With access to public decision processes, people may readily seek escape from pain, compensation for loss of security, and protection against adjustment. This in turn may overload the newly developing democratic systems with shorter-term complaint demands that keep its agenda from focusing on the longer-term and more difficult institutional and infrastructural developments that are needed for the post-transition periods.

Is there a lesson in this for NAFTA? Perhaps in the better understanding of how the existing "people" systems are structured to be capable of absorbing change. On the surface, the Mexican system appears to be the one more vulnerable to open systems transitions. Ironically however, its traditional one-party system might provide a better discipline and stability for transition as pain avoidance and internal cost sharing are dealt with within traditional party structures and decision processes. The U.S. system itself may appear to be quite stable as it has periodically absorbed change in new administrations. However, there are enough indications that even this decision system will be taxed in making decisions that support NAFTA over domestic interests. And Canada has its constant federalism problems which promise to make NAFTA issues a continuing challenge to its decision-making institutions.

Thus NAFTA debate should spend an equal amount of time thinking, discussing, and planning the "people" changes as it does the more impersonal technological physical systems changes. The two can complement each other or not depending on how well they are accounted for in the debate.

Power Imbalance and Instability

Triads are historically the most unstable type of relationship. The possibilities of side deals, exclusion tactics, "ganging up," and the like create uncertainties that lead to mixed motive commitments and unstable alliances. Thus the alliance of Canada, United States, and Mexico is subject to the machinations of triad situations.

And being on a single unitary continent does not guarantee a stable relationship. Modern communications and transportation make the barriers of oceans a less effective guarantor of forced loyalty and commitment based on geographic determinism. In addition, the physical location of the United States between its partners suggests a hidden advantage of location that naturally divides and conquers. Like the proverbial eight hundred pound gorilla, the United States is probably not very sensitive to the needs of its partners. What comes together, can come apart.

In addition, there are significant size and power differentials that put some doubt into attempts to project NAFTA as a negotiations and adjustment process among equal partners. Power in this case is based on a simple resource dependence equation. The more party A has of quantity X that party B needs, and the more dependent B is on A to provide X, the more power A has over B.[6] Power among nations at least is often founded on the resource dependencies of other nations. The examples of Middle East oil, Japanese capital, or U.S. markets immediately come to mind.

This plays a role in both negotiations and long-term relationships. One is treated as an equal (and perhaps nicely) as long as one has something the other parties want. That could be oil, cheap labor, untapped mineral wealth, or vast markets and capital resources, all present in NAFTA countries. Thus it pays to assess why one is being courted so assiduously and what one has to do to remain an attractive investment.

The history of alliances shows mixed motives and situation-bound relationships. For this reason, the institutionalization of relationships, whether it be marriage or common markets, becomes a critical issue in maintaining integrated systems. For then the centripetal force of institution counteracts the centrifugal forces of independent solution seeking. This alone probably explains why certain parties want to move ahead so quickly with formalizing the Agreement.

Change theory provides further insight into this matter of

imbalance and instability.[7] Any social system represents a relative equilibrium of forces at work. Change occurs in the level of activities, but the kinds of activities may remain the same—such as increased trade of certain goods, but not the mix of goods. When decisions are made to change the system, the present relationship of forces must first be "unfrozen." This stage represents an uncomfortable disequilibrium that allows for adjustments, modifications, and terminations of former activities and their supporting structures.

It is also a temporary "window of opportunity." For nature and human social systems tend to abhor a disequilibrium. They will try to reestablish a new equilibrium immediately. Thus change in attitudes, beliefs, and values as well as activities do not remain in play indefinitely. Once a new agreement is reached, a new equilibrium comes into being that is resistant to further change for a period of time.

NAFTA has all of these change processes ongoing. All three state systems are now in the process of "unfreezing" their expectations about traditional interstate relations. Mexico dramatically shifted its policy of closed border state protectionism. The United States signaled interests in bilateral agreements with the United States. These represent a changing set of expectations for important national constituencies.

NAFTA accords thus mark a point of explicit public agenda that is signaling the various internal constituencies, businesses, labor and regional governments that there is change and adjustment. Like the game of musical chairs, all of the interested parties are marching around keeping eyes fixed on the chairs of opportunity and cost. Their ears are attuned to the music of the negotiations. When the music stops, the scramble for chairs will leave winners and losers of the game. A new relative equilibrium is established until a new game is played.

For these reasons, NAFTA debate is critical. Once agreements are made, significant changes and challenges to the new equilibrium will be difficult and costly. Thus an analysis of the change dynamics and power balance issues remains an important agenda.

Cost-Benefit Sharing of Adjustments

A related issue to power is that of deciding on the sharing of costs and benefits. Any integration involves dislocation effects as trade and investment opportunities are both created and destroyed. The degree of adjustment required, the ability to absorb the costs of adjustment, and the existence of cost sharing options all contribute to the lasting permanence of any integrated market relationship. At this time, all that is known is that the major adjustments will take place in Mexico.

It is important to note that less than ten years ago, Mexico was considered a Third World nation of high economic and investment risk because of its apparently intractable debt and structural and political decision process problems. Now, however, Mexico claims that it is both fully willing and able to make the adjustments necessary for the creation of integrated markets. In some ways, Mexico has no choice but to "go international" and seek a solution to its huge domestic development problems via international linkages. There is modern evidence in Chile, Korea, Spain, and Hong Kong that opening borders does lead to significant opportunities for growth.

However, the kinds of adjustments by Mexico, in comparison to the United States and Canada, seem to be very large; and Mexico also has problems of development that are different in kind as well as magnitude. Its population is largely youthful and undereducated. Its traditional agriculture cannot compete with agribusiness interests. Its infrastructure is uneven and poorly developed. This might create strains beyond the limits of both Mexico and joint-NAFTA institutions. Such a situation calls for identifying a process, *a priori,* to study and prepare strategic options for explicit sectoral adjustments as in the case of energy, real estate development, and insurance/banking services. A multidisciplinary team with a specific NAFTA institutional mandate could be assembled to do this analysis now, before the problems and issues of adjustment fully develop. Negotiations experience shows that preplanning is the most critical determinant of success in international agreements.

Investment-Trade Linkage and the Maquiladora Corridor

One cannot understand investment patterns and the motives that created them in a vacuum. From the international product life-cycle theory, value chain analysis and exchange rate theory, one knows that investment is tied to trade and vice versa. One must look at trade patterns and issues simultaneously to get a fuller understanding of the deeper issues involved in integrated markets.

In addition, macroanalyses of larger investment patterns tell only a limited story that is useful largely for public policy purposes. Investment decisions are made based on expectations and knowledge of market conditions and potentials. They are made by business people with complex, mixed motives and profit/performance expectations, not impersonal corporate entities or government agencies. Thus a business motive must be kept constantly in view when making policy analysis and recommendations. This means that market development, structure, and potential are a fundamental part of investment analysis.

Finally little has been said of impacts of NAFTA on the maquiladora corridor that exists on the U.S.-Mexican border. On the surface, NAFTA agreement seems to make this development a moot point and an effort that is no longer useful. Such an attitude would be both short-sighted and ignorant. The maquiladora development represents a significant investment in both size, institution building, cross-cultural learning, and real impact on lives. However, and perhaps more importantly, this long-term experiment might provide useful transitional learning for the stages of development that NAFTA will inevitably go through as well as provide a model for specific developments in other regions of Mexico.

Related to the investment issue, it has been suggested that NAFTA may provide the impetus for developing the equivalent of GATT for investment in the form of a comprehensive international set of rules. Given the importance of property rights and ownership agreements, and technology transfer in most direct investment decisions, this organization might be labeled GATPO-General Agreement on Technology, Property, and Ownership. A parallel organization might be created to deal with the coordination of the specifics of portfolio investment policy and practice. It is generally agreed that the U.S.-Canadian Free Trade Agreement provided some very important precedents in the development of sectoral rules that have been further improved upon in NAFTA accord. Perhaps the lessons have merit for further international institution building.

A Fundamental Assumption: NAFTA Will Evolve

As with any new institutional idea, there is a tendency to prematurely treat the idea-in-becoming as the actual institutional realization of that idea. In doing so, people often become locked into an early version of an idea. This limits the debate's purpose to discover and refine emerging institution's qualities. In this case, NAFTA document is treated as an institution itself rather than the proposal and common discussion agenda it represents.

In addition, people appear to be making decisions based more on the promise than the deed. This further feeds expectations to move from general interests to specific needs based on an early interpretation of the document. Self-fulfilling development potentially comes into play as parties push for specific interpretations of clauses that meet their initial expectations and early interpretations of the document. In folk wisdom terms, this might be a case of putting a wine to market before its time.

In reality, the signing of a document attests to a serious intention to build an institution. Such a document serves as the negotiating agenda for the real institution that is to evolve. It is not a tight contract but a working document. The various sections of the treaty do not have a separate reality other than that imposed by the negotiators through discovery, fiat, and demand. These sections merely act to guide and put workable limits on the task of turning intentions into realities.

NAFTA creates potential problems for expectations, growth, adjustment, and evaluation in the implementation of ideas. In a related example, few seasoned and realistic observers would venture the proposition that the platform of a newly elected political party ought to be the same as its realized achievements. Nor that marriage vows at the altar are the marriage itself. The platform and the vows are commitments and intentions to achieve some stated aims, both clear and otherwise. Both involve promises based on imperfect information, some informed guessing, and much hope. Both had imperfect models from other times and places to provide guidance. And both need the value of ambiguity of issues that allows for flexible adjustment in the continuing conflict resolution that leads to institution building. There is much adjusted experience and time needed before one can declare a marriage as good or a government as successful. The point here is that ideas-in-becoming face considerable pressures to meet conflicting economic and political agendas. Unless a continuing debate is allowed to create open and flexible interpretations of interests, the implementation of the ideas may be less than optimal. Thus the debate remains the major reality that merits attention.

Summary

There can be no final conclusions about NAFTA. What one knows about NAFTA remains inconclusive and imminent for some time to come. It is a very large-scale experiment in the making by three cultures with mixed experience in integrating their own countries. There is both theory and experience that suggests that it can be a successful venture. And there seems to be the will to deal with the issues that grow from its further development. Those who study these phenomenon of cooperation and integration have a special opportunity and duty to choose their efforts well so that they may add the most relevant and helpful insights into the institutions developments. This book will be seen as one of those contributions.

Notes

1. Joseph A. Schumpeter, *The Theory of Economic Development* (Cambridge, Mass.: Harvard University Press, 1961).

2. James Flanigan, "After all the talk, NAFTA will be about vision," *Los Angeles Times,* 16 May 1993, D1.

3. Paul R. Lawrence and Davis Dyer, "Toward a Theory of Organizational Adaptation and Readaptation" in their book, *Renewing American Industry: Organizing for Efficiency and Innovation* (New York: The Free Press, 1983) and Robert Chin and Kenneth D. Benne, "General Strategies for Effecting Changes in Human Systems" in Warren G. Bennis, Kenneth D. Benne, Robert Chin, and K. E. Corey, eds., *The Planning of Change* (New York: CBS College Publishing, 1985).

4. Tad Szulc, "Democracy's Light Grows Fainter in Eastern Europe," *Los Angeles Times,* 6 June 1993, M2.

5. Noel Tichy, *Managing Strategic Change: Technology, Politics and Cultural Dynamics* (New York: J. Wiley and Sons, 1983).

6. Jeffrey Pfeffer and G. Salancik, *The External Control of Organizations* (New York: Harper and Row, 1979).

7. Warren G. Bennis, Kenneth D. Benne, Robert Chin, and K. E. Corey, *The Planning of Change* (New York: CBS College Publishing, 1985).

ADDENDUM TO CHAPTER 2: "THE POLITICS OF NAFTA"

by Susan W. Liebeler

The side agreement negotiations continued until mid-August of 1993 when the three parties reached agreement. The side pacts provide for two trilateral commissions on environmental and labor cooperation.

The commissions will be comprised of a council with each country represented by a cabinet-level official with responsibility for labor or environmental matters, a secretariat, and in the case of the environmental commission, a joint public advisory committee. In addition to monitoring labor and environmental conditions and enforcement in each country, the commissions have dispute settlement authority in the event of a party's persistent pattern of failure to enforce effectively its environmental laws or its labor laws with respect to health and safety, child labor and minimum wage. Where consultations fail to resolve such disputes, a neutral panel of independent experts can be established by a two-thirds vote of the parties. If a panel finds such a persistent pattern, it can formulate a corrective action plan. If the offending country fails to remedy the matter, the commissions are empowered to impose a monetary assessment against the offending country in an amount not to exceed $20 million (U.S.) for the first year, and thereafter, no greater than .007 percent of the total annual trade in goods between the parties. If a party fails to pay a monetary enforcement assessment or continues its failure to enforce its laws, the party is liable to ongoing enforcement action and, in the case of Mexico and the United States, trade sanctions where the complaining party may suspend NAFTA benefits based on the amount of the assessment. For Canada, the commission will collect the monetary enforcement assessment and enforce an action plan in a summary proceeding before a Canadian court.

The side agreement on safeguards set up the Working Group on Emergency Action to consider issues relating to the use of safeguards and consult with a party on import surges.

Concluding the side agreements failed to turn the tide in favor of NAFTA in the United States. The labor agreement did not pacify organized labor which continued its all-out opposition. Likewise, several environmental groups were dissatisfied with the environmental agreement and continued to attack NAFTA. Mr. Clinton still lacked the votes he needed to secure Congressional approval.

Rather than focusing on NAFTA's benefits, Mr. Clinton played to environmentalists and organized labor and kept a low profile during the sidebar negotiations. Unfortunately, this strategy allowed the critics to set the stage and keep the administration on the defensive. Distracted by the battle to get his budget through Congress and by foreign policy problems in Somalia and Haiti, the president ignored NAFTA for several additional weeks while NAFTA critics gathered votes from House Democrats. Not until mid-September did the president focus on NAFTA. At this point, he faced an uphill battle. While Senate passage was assured, a majority of the Democrats in the Democrat-controlled House of Representatives opposed NAFTA, including house majority leader Richard Gephardt and house majority whip David Bonior. This meant the president would have to bypass the Democratic House leadership and rely on Republication support. Unless the president could deliver 100 Democratic votes, the house Republican whip could not deliver the additional 118 Republican votes needed for approval. In an effort to solidify Republican support, the president promised he would defend Republicans in the 1994 elections from Democratic attacks for pro-NAFTA votes.

Anti-NAFTA forces held the upper hand in the House of Representatives until the last minute when Mr. Clinton mounted a highly visible campaign for NAFTA. In order to sway public opinion and discredit Ross Perot, Vice President Gore debated Perot on national television on November 9. Mr. Gore trampled his opponent and the administration's NAFTA campaign began to gather momentum. In the final days Mr. Clinton mounted a full court press and brought the rather considerable powers and coffers of the presidency to bear in persuading the U.S. House of Representatives to vote yes on November 17. However, during this process the text of NAFTA was not altered in any way.

By November 17, Mr. Clinton had garnered enough votes to push NAFTA through the House of Representatives by a vote of 234200. Three days later the Senate approved the agreement 6139. On December 8, 1993 President Clinton signed the NAFTA implementing legislation into law.

In Canada, the Conservative government which had negotiated NAFTA and the side agreements lost the final election in October 1993. Canadian prime minister Jean Chretien, head of Canada's new Liberal government, had distanced his party from the treaty during the campaign. Elected after the Canadian parliament had approved NAFTA in Spring 1993, he withheld the final act of proclamation as a lever to persuade the United States and Mexico to alter the agreement. His concerns had to do with rules on unfair trade and security for Canada's water resources and energy supplies. On unfair trade, the three countries agreed to a two-year negotiation on a common definition of what constitutes below cost dumping and unfair export subsidies. (The United States and Canada made a similar agreement in 1989 with the enactment of the U.S.-Canadian Free Trade Agreement.) On energy, Canada settled for a unilateral declaration of Canada's intent on energy—in time of shortage Canada will interpret and apply NAFTA so as to maximize energy security for Canadians. On water, the three nations issued a statement that NAFTA doesn't require any member to export its natural water resources. Mr. Chretien abandoned his campaign reservations and on December 2 announced his government would enact NAFTA.

In Mexico the Senate voted to approve NAFTA in early December 1993, so in the end all three parties agreed to enact

NAFTA to meet the deadline. The final obstacles overcome, the historic North American Free Trade Agreement went into effect on January 1, 1994. Despite the last-minute wheeling and dealing, overall, NAFTA will increase trade and foster economic growth throughout North America.

CONTRIBUTORS

David W. Edgington, Department of Geography, University of British Columbia.

W. Mark Fruin, Institute for Asian Research, University of British Columbia.

Michael Gestrin, Faculty of Management, University of Toronto.

Steven Globerman, Department of Economics, Simon Fraser University.

Edward M. Graham, Institute for International Economics, Washington D.C.

Daniel A. Hagen, Department of Economics, Western Washington University.

Steven E. Henson, Department of Economics, Western Washington University.

Susan W. Liebeler, Irell and Manella, Los Angeles, California.

David E. Merrifield, Department of Economics, Western Washington University.

Alan Nymark, Investment Canada, Ottawa.

Edgar Ortiz, Universidad Nacional Autónoma de México, Mexico City.

Don G. Roberts, Levesque, Beaubien, Geffrion, Inc., Montreal.

Alan M. Rugman, Western Washington University and the University of Toronto.

Robert Spich, Western Washington University and University of California at Los Angeles.

Alain Verbeke, Solvay Business School, University of Brussels.

Emmy Verdun, Investment Canada, Ottawa.

Ilan Vertinsky, FEPA Research Unit, University of British Columbia.

Leonard Waverman, Department of Economics, University of Toronto.

INDEX